IXP2400/2800 Programming

The Complete Microengine Coding Guide

Erik J. Johnson
Aaron R. Kunze

INTEL
PRESS

ISBN 0-9717861-6-X

Publisher: Rich Bowles

Managing Editor: David B. Spencer

Assistant Editor: Lynn Putnam

Text Design: Marianne Phelps

Page Composition: Octal Publishing, Inc.

Graphic Art: Donna Lawless (illustrations), Ted Cyrek (cover)

Printed in the United States of America

10 9 8 7 6 5 4 3 2

First printing, April 2003

Contents

Acknowledgments

Between the pages of every book are the many people who helped work the text into its final form. All of the people acknowledged on these pages have done just that for us and, thus, have earned our thanks. We are sincerely thankful to be able to work with and learn from all of you.

In addition to countless reviews, Raj Yavatkar, Bernie Keany, Alan Crouch, and Abel Weinrib contributed the most valuable help in the development of this book in that they got us started and kept us going. We acknowledged these same people in our *IXP1200 Programming* book, and for good reason, as they made both books possible through their encouragement, time, expertise, and, lest we forget, their sponsorship.

Both Larry Huston and Jamie Jason deserve gold stars for their front-to-back technical reviews. How they were able to find inconsistencies in code formats between pages 14 and 352 while also providing suggestions for improving the flow of each and every section amazes us.

Our thanks also go out to our team of expert reviewers: Mark Ramos, Roy Larsen, Chandramouli (Mouli) Narayanan, Don Hooper, and Bill Carlson for being early reviewers; Dale Paige and Liang-min (Larry) Wang for resolving our SPI-4 RBUF overflow issues and providing code for initialization of the flow control mechanisms; Justin Cox for explaining what we were doing wrong with "mode 3" enqueue operations;

Regis Cheval, Ram Huggahalli, and the IXAC team of Winnie Shao, Charles Han, Henry Yuan, Jim Tang, Tony Dou for validating the final versions.

We would also like to thank Mark Stair, Gene Nomicos, and Evan McLain from Consystant, as well as Ben Hardekopf from the University of Texas at Austin for their insightful comments and unique perspectives.

Finally, thanks to the entire Network Platforms team for all their help and support during this process.

Chapter 1

You've Got an IXP2XXX Processor, Now What?

Theory can leave questions unanswered, but practice has to come up with something.

—Mason Cooley

Whether you are looking to use the IXP2XXX[1] series of Intel's network processors to build a modest single-box switch or a fully-redundant, multi-blade, content-aware, packet processing system, this book is your programming guide. The IXP2XXX processors offer a wide range of programmability through programmable processors and co-processors specifically tuned to network programming. Due to this specialization, the IXP2XXX processors can provide flexible programmability without sacrificing performance as might be expected with general-purpose processors.

At the same time, the new programming model presented by any network processor, including the IXP2XXX processor, can be daunting. For example, say you want to write a network address translation (NAT) function for the IXP2800, which has seventeen programmable processors and at least four different types of memory. How many, and which,

---

[1] The IXP2XXX designation represents a family of three processors: the IXP2400, the IXP2800 and the IXP2850. All of the information contained in this book applies to all processors, except where noted.

processors would you devote to performing the NAT function? Which memory would you use to hold your data structures, and how would you best organize your data structures? For answers to these questions, keep reading!

As you begin programming the IXP2XXX processor, accomplishing seemingly trivial tasks, such as receiving or transmitting packets, has been known to invoke an all-out engineer's victory dance. This initial programming experience can be especially frustrating for programmers already well versed in the standard write-debug-optimize programming methods. Optimizing code is less about finding ways to execute fewer lines of code and more about understanding ways to offload work to the hardware.

Why Use the IXP2XXX Network Processor?

The IXP2XXX processors and network processors in general, enable you to add, through software, the latest-and-greatest network services while maintaining high packet[2] throughput and low packet latency. Simply put, the IXP2XXX processors offer performance and flexibility for implementing network services. It is this promise of performance and flexibility that differentiates network processors, including the IXP2XXX, from general-purpose processors and hardware-based solutions, such as Application Specific Integrated Circuits (ASICs).

General-purpose processors certainly meet the flexibility requirements of modern networking services, but often fail to meet the performance requirements of these services. The flexibility of general-purpose processors comes from the availability of modern operating systems and programming tools, such as C compilers, which enable you to create any network application you can dream up. In addition, the software community is fairly successful at keeping up the steady stream of new network applications, so you can leverage those implementations. However, general-purpose processors are not capable of meeting the high-end performance requirements of modern networks. Modern networks commonly support multiple gigabits of data speeds, and, in extreme cases, a single interface can run at ten gigabits per second. Unfortunately, these network speeds are approaching the memory interface speeds of general-purpose processors, meaning even a single memory

---

[2] The term 'packet' is used generically and might include IP datagrams, Ethernet frames, ATM cells, CSIX CFrames, or any other similar unit of network data. We use packet in this generic sense throughout the book.

reference can significantly impact the performance of a network application on a general-purpose processor. To make matters worse, the memory caching solutions on general-purpose processors rely on temporal locality of the incoming data—something less and less present in today's high-speed, aggregated networks.

ASICs, on the other hand, can meet your network performance requirements by designing circuitry with strict guarantees on latencies and throughput using embedded memories or pipelined architectures. However, the flexibility of ASICs is nowhere near that of network processors. Implementing complex algorithms, such as NAT connection establishment in a finite-state machine, can be tricky on an ASIC. In addition, ASIC design cycles, which can take years, cannot keep up with the rapid changes in network services. And even then, are you positive your solution is correct and is acceptable to the market? If not, then using an ASIC as a prototype vehicle is an expensive proposition.

Network processors, such as the IXP2XXX processor, meet network performance and flexibility requirements through highly parallel, programmable architectures. For example, you can write software for your new security-enabling NAT device to take advantage of the multiple cores, multiple threads, and built-in queueing and hashing hardware to accelerate the performance of the software.

The parallel nature of the IXP2XXX processors allows processing of multiple packets simultaneously, which can greatly increase the throughput of the processor. Parallel processing works well for packets that are independent, but requires high-speed synchronization and communication primitives when packets are dependent on each other. For example, packets being compressed and decompressed by two gateways in the Internet represent an order dependency. These packets must be processed in a particular order or the decompression function corrupts the data. The IXP2XXX processors provide many choices for high-speed synchronization and communication specifically designed for these situations.

The IXP2XXX processors offer flexibility through upgradeability, libraries, and programmability. Upgradeability, while maybe not your first concern as a programmer, is a handy feature when you consider it also enables you to fix bugs easily. Libraries of code, just like those provided with general-purpose processors, can ease the burden of developing everything from scratch. Finally, programmability means new services are delivered via software, as opposed to hardware, such as ASICs, which means these latest-and-greatest network services should get out faster, right?

In theory, it should, but in practice, the time-to-market advantages provided by implementing a new network service in software on a network processor can be offset by the steep learning curve for programmers of the network processor. The new programming model typically prevents you from simply taking your existing general-purpose code base and recompiling it for the network processor. Often times, it is the very thing that gives network processors their performance advantage (multiple cores and threads) that humbles even the most experienced programmer. The IXP2XXX processor is no exception.

Not to Worry

If we have now frightened you about the prospect of network processor programming, don't worry, you've got this book to help. Here, we'll show you how to program the IXP2XXX processor. We learned how. We're confident that software people, like you, can learn to program it too. While the multi-core-parallel-processing programming model may be unfamiliar, the tools, languages, and even programming constructs, such as threads, mutexes, critical sections, and signals, are all very familiar. The trick is to filter the information about the hardware to present what is relevant to a programmer. This is one of the purposes of this book.

What is familiar to most network programmers when programming the IXP2XXX processor is the basic packet flow of receive, process, and transmit. The process step can range from simple operations like bridging, switching, or routing to more complex quality-of-service (QoS) metering, marking, and policing, to enforcing access control lists (ACLs) and other forms of deep packet inspection. In theory, implementing the latest-and-greatest network service on the IXP2XXX processor means adding more code to the packet-processing step within this basic packet flow. In practice, implementing the latest-and-greatest network service on the IXP2XXX processor means understanding what the IXP2XXX hardware can do for your code. Hiding memory latencies and proper data structure design is the kind of practical knowledge you need.

Luckily, all of this knowledge can be learned without resorting to reading hardware schematics or wheeling a logic analyzer into your cubicle. You'll gain this knowledge as we present the details as they relate to your software. So if you are interested in the practice of effective IXP2XXX microengine programming, this book takes you from start to finish and along the way hopefully find time for a few victory dances.

Is This Book For You?

Presumably, you are reading this book because you have already invested in the IXP2XXX processor. Perhaps you have been asked to develop, or evaluate the suitability of, the next great network product using the IXP2XXX processor. Or, you may be transitioning a design from the IXP12XX processor family to the IXP2XXX processor.

If you are not familiar with the IXP12XX processor, you may have tried to read the IXP2XXX data sheet and various reference manuals. Perhaps you downloaded and installed the IXP2XXX Software Development Kit (SDK), but exploring the complete microengine assembly reference designs left you wondering where to begin. And if you did get started with the reference designs, you might still be wondering why the code works the way it does.

If you are familiar with the IXP12XX processor, the first order of business is cataloging the newly added (and removed!) features of IXP2XXX processor. Given this understanding, the questions become how to use these features, and even more important, when is it appropriate to use them.

Whether you are familiar with the IXP12XX processor or new to Intel network processors, this book provides practical advice on programming IXP2XXX processors.

A Guide to the Rest of the Book

Depending on your background and goals, you may not need to read every chapter of this book straight through. Some of the chapters can be read independently, while others build upon previous chapters and should be read in sequence. Furthermore, some chapters can be skimmed or skipped, depending on your familiarity with the IXP2XXX processor, IXP12XX processor and your goals. Here is how we recommend different readers use this book:

■ *IXP12XX programmers looking to begin IXP2XXX programming:* If you are an IXP12XX programmer, Chapter 2, which covers the IXP2XXX hardware, should be skimmed first so that you are familiar with the changes between the IXP12XX and IXP2XXX hardware. Chapters 3 and 4 can be skimmed or even skipped as they cover tools and the framework provided for programming, all of which is similar to the IXP12XX. Chapters 5 and 11, which cover the receive and the transmit operations, can be read or skimmed, depending on your desire to understand these operations on the IXP2XXX processor. The receive and the transmit operations are quite different (and simplified!) from the IXP12XX processor, so don't assume they are the same. Chapters 6 through 10 build a working quality-of-service application and should be read as they present examples of programming with nearly all of the IXP2XXX processor features. Finally, Chapters 12 and 13 present special programming examples, tips and tricks, and can be skipped unless you need these special features in your application.

Also, we use notes, like the following one, to point out differences and similarities between programming the IXP12XX and IXP2XXX processor.

IXP1200 Note

> For readers familiar with programming the IXP12XX processor, these notes point out differences and similarities between the IXP12XX and IXP2XXX processor.

■ *IXP2XXX programmers looking to improve their understanding of IXP2XXX programming:* If you are already an IXP2XXX programmer, you can safely skip Chapters 2 through 4, although skimming these chapters, especially Chapter 2 probably won't hurt, just to make sure you are familiar with all of the hardware. Chapters 5, 6, and 11, which cover receive, transmit and single-threaded processing, can be skimmed or skipped depending on how confident you are with IXP2XXX programming. Chapters 7 through 10 detail the methods of unordered and ordered thread execution, as well as context pipeline stages, and should be read, in order. Finally, Chapters 12 and 13, which cover the crypto unit, CRC, and CSIX interfaces, among other things, are worth reading to help broaden your knowledge of IXP2XXX programming.

■ *Programmers new to the IXP2XXX processor and IXP12XX processor:* If you fall into this category, you should read Chapters 2 through 10, in order. But don't despair that you have to read more than IXP12XX programmers because, after all, we wrote this book primarily for people like you. Once you finish Chapter 10, you will be ready to tackle your own IXP2XXX applications, or read Chapters 11 through 13, which cover advanced, specialized topics, as you find necessary.

Conventions

Throughout the book we use the terms byte, word, long-word, and quad-word to represent 8, 16, 32, and 64 bits of data respectively.

All but the most trivial code examples are available on the accompanying CD-ROM. To help you correlate the code in the book to the proper file on the CD-ROM, the format for most code examples contains locator information. The following is an example of the code format used in the book.

compute_answer_to_universe()

```
     File: ChapterX\<directory…>\<filename> -- if appropriate
     Project: ChapterX\<directory…>\<filename> -- if appropriate
256  /* Code conventions */
257  int compute_answer_to_universe()
258  {
259     return 42;
260  }
```

Lines 256 – 260:

These lines compute the answer to the universe, but not the question. The line numbers are absolute and correspond to the line in the associated file.

The file and project names are provided when appropriate. Each line of code has a line number to make it easy to dissect the code and refer to individual code segments in the text. The line numbers correspond to the same lines in the source file on the accompanying CD-ROM.

The include paths within the sample projects have been defined so that the example code can be compiled, without modification, from a sibling directory of the Intel IXA SDK 3.0 directory. Thus, if you installed the Intel IXA SDK 3.0 in the default directory, c:\ixa_sdk_3.0, you can copy the CD-ROM directory of the CD-ROM into c:\ixp2k_prog_book, for example, and compile the examples without modification. If you copy the contents of the CD-ROM into a non-sibling directory of the Intel IXA SDK 3.0 directory, you must update the include paths in each of the projects to compile the code.

Chapter 2

IXP2XXX Hardware

The programming model of the IXP2XXX processor differs from traditional programming models, such as those used in a Windows- or Linux-based environment. In traditional programming models, operating systems abstract the concepts of threads and memory hierarchies and thus "virtualize" most, if not all, of the hardware. However, when programming the IXP2XXX processor, you must be aware of the hardware, including threads and different memory types, to produce optimized code and let the hardware do what it was designed to do.

Understanding the IXP2XXX programming environment goes beyond just learning another set of software programming interfaces. Understanding the IXP2XXX programming environment means understanding the processor architecture. But consider the upside. By taking advantage of the IXP2XXX hardware, you can offload work to it. One less thing to write and debug is always a win.

This chapter describes the components of the processor's architecture relevant to programmers. Typically, such descriptions provide good reference material, but can be difficult to remember. So, to put the pieces of the processor architecture into perspective, the description is followed by a practical, and hopefully memorable, explanation of a day in the life of a packet in the IXP2XXX hardware.

Programmable Processing Units

As shown in Figure 2.1, the IXP2850 consists of 17 programmable processors: one Intel® XScale™ core and 16 second-generation micro-engines[1] all on the same die. The Intel XScale core is an Advanced Reduced Instruction Set Computer (RISC) machine that is compliant

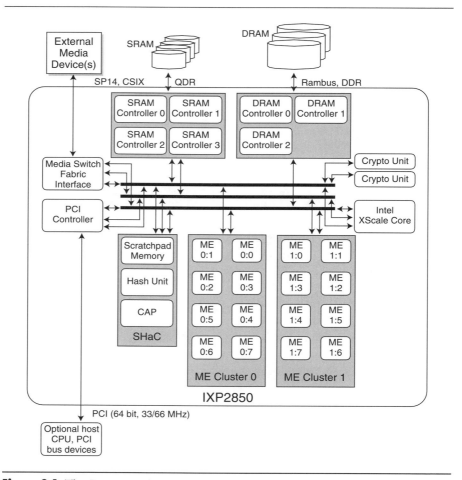

Figure 2.1 The Functional Units of the IXP2850

---

[1] The second-generation of microengines are also referred to as MEv2. Microengine and MEv2 are used synonymously in this book.

with ARM[†] Architecture V5STE, general-purpose processor. The micro-engines are RISC processors optimized for fast-path packet processing.

The IXP2400 and IXP2800 differ from the IXP2850 in a few ways, as summarized in Table 2.1.

Table 2.1 The Major Components of the IXP2400, IXP2800, and IXP2850 Processors

Feature	IXP2400	IXP2800	IXP2850
XScale core	Yes (600MHz max.)	Yes (700MHz max.)	Yes (700MHz max.)
Microengines	Yes (8 @ 600MHz max., organized into two clusters of 4)	Yes (16 @ 1.4GHz max.)	Yes (16 @ 1.4 GHz max.)
SHaC Unit	Yes	Yes	Yes
MSF	Yes (SPI-3, Utopia, CSIX-L1)	Yes (SPI-4 Phase 2, CSIX-L1)	Yes (SPI-4 Phase 2, CSIX-L1)
PCI Controller	Yes	Yes	Yes
SRAM Controller	Yes (2)	Yes (4)	Yes (4)
DRAM Controller	Yes (1, DDR)	Yes (3, Rambus)	Yes (3, Rambus)
Crypto Unit	No	No	Yes (2)

Intel® XScale™ Core

The Intel XScale core on an IXP2XXX processor is compliant with the ARM V5TE architecture as defined by ARM Limited. The "T" in "TE" indicates support for ARM's thumb instructions. Thumb instructions allow the Intel XScale core to switch back and forth between the standard 32-bit instruction set and a 16-bit instruction set for better memory performance. The "E" in "TE" indicates support for Digital Signal Processing (DSP) enhancements to the instruction set. Intel has also gone through a fair amount of effort to improve the internal pipeline in the Intel XScale core, as compared to other ARM V5TE implementations, to improve the memory-latency hiding abilities of the core. The Intel XScale core does not implement the floating-point instructions of the ARM V5 instruction set.

Programming the Intel XScale core is not much different from programming any other embedded general-purpose processor. The availability of operating systems, such as Linux* and VxWorks*, C/C++ cross-compilers, debuggers, and integrated development environments (IDEs), make the core familiar territory for programmers. With a wealth of information available on this topic, we only cover programming the Intel XScale core inasmuch as it supports microengine programming.

Microengines

Figure 2.2 shows the functional blocks in each microengine.

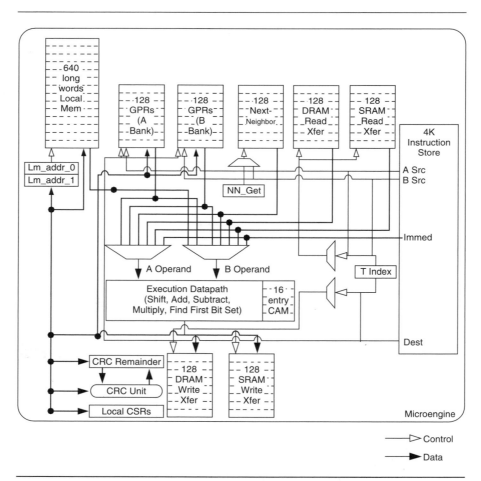

Figure 2.2 IXP2XXX Microengine Block Diagram

The microengines have an instruction set specifically tuned for processing network data. The instruction set consists of over 50 different instructions including arithmetic and logical operations that operate at bit, byte, and long-word levels, and can be combined with shift and rotate operations in a single instruction. The microengines have an integer multiplication instruction but no division or floating-point operations.

Each microengine has an independent instruction store large enough for 4K, 40-bit instructions. Code on the Intel XScale core initializes this instruction store before the microengines begin running. Once the microengines are running, the instructions are executed in a six-stage pipeline and on average take one cycle to execute when the pipeline is full. When instructions block during memory or device access, or when branch instructions force some instructions in the pipeline to be aborted, the average instruction execution time is longer than one cycle.

Threads and Thread Arbitration

Each IXP2XXX microengine has eight hardware-assisted (i.e., zero-overhead context switch) threads of execution. The term "zero-overhead" context switch implies that the microengine has duplicate states (e.g., registers and program counters) for each thread and can quickly switch from executing one thread to another thread in the microengine. We'll discuss this in greater detail later in this chapter and throughout the book as this feature is critical to the IXP2XXX processor's ability to hide memory latencies and achieve high performance.

You can configure each microengine to use either all eight threads or only four threads. When only four threads are enabled, the even-numbered threads execute while the odd-numbered threads are inactive.

All threads in a particular microengine execute code from the single instruction store on the microengine. Strictly speaking, all threads on a microengine execute the same code. However, this statement is misleading because you can have different threads on the same microengine performing different tasks. For example, consider the following pseudocode:

```
if (ctx() % 2) { // All even-numbered threads
    while(1) {
        task1();
    }
```

```
    } else {  // All odd-numbered threads
        while (1) {
            task2();
        }
    }
}
```

In this example, all of the even-numbered threads perform task1, while all odd-numbered threads perform task2. All of the code shown (including the if, while and both tasks) is part of the single instruction store on the microengine and, strictly speaking, all threads execute this same code. However, because the code branches based on the thread number, different threads perform different tasks. Branching based on thread number reduces the effective size of code that each thread can execute because the total amount of code must still fit within the single instruction store on the microengine.

The threads of a microengine are non-preemptive, which means the currently active thread must explicitly release control of the processor before another thread can run. Many operating systems have preemptive threading models, in which the developer cannot control or predict when a particular piece of code gets interrupted to let another piece of code run. Microengine threads, however, are not preemptive. The code must explicitly give up control of the microengine before another thread is allowed to run.

The non-preemptive nature of threads simplifies synchronization within a microengine. For example, to do computation on a register and maintain mutual-exclusion, simply avoid instructions that give up control of the microengine. The hardware then maintains mutual exclusion for you. Just make sure your code releases control once in a while, or else no other thread gets to run.

The IXP2XXX processor also contains a thread arbiter that swaps between threads in a microengine in round-robin order, only activating threads that are ready to run. Round-robin means the arbiter keeps track of which threads are ready to run and when one thread gives up control of the microengine, it searches in thread ID order for another thread in the microengine that is ready to run.

Registers

Microengines have four types of registers: general purpose, Synchronous Random Access Memory (SRAM) transfer, Dynamic Random Access Memory (DRAM) transfer, and next-neighbor (NN).

Microengine registers do not need to be flushed to memory when the control of the microengine switches from one thread to another, as is the case for most registers in general-purpose processors. Register flushing is avoided because the hardware allocates an equal portion of the total register set to each microengine thread. Although any thread can access any register on the microengine, by default, each thread accesses its own subset of the registers. Because register flushing is unnecessary, the latency experienced for a context switching—switching control of the microengine from one thread to another—is therefore the same as an instruction that causes the pipeline to abort the current execution, about four clock cycles.

The IXP2XXX microengines also have access to many control status registers (CSRs). These CSRs are used for a wide variety of control and configuration tasks, so we'll cover their usage and meaning as we go.

General-Purpose Registers

Each microengine has 256, 32-bit general-purpose registers (GPRs), allocated into two banks of 128 registers. The two banks are called the A and B banks. Any instruction that allows two GPR's as input requires one of the GPRs to be from the A bank and the other from the B bank. The bank in which a register exists is not important until you inadvertently require a particular variable to be in both banks. For example, the following code is not valid:

```
/* x, y, z are GPRs */

op(x, y); /* Requires x and y to be in opposite banks */

op(x, z); /* Requires x and z to be in opposite banks */

op(y, z); /* Requires y and z to be in opposite banks
             IMPOSSIBLE */
```

This example has three GPRs: x, y, and z. If x and y are used together in an instruction, x and y must be in different banks. The banks they are in are not important. If x and z are together in an instruction, x and z must be in opposite banks. Considering the requirement imposed by the first instruction, y and z must be in the same bank. Thus, any instruction using y and z in the same instruction results in code that cannot execute on the IXP2XXX processor. In practice, this problem is rare, and you can easily work around it by copying one of the variables into a temporary variable before use.

The 256 GPRs per-microengine can be accessed in thread-local or absolute mode. In thread-local mode, each thread accesses a unique set of GPRs. If configured to execute eight threads, a total of 32 GPRs are allocated to each thread—16 A bank GPRs and 16 B bank GPRs. If the microengine is configured to execute four threads, 64 GPRs are allocated to each thread—32 from each bank. In absolute (also called global) mode, a GPR is accessible by any thread on the microengine. Absolute registers are useful for inter-thread communication within a microengine.

Each GPR can be accessed in either an absolute or thread-local manner, as determined at compile-time by the programmer. For example, eight GPRs may be designated as absolute by the programmer and the remaining 248 GPRs are thread-local. Accesses to the absolute and thread-local GPRs can be made within a single microengine program. Indeed, as many instructions only operate on thread-local GPRs, programs often move values from absolute registers into thread-local registers, perform the desired operation, and then move the resulting value from the thread-local register back into the absolute register.

SRAM Transfer Registers

Each microengine has 256, 32-bit SRAM transfer registers. SRAM transfer registers are used to read from and write to all functional units on the IXP2XXX processor except for the DRAM unit. Therefore, SRAM transfer registers are used to read and write data to and from the SRAM unit as well as the SHaC—Scratchpad, Hash and CSR Access Proxy (CAP)—unit, the Media and Switch Fabric (MSF) unit, and Peripheral Components Interconnect (PCI) interfaces.

SRAM transfer registers, and transfer registers in general, are the primary mechanism for dealing with asynchronous memory operations. When data is read from these other functional units, it is placed in SRAM transfer registers, and when microengine code writes data to these units, it must first be placed in transfer registers. Half of these registers are write-only, and the other half are read-only. For example, to write to SRAM, the microengine code must put data in a write-only SRAM transfer register, and to read data from SRAM, the code must read from a read-only SRAM transfer register. Thankfully, the microengine assembler and the microengine C compiler prohibit the programmer from using read-only and write-only transfer registers improperly. However, you can still get confused when dealing with the read-only and write-only distinction of transfer registers. When reading microengine assembly code, be sure to remember that read and write transfer registers can share the same names. Writing to the register name places the data into the write-only transfer register; reading from the register gets the data from the read-only transfer register. The following example illustrates a trap we have fallen into numerous times:

```
// Setup a value to write into memory
.reg $my_xfer_reg // Declares both a read and write xfer

// First, set bit 31 in the write xfer
alu_shf[$my_xfer_reg, --, B, 1, <<31]

// Second, OR in the context number into bits 2 - 0.
alu[$my_xfer_reg, $my_xfer_reg, OR, ctx] // Wrong!
```

But this code is wrong! The first alu_shf instruction modifies the *write* transfer register called my_xfer_reg. However, the second instruction logically ORs the context number with the *read* transfer register and places the results into the write transfer register. One correct way to write this piece of code would be with a GPR, as follows:

```
.reg $my_xfer_reg temp // Declares both an xfer and GPR

// Setup a value to write into memory
alu_shf[temp, --, B, 1, <<31] // Write into the GPR
alu[$my_xfer_reg, temp, OR, ctx] // OR with the GPR
```

Like GPRs, when transfer registers are accessed in a thread-local manner, each thread accesses an equal, unique, set of these registers. SRAM transfer registers can also be addressed globally, through an indirect register. Microengine threads can access any transfer register by number as follows: the T_INDEX register is first loaded with the transfer register number to access—between 0 and 127.[2] Then, the pseudo-register *$index is used to access the SRAM transfer register indicated by the T_INDEX register.

Only one T_INDEX register exists per microengine. This fact has several implications. First, the T_INDEX register simultaneously refers to four different transfer registers: an SRAM read-only, an SRAM write-only, a DRAM read-only, and a DRAM write-only. Second, because any thread can modify the T_INDEX register, threads should reload this register with the desired value before accessing it and after every context switch. Finally, threads should be careful to not inadvertently access other

---

[2] If you are wondering how there can be 256 SRAM transfer registers and only 128 numbers, recall that the SRAM transfer registers are split into 128 read-only and 128 write-only registers. So, to identify an SRAM transfer register, the hardware needs to know whether it is read-only or write-only, and the register number between 0 and 127.

thread's transfer registers. A T_INDEX value of zero indicates the first transfer register in the global set, not the first transfer register local to the current thread.

The advantage of having separate transfer and general-purpose registers is that the microengine can continue processing with GPRs while other functional units of the IXP2XXX processor read and write the transfer registers. Later chapters explore this capability in more detail.

DRAM Transfer Registers

Each microengine has 256, 32-bit DRAM transfer registers divided equally into read-only and write-only. DRAM transfer registers are used for communication between the microengines and the DRAM unit and can be used for read-only communications with the other hardware unit. In other words, DRAM read transfer registers can be used in place of SRAM read transfer registers, however, this is not true for DRAM write transfer registers.

Like SRAM transfer registers, DRAM transfer registers can be accessed in thread-local and indirect global manners. Thread-local access to DRAM transfer registers uses the syntax $$reg_name. The T_INDEX register can be used to access these registers in an indirect global manner using the psuedo-register *$$index.

Next-neighbor Registers

Each microengine has 128, 32-bit next-neighbor registers. These registers can be used in one of two modes. The first mode makes data written in these registers available in the next microengine, numerically, as shown in Figure 2.3. In this mode, if code on microengine 0 writes into a next-neighbor register, code on microengine 1 can read the data from its next-neighbor register, and so on, except for the first and last microengines, which have no previous and next neighbors, respectively.

In the second mode, these registers are used as extra GPRs. Data written into a next-neighbor register is read back by the same microengine, however, you must account for a delay (16 clock cycles) between the time data is written and when it is available to be read.

Two CSRs in each microengine allow the code to treat the next-neighbor registers as a 128-entry queue when they are configured in the first mode. These CSRs are NN_GET and NN_PUT and can be used as the consumer and producer indexes into the array of 128 next-neighbor registers. A pair of status signals helps microengine code treat these registers as a queue. When NN_GET for the current microengine and NN_PUT for the previous microengine are equal, the NN_EMPTY signal is asserted.

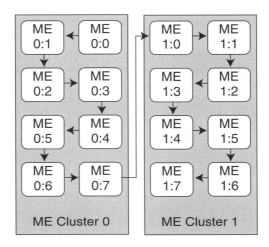

Figure 2.3 IXP2XXX Next-Neighbor Register Connectivity

And when NN_PUT for the current microengine minus NN_GET for the next microengine is 96 or more, the NN_FULL signal is asserted. The NN_FULL signal asserts before the queue is actually full (i.e., when the queue is 3/4 full) because it takes a few cycles for it to actually assert. This early signal helps to avoid a race condition where the queue is actually full, but the indication has not yet propagated into the microengine's status registers.

Note You might be worried that the unidirectional nature of next-neighbor registers limits how you can program the IXP2XXX processor, but that is not the case. Next-neighbor registers are only one of many inter-microengine communication mechanisms, and so they do not constrain your code to running sequentially on all 16 (or 8) microengines. Next-neighbor registers are useful when two context pipeline stages (Chapter 8) are communicating, but should not be used for all inter-microengine communications.

Generalized Thread Signaling

Each microengine thread has 15 numbered signals. Most accesses to functional units outside of the microengine can cause a signal represented by any one of these signal numbers. Some functional unit accesses, like DRAM, generate two signals, represented with consecutive signal numbers. The signal number corresponding to the signal generated for any functional unit access is under the programmer's control.

A microengine thread can test for the presence or absence of any of these signals, which can be used to control execution flow by branching on the signal presence or by specifying to the thread arbiter that a microengine thread is ready to run only after the signal is received.

For example, when reading a value from SRAM memory, the programmer specifies both the address to read from and a signal to send to the requesting thread when the read operation is complete. The following pseudocode illustrates this concept.

```
// Read SRAM at address addr into variable x. x is not
// valid until the signal, signal1, is received
SRAM(read, x, addr, signal1);

// Do other work, but do not use x!
wait_for_signal(signal1);

// Now x is valid and can be used
```

In the example code, the programmer requests a read of SRAM memory and specifies that the value at the given address (addr) should be stored in a particular transfer register (x). This instruction, however, does not block the microengine thread while the memory is read. Instead, the programmer specifies a signal (signal1) to be sent to the microengine when the read is complete. Before the programmer can safely use the value in x, this signal must be presented to the microengine thread by the SRAM controller.

Decoupling signals from functional units is beneficial because software can have multiple outstanding references to the same unit and can wait for all of them to complete using different signals. The following pseudocode illustrates this idea.

```
SRAM(read, x, addr, signal1);
// Other work here, but do not use x

SRAM(read, y, addr, signal2);
// Other work here, but do not use x or y

Wait for signal(signal1);
// Other work here, can use x, but do not use y

Wait for signal(signal2);
// Can use both x and y here
```

The ability to wait on multiple signals is also a big help in cases where multiple signals are outstanding.

IXP1200
Note

IXP1200 programmers, especially, should appreciate these properties of generalized thread signaling. In the IXP1200, each functional unit generated its own signal, and each signal had to be waited on separately. On the IXP2XXX processors, any functional unit can generate any signal.

The non-preemptive threading, along with generalized thread signals, makes it possible for microengine threads to deal with memory and other functional units asynchronously. A microengine thread can choose to explicitly release control of the microengine while, say, waiting for a memory operation; it can also choose not to release control. For example, a microengine thread issues a memory read request and then continues any processing that does not rely on the result of the memory read. In this case, the processing is occurring simultaneously with the memory access, hiding some, or all, of the memory access time.

Alternatively, while a thread is accessing memory—an operation that can take tens or hundreds of cycles—the thread can swap out and allow another thread to run while waiting for the memory access to complete. This thread swap helps to hide the memory access time and maximizes the work the microengine is doing, as shown in Figure 2.4. In this figure, the completion of each memory read request is reported back to the microengine thread using thread signals, and the thread arbiter uses these signals to determine which threads are ready to run.

Asynchronous memory access is a key differentiator between microengines and most general-purpose processors and is covered a lot throughout the book.

Local Memory

Each microengine has 640 long-words of local memory. Data in this memory can be accessed by any thread in the microengine with at most a 3-clock-cycle latency, much faster than the scratchpad, SRAM, or DRAM memory discussed in the next section. To read or write local memory, one of two microengine-local, per-thread, CSRs—lm_addr_0 or lm_addr_1–is written with the address of the memory location, then three clock cycles later the local memory location can be used as a source or destination register. This extra step—first loading one of the

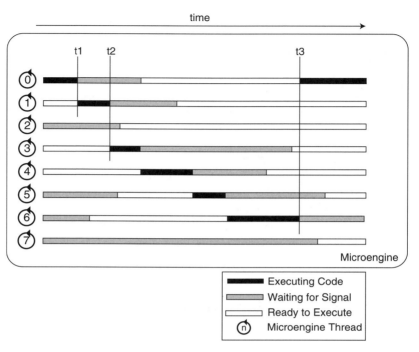

Figure legend:
- ■ Executing Code
- ▨ Waiting for Signal
- □ Ready to Execute
- ⓝ Microengine Thread

This diagram shows a timeline of thread activity on one microengine. At the beginning of the timeline, thread 0 is running code, and the other threads are either waiting for responses from other hardware units or ready to run. At the time marked t1, thread 0 issues a memory read and explicitly releases control of the microengine to wait for that memory access to complete. At the same time, the arbiter determines that the next thread, thread 1, is ready to run and starts it running. At the time marked t2, thread 1 issues a memory access and explicitly releases control of the microengine to wait for that memory access to complete. The arbiter then tries to run thread 2, but thread 2 is waiting for an I/O access that hasn't been completed. So the scheduler runs thread 3, since it is ready to run. This round-robin scheme continues through all eight threads concluding at the time t3 when thread 6 issues a memory reference and explicitly releases control of the microengine. The arbiter then runs thread 0 because it is the next ready thread.

Figure 2.4 Sample Timing Diagram for Microengine Threads

local memory address registers—may seem confusing at first, but the following example pseudocode should help make local memory access clear:

```
// Read local memory address 8, and write addr 32
lm_addr_0 = 8;
lm_addr_1 = 32;

// Wait lm address registers to update,
// could do other work
nop;
nop;

val = read_local_mem_addr_0(); // Read addr 8
write_local_mem_addr_1(7); // Write addr 32 with value 5
```

When accessing local memory, the lm_addr_0 and lm_addr_1 CSRs can be post-incremented or post-decremented. This feature is handy for sequentially traversing data structures placed in local memory. Additionally, these CSRs can be used with a compile-time offset in the range 0 to 15, which enables local memory to be accessed like an array of up to 16 32-bit elements, as shown in the following pseudocode:

```
// Load one of the address registers
lm_addr_0 = 0;

// Access local memory like an array of 16 32-bit
// elements
lm_addr_0[4] = 5 + lm_addr_0[8];
```

When using local memory with offsets, you can only use constant offsets, thus, lm_addr_0[i] is not legal. The offset value is logically ORed with the value of the address register and so you must be careful with the alignment of the value in the address register. For example, if you use offsets up to 15, the value in the address register must be a multiple of 64.

Unlike the T_INDEX register, the local memory address registers are per-thread. In other words, each thread can access two of sixteen total local memory address registers. If your application requires it, the microengine can be configured so that all threads access the same two local memory address registers.

Content-addressable Memory

In addition to local memory, each microengine contains content-addressable memory (CAM). As shown in Figure 2.5, the CAM is an array of 16 entries. Each entry has a 32-bit tag and a 4-bit state.

A CAM_LOOKUP instruction takes a tag value as input and returns a 9-bit return value. When CAM_LOOKUP is executed, the specified tag value is compared with all 16 tag values in the array. If the specified tag value matches one of these stored tags, the 9-bit return value uses one bit to indicate a hit, four bits for the state from the CAM entry, and four bits to indicate which CAM entry matched. The state bits are controlled by

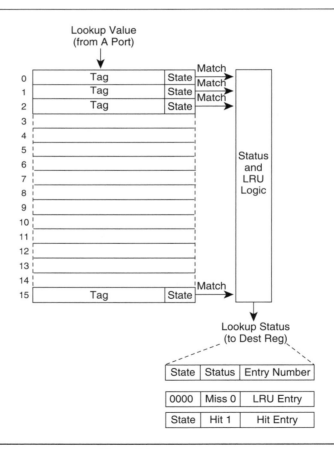

Figure 2.5 MEv2 Content-addressable Memory

software. When an entry is added to the CAM, the state bits are provided by the software as part of the instruction itself. When an entry is matched on a lookup, the interpretation of the state bits is under software control.

If the specified tag does not match any of the stored tag values, only 5 bits of the return value are useful: one to indicate a CAM miss, and four to indicate the Least Recently Used (LRU) CAM entry. A CAM entry is "used" when a lookup matches it, or when it is written using CAM_WRITE.

The CAM is a great way to implement a cache. In fact, the combination of the local memory and the CAM can provide the storage and control structures for a cache. The CAM can also be used for a locking mechanism similar to the mechanism that existed in the SRAM unit on the IXP12XX. However, only locking between threads on a single microengine is possible with the IXP2XXX CAM.

Cyclic Redundancy Check Calculations

Cyclic Redundancy Check (CRC) calculations on the microengine are possible using the CRC unit and CRC_remainder register. To compute a CRC, first, the CRC_remainder register is initialized. The initial value is either zero or the remainder saved from a previous partial calculation. Next, the CRC unit is provided with a 32-bit input value, either from a GPR, transfer register, or local memory. The CRC unit then uses this input and the current CRC_remainder register to compute the new CRC value. The result is stored in the CRC_remainder register. In effect, a CRC is computed over a stream of data fed to the CRC unit 32-bits at a time.

Only one CRC_remainder register exists in each microengine. Much like the T_INDEX register, the implication is multiple threads must ensure the register is loaded and stored after any context switch operation because another thread may have modified the register.

IXP1200
Note

The CRC hardware has moved from the SDRAM unit into each microengine. CRCs can be calculated over any data available to the microengine, not just DRAM data. In addition, different microengines can compute different CRCs simultaneously.

Other Functional Units

In addition to the microengines and the Intel XScale core, Figure 2.1 shows five other functional unit types on the IXP2XXX processor. The SRAM and DRAM units, or controllers, provide access to different external memory types. The Peripheral Components Interconnect (PCI) unit provides an interface to an external industry-standard PCI bus, like those found in all personal computers today. The Media Switch Fabric provides access to a high-speed external data bus where packets come and go. The SHaC unit has a small amount of on-chip SRAM memory, called scratchpad memory, chip-wide control status registers, and a hash generator. The IXP2850 processor contains two cryptography ("crypto") units. Each one capable of performing bulk encryption and decryption as well as keyed message digests.

Memory Interfaces and Types

The IXP2XXX processor can access four different memory types: local memory, scratchpad, SRAM, and DRAM. Local memory can only be accessed by a single microengine whereas the other memory interfaces are shared by all microengines as well as the Intel XScale core processor. Table 2.2 shows the tradeoffs of each memory in terms of size, latency, logical width, and special operations. Local memory, discussed previously, has the smallest size with the lowest latency available on the IXP2XXX processor. Of the shared memories, scratchpad has the smallest size, with the lowest latency. DRAM is the largest memory interface, with the highest latency and is optimized for bulk sequential accesses. The SRAM memory interface takes the middle ground between scratchpad and DRAM in both size and latency.

Each memory type implements a unique set of special operations summarized in the final column of Table 2.2. Most of the special operations are targeted at managing multithreading in the microengines. Thus, like any multithreaded programming, synchronization primitives and atomic operations are key to programming the microengines. Synchronization mechanisms, such as the atomic test operations provided by the scratchpad and SRAM units, allow multiple threads to coordinate access to shared data structures.

Table 2.2 The Properties of the Four IXP2XXX Processor Memories

Memory	Logical width in bytes	Size in bytes – IXP2800/ IXP2400	Approx. unloaded latency in clks (IXP2800/ IXP2400)	Special Operations
Local Memory	4	2560/2560 (per-microengine)	3	Indexed addressing with post increment and decrement.
Scratchpad	4	16K/16K (on-chip)	60/60	Atomic operations including atomic subtract. 16 rings, with atomic get and put operations.
SRAM (QDR)	4	256M/128M (addressable, 64MB per-channel)	150/90	Atomic operations, excluding atomic subtract. 64-element queue array, with atomic enqueue, dequeue, get and put operations.
DRAM (Rambus/DDR)	8	2G/1G* (addressable, 1 GB per-channel)	300/120	Direct path to and from the MSF, which allows data to be moved between the two without first going through one of the processors.

The IXP2400 can address 2 gigabytes of DRAM memory, but the single DRAM channel can only be populated with 1 gigabyte of memory. The IXP2800 can address 2 gigabytes of DRAM memory, and each of the three channels can be populated with 1 gigabyte of memory. Thus, it is not possible to populate all three channels of the IXP2800 DRAM controllers to their maximum extent and simultaneously access all the resulting memory.

Scratchpad

Scratchpad memory is 16 kilobytes of on-chip memory. Scratchpad provides a small, low-latency memory interface to all of the microengines. Scratchpad memory is physically located within the SHaC, but that fact is usually interesting only to people who worry about transistor counts and power consumption.

Note

> Sometimes, the fact that scratchpad physically resides in the SHaC might be an issue. Because the SHaC is responsible for other tasks, adding a large number of scratchpad accesses to the SHaC's workload might deteriorate overall system performance.

In addition to random-access reads and writes, scratchpad also provides atomic operations for bit-test-and-set, bit-test-and-clear, bit-test, bit-clear, add, subtract, test-and-add, test-and-clear, swap, increment, and decrement. These operations are ideal for keeping counters across multiple microengine threads as well as synchronizing access to data structures across microengines. Also, the scratchpad unit supports 16 rings, each of which supports atomic put and get operations.

SRAM

Unlike scratchpad memory, SRAM is off-chip. The IXP2XXX processor only provides an interface to quad-data rate (QDR) SRAM memory. This interface is embodied in the SRAM unit. Each SRAM unit—two exist on the IXP2400 and four exist on the IXP2800 and IXP2850—provides an interface for up to 64 megabytes of medium-latency memory. Each unit is addressed in a non-overlapping fashion. For example, assume each SRAM channel is populated with 2 megabytes of memory. The addresses 0x00000000 through 0x3FFFFFFF would access the first SRAM unit, the addresses 0x40000000 through 0x7FFFFFFF would access the second SRAM unit, and so on. No single access may cross an SRAM address boundary.

The SRAM unit provides the same atomic operations as the scratchpad unit, with the exception of atomic subtract and test-and-subtract, which the SRAM unit does not support. In addition, each SRAM unit contains a 64-element queue array. Each queue array element can be configured as a queue or ring. (For more information on queues and rings, see Chapter 10.) Atomic enqueue and dequeue (put and get) operations are supported on each queue (ring). Chapter 10 contains detailed information and examples of how to use both scratchpad rings as well as SRAM queue arrays.

DRAM

Like SRAM memory, DRAM memory is external to the IXP2XXX processor. Each DRAM unit—one exists on the IXP2400 and three on the IXPP2800—provides an interface for up to one gigabyte of high-throughput memory (Rambus DRAM on the IXP2800 and IXP2850 and double-data rate DRAM on the IXP2400). The DRAM unit does not accommodate the atomic bit operations like scratchpad and SRAM. Instead, the DRAM unit's unique functionality lies in the ability to move data to and from the MSF unit without the data going through the microengines. For those of us writing software, this feature means one less thing to write and debug, one less bus transfer, and more time for the microengines to be performing other useful work.

On the IXP2800 when multiple DRAM units are populated with memory, the hardware stripes, or interleaves, the DRAM addresses across the available memory. This interleaving helps balance the load placed on each bank of memory. The hardware performs this interleaving automatically and the software rarely, if ever, needs to be aware of it.

Logical Width

While all of the memory interfaces on the IXP2XXX processor use byte addresses, it is not possible to read or write any arbitrary byte in memory. Rather, each memory has a logical width that determines the minimum number of bytes that are accessed during any memory operation. All accesses to a particular memory type must be aligned to the memory's logical width. You must understand these logical widths because they are not hidden by the assembler or compiler. In fact, the hardware controller for any particular memory accepts byte addresses, but then simply masks off some number of the least-significant bits in the address before performing the requested memory operation.

The logical width of local memory, scratchpad, and SRAM is 32 bits, or 4 bytes, of data. So, only byte addresses 0, 4, 8, etc. make sense when accessing these memories. DRAM's logical width is 64 bits, or 8 bytes, of data, and hence only byte addresses of 0, 8, 16, etc. make sense when accessing DRAM. In addition two, 32-bit transfer registers are required to read (write) data from (to) a single DRAM address.

For example, consider trying to read the destination Internet protocol (IP) address (DIP) of an IP packet encapsulated in an Ethernet II frame. Remember that DRAM has a direct connection to the MSF, so packet data is placed in DRAM memory. Figure 2.6 shows such a frame in DRAM memory along with the logical width boundaries of the memory. The DIP, a 4-byte quantity, spans a logical width boundary. Therefore, two DRAM reads are needed to get the DIP: one read for the quad-word starting at byte address 0, and a second for the quad-word starting at byte address 4. Each read requires two registers, for a total of four, 32-bit registers needed to get the 32-bits desired.

On the positive side, these two memory reads can be combined into one instruction, and extracting the final destination IP address from the 4 transfer registers can be accomplished in two alu instructions. Chapter 6 shows how to design data structures and code that deal with the logical memory widths of the IXP2XXX memory.

Memory Command Queues

As discussed earlier, the microengine threads are non-preemptive. The active thread on any microengine is responsible for releasing control of the microengine. This control means software can be written that

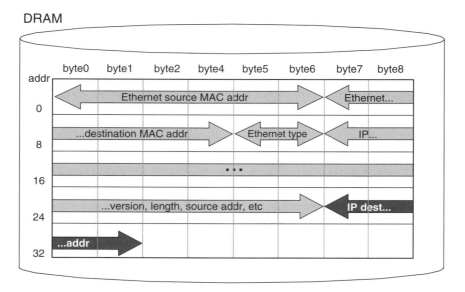

To read the destination IP address from an Ethernet II frame carrying an IP packet in DRAM requires 2, 8-byte reads because of the logical width of the memory.

Figure 2.6 The Effects of Logical Memory Widths on Microengine Code

allows hiding memory latencies by issuing read, write, and other special commands on the memory interfaces and then continuing to perform work while the memory interface services the command. Now this memory-latency-hiding thing is cool, but it gets even better. Each of the three shared-memory interfaces queues incoming command requests, and nothing prevents a single microengine thread from having multiple requests outstanding in one of these queues.

For example, microengine assembly can be written that initiates a packet transfer from the MSF into DRAM, reads that same packet data from the MSF into registers in the microengine so the packet header can be processed, and increments a global packet counter in scratchpad memory, all at the same time. Now imagine performing these operations in parallel across many microengine threads and some of the unique programming opportunities of the IXP2XXX processor start to emerge.

Media Switch Fabric Unit

The MSF is the programmer's interface for data movement into and out of the IXP2XXX processor. Packet reception and transmission on the IXP2XXX processor is a unique, complex act of reassembling and segmenting small partial-packet data chunks called mpackets. The receive and transmit state machines control the basic processes of receiving and transmitting packets and mpackets on the IXP2XXX processor.

Understanding Mpackets

All data movement into and out of the MSF is in fixed-sized chunks called mpackets. By splitting packets into (potentially) smaller mpackets, the MSF presents the programmer with an interface to the tasks of receiving and transmitting packets that is (mostly) independent of the physical MSF device or packet format.

Receive and transmit mpacket sizes are determined by the receive buffer (RBUF) and transmit buffer (TBUF) sizes, respectively. RBUF and TBUF sizes are independently configurable to 64, 128, and 256 bytes by writing the appropriate MSF CSRs.

IXP1200 Note

The IXP1200 has 64-byte RFIFOs and TFIFOs; however, the RBUF and TBUF size in the IXP2XXX MSF can be configured to be 64, 128, or 256 bytes. In fact, the RBUF size can be configured independently from the TBUF size on the IXP2XXX processor.

The receive and transmit tasks can be made more efficient by configuring the RBUF and TBUF sizes to suit the physical interface. For example, the RBUF and TBUF sizes can be matched with the average or maximum physical packet size to avoid reassembly and segmentation in many cases.

When the physical media frames carry packets larger than an mpacket, the microengines must reassemble incoming mpackets back into complete packets. Similarly, the microengines must segment outgoing packets into mpackets before the MSF can transmit them.

So how do the microengines know whether an incoming mpacket represents the start of a new packet or the continuation of a previous packet? And how does the MSF know the same information for outgoing mpackets? The answer is that each mpacket is identified as the start of the packet (SOP), the end of packet (EOP), both, or neither.

Figure 2.7 shows examples of how the MSF breaks incoming packets into mpackets. In this figure, the MSF has been configured to use 64-byte RBUFs. In the first example, the MSF receives a 64-byte packet that is placed entirely in one mpacket. In this case, the mpacket is both the start and end of the packet, so the MSF marks it SOP and EOP. In the

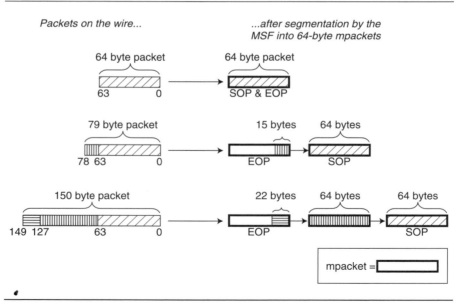

Figure 2.7 Examples of 64-byte Mpacket Segmentation

second example, the MSF receives a 79-byte packet that is segmented into two mpackets. The first mpacket contains the first 64 bytes of data and is marked SOP. The second mpacket contains the last 15 bytes of the packet and is marked EOP. Finally, for a 150-byte packet, three mpackets are produced. The first mpacket, marked SOP, contains the first 64 bytes of packet data. The second mpacket, not marked SOP or EOP, contains the next 64 bytes of packet data, and finally the last mpacket, marked EOP, contains the last 22 bytes of packet data.

For outgoing mpackets, the microengines perform an analogous marking of mpackets as SOP, EOP, both, or neither so that the MSF can properly transmit the packet.

The Receive State Machine

Receiving packets using the MSF interface is done through an array of RBUF elements, which are very much like the RFIFO elements in the IXP12XX processors. The RBUF holds 8 kilobytes of data.

Besides the RBUF elements, the MSF interface has two internal data structures that control the receive process. These data structures are the RX_THREAD_FREELIST and the FULL_ELEMENT_LIST. The RX_THREAD_FREELIST is a list of threads waiting to handle received mpackets, and the FULL_ELEMENT_LIST is a list of mpackets waiting to be handled by threads.

From the software's perspective, receiving an mpacket is done in four easy steps.

1. Put the current thread on the RX_THREAD_FREELIST.

2. Wait for a signal from the MSF interface indicating it has data in a RBUF element.

3. When the MSF interface signals the thread, read the receive-status words (e.g., the SOP, EOP, and error bits) from the thread's transfer registers.

4. Copy the data into memory and notify the MSF interface that you are done with the RBUF element.

Two example packet receptions are shown in Figure 2.8 and Figure 2.9. Figure 2.8 shows what happens when a thread is ready for an mpacket before the mpacket arrives. Figure 2.9 shows what happens when an mpacket arrives before a thread is ready for it.

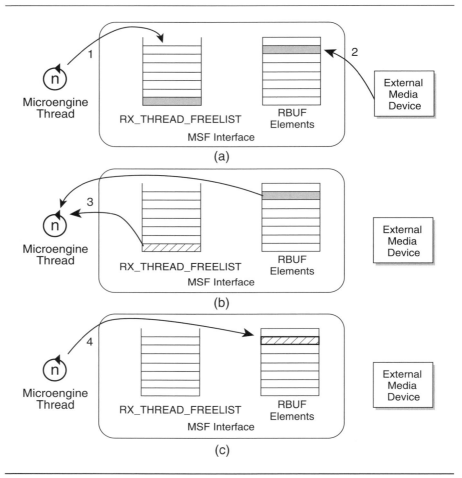

Figure 2.8 Receive Sequence of Steps When Receive Thread is Ready Before Mpacket Arrives

Steps for Figure 2.8 are:

1. When a thread is ready for an mpacket before one arrives, the thread places itself on the RX_THREAD_FREELIST.

2. When an mpacket arrives, the MSF interface puts the mpacket into an RBUF element and writes the Receive-Status Words (RSW) (SOP, EOP, and mpacket status) into transfer registers of the thread in the RX_THREAD_FREELIST.

3. The thread in the RX_THREAD_FREELIST is notified that data is available, and it copies the data from the RBUF element.

4. The thread notifies the MSF interface that it is done with the RBUF element.

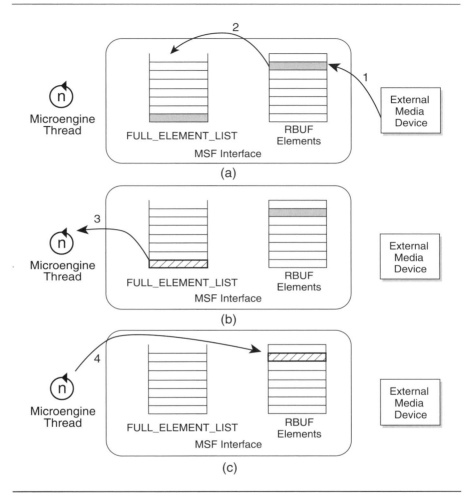

Figure 2.9 Receive Sequence of Steps When the Mpacket Arrives Before a Receive Thread is Ready

When an mpacket arrives before a thread is ready to process it, the steps are a little different as shown in Figure 2.9.

1. The mpacket arrives and the MSF interface puts it into an RBUF element.

2. Because the RX_THREAD_FREELIST (not shown) is empty, the MSF interface puts the RBUF element information on the FULL_ELEMENT_LIST.

3. When a thread is ready to process an mpacket, it attempts to add itself to the RX_THREAD_FREELIST, and the MSF interface instead updates the receive-status words of the thread with the information in the FULL_ELEMENT_LIST and signals the thread that an mpacket is available.

4. After the receive thread has copied the data from the RBUF element, it notifies the MSF interface that it is done with the element.

The Transmit State Machine

In an analogous fashion to receiving packets, transmitting packets uses an array of TBUF elements, which is 8 kilobytes in size. The MSF handles all of the communication between the chip and the MAC devices. The microengine code just has to give data to the MSF in the TBUF elements, and the hardware handles the mpacket transmission from there.

Like the receive task, the transmit task must understand both packets and mpackets. Of course, the transmit task segments packets into mpackets as opposed to reassembling mpackets into packets. In addition, the transmit task must also be concerned with flow-control issues on the transmission link. For example, the transmit task must not under- or over-flow the transmit link.

Each mpacket is placed in a TBUF, which the MSF uses to physically transmit the mpacket. How the MSF uses TBUFs, and, thus, how the microengines must place mpackets into TBUFs, is controlled by the transmit state machine (TSM) within the MSF. Figure 2.10 shows the major components of the TSM.

The TSM maintains a pointer to the TBUF element to be transmitted next. The TSM waits to transmit the current TBUF element until it has been marked valid by the microengines. When the current TBUF element has been marked valid, the TSM examines the TBUF element's control word to determine the port to which the data should be sent. The control word also tells the TSM whether the mpacket contained in the TFIFO element is the start of a packet (SOP), the end of a packet (EOP), both, or neither. It then transmits the data out the proper port with the SOP and EOP lines properly set, marks the TBUF element as invalid, and advances the transmit pointer.

SHaC

In addition to housing scratchpad memory discussed previously, the SHaC also contains logic to interface with Intel XScale core peripherals such as "slow port" memory and external timers, a hash generation unit, and the CAP unit.

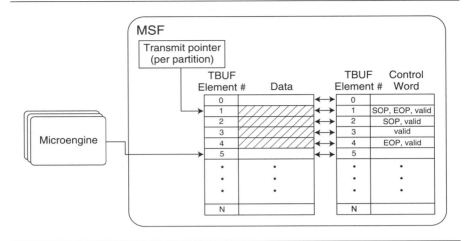

Figure 2.10 The Components of the Transmit State Machine

The hash unit is capable of generating 48-, 64-, and 128-bit hashes from keys of the same sizes. In addition, any single hash request can contain three keys to hash. The hash algorithm parameters are configurable through the CAP.

The CAP unit provides an interface to all of the chip-wide CSRs. In addition, it provides the implementation of inter-thread signals and messages across microengines, a mechanism for the microengines to interrupt the Intel XScale core, as well as a register reflector. The register reflector allows any thread to read or write the SRAM transfer registers of any other thread, including threads on different microengines.

The Crypto Unit

The IXP2850 contains two crypto units, each of which implements the following functionality:

■ Advanced Encryption Standard (AES) and triple Data Encryption Standard (3DES) symmetric-key ciphers for bulk encryption and decryption. Symmetric ciphers are commonly used in both Virtual Private Network (VPN) gateways to ensure the privacy of network packets between, say, a remote employee and the corporate computers, as well as in Transport Layer Security (TLS[3]) for providing privacy for packets containing such information as credit card numbers, passwords, and other personal information.

---

[3] Also known by the earlier, and more common, Secure Sockets Layer (SSL) name.

- Secure Hash Algorithm (SHA-1) for computing a one-way hash function[4] over input data. SHA-1 computes a 160-bit hash of a given input stream with the property that two different input streams almost always produce two different SHA-1 hash values. This property allows one-way hash functions to be combined with private information (e.g., a key) to ensure the integrity (but not the confidentiality) of exchanged information.

- Hashed Message Authentication Code (HMAC) for computing a keyed message digest over input data. An HMAC concatenates some private information (e.g., a key) into the message data before computing some one-way hash over the data. The resulting hash value represents an integrity check for the data because the data cannot be modified in transit without changing the value of the HMAC. The HMAC computation in the IXP2850 crypto unit is part of each SHA-1 hardware block and, thus, the computed HMAC uses the SHA-1 hash function (i.e, the results are the HMAC-SHA1 message digest).

- A checksum accumulator used to compute checksums over any data passing through the crypto unit.

The hardware necessary to achieve the above functionality is shown in Figure 2.11. Command requests (e.g., encrypt data and initialize state information) enter the crypto unit via the command bus into two command queues: a read and a write command queue. The crypto unit removes commands from these queues and processes them. Two separate queues enable the hardware to process commands from one queue while waiting to complete commands from the other queue.

The input for many of the crypto unit's blocks can come from a 128-quadword (1 kilobyte) input RAM. This RAM can be loaded—either from RBUF elements or microengine transfer registers—with information, such as the data to encrypt or decrypt, initialization vectors, shared keys, or other configuration information.

Each crypto unit contains one AES block and two independent 3DES blocks (referred to as the two 'banks' of the crypto unit), which are used for the AES and 3DES ciphers respectively. Each 3DES block has access to three initialization vectors (IVs) and three keys. The AES block has access to six IVs and six keys, which physically are the same resources that supply the IVs and keys for the 3DES blocks. Of course,

---

[4] Sometimes referred to as a message digest

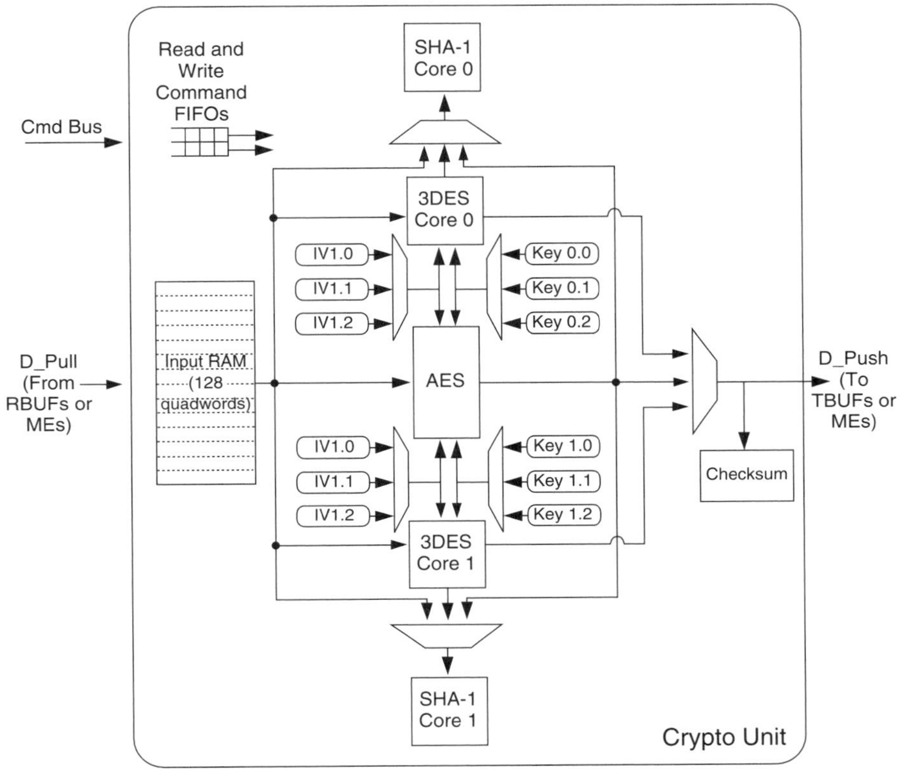

Read and
Write
Command
FIFOs

Cmd Bus

SHA-1
Core 0

3DES
Core 0

IV1.0   Key 0.0
IV1.1   Key 0.1
IV1.2   Key 0.2

D_Pull
(From
RBUFs or
MEs)

Input RAM
(128
quadwords)

AES

IV1.0   Key 1.0
IV1.1   Key 1.1
IV1.2   Key 1.2

3DES
Core 1

SHA-1
Core 1

D_Push
(To
TBUFs or
MEs)

Checksum

Crypto Unit

Figure 2.11 An IXP2850 Crypto Unit

the IVs and keys are different lengths for the different algorithms. The AES block supports 128-bit IVs and keys of length 128, 192 and 256 bits, while the 3DES block supports 64-bit IVs and 192-bit keys (in which every 8th bit is used for parity and is ignored).

Each crypto unit also contains two independent SHA-1 blocks (again on in each bank), used in the computation of SHA-1 hashes and HMACs. These blocks contain internal state registers that can be written by the microengines to initialize the hash operation.

Finally, the crypto unit also contains a checksum unit which maintains independent checksums for data exiting both banks of the crypto unit. These checksums can be read and reset by the microengine software.

The basic operation of the crypto unit is as follows:

1. The microengine initializes the unit, including writing the SHA-1 state, resetting checksums, writing IVs and keys from microengine transfer registers. Both the IVs and keys can also first be written into input RAM and then written into the IV and key registers.

2. The microengine transfers data to encrypt, decrypt, or hash from either RBUF elements or transfer registers into input RAM.

3. The microengine issues the appropriate encrypt, decrypt, or hash command referencing the previously-established input RAM address. When specifying the command, the algorithm (i.e., AES, 3DES, SHA-1 or HMAC) and the bank (i.e., 0 or 1 for 3DES and SHA-1) are provided, as well as the resulting location of the operation (e.g., write to TBUF elements or microengine transfer registers)

Furthermore, given the multiple banks of each crypto unit, multiple commands can be issued to the crypto unit simultaneously, thus improving the throughput of the application.

Chapter 11 provides a simple example of using the crypto units of the IXP2850, but nowhere in this book do we attempt to cover the basics of cryptography or its network-specific applications. See *Applied Cryptography* (Schneier 1996) for more information on cryptography.

Clusters and Buses

As you can see in Figure 2.1, the microengines are grouped into clusters. The IXP2400 has two clusters of four microengines each and the IXP2800 has two clusters of eight microengines each. Each cluster gets an independent command bus and SRAM bus, and all clusters share the same DRAM bus. Although clusters do not affect how you write code, they might affect how you allocate the microengines to specific tasks. For example, if you dedicate two microengines to tasks that are heavy on SRAM references, you might decide to put them on separate clusters to better use the bandwidth of the buses between the microengine clusters and the SRAM controllers.

A day in the life of a packet

So now that you have read through the description of the IXP2XXX hardware, if you still can't explain how a packet enters and leaves the IXP2XXX processor, don't worry. From a programmer's perspective, the best way to learn about the IXP2XXX hardware is through an example of the "big picture". This example of a day in the life of a packet examines how a single packet makes its way through the various functional units of the IXP2XXX processor. Nearly every part of the IXP2XXX hardware that programmers care about is covered by following a packet through the hardware.

Figure 2.12 shows the functional units of the IXP2XXX processor with numbers corresponding to the units visited during the packet reception, packet processing, and packet transmission.

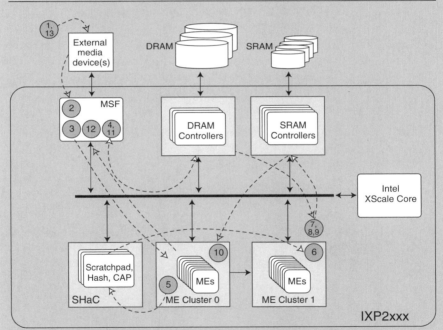

Note: The numbers correspond to the path of a packet through the hardware during packet reception, processing, and transmit.

Figure 2.12 The Functional Units of the IXP2XXX Processor

In the morning: packet reception

1. The packet's day begins when it is received by one of the physical media devices attached to one of the MSF interfaces. A physical media device is a piece of hardware, external to the IXP2XXX processor that converts some physical media type to one of the MSF interface types, such as SPI-4 Phase 2 or CSIX-L1. The physical media types can be anything including Ethernet, Asynchronous Transfer Mode (ATM), and Synchronous Optical Network (SONET).

2. The MSF retrieves the next available RBUF element from the RBUF_ELEMENT_FREELIST and places an mpacket's worth of the data into this RBUF element.

3. The MSF obtains an available thread to service the RBUF from the THREAD_FREELIST. Using the information from the THREAD_FREELIST, the MSF writes the receive status words into the thread's transfer registers and signals the thread.

4. The signaled thread wakes up, reads the receive status information from its transfer registers and moves the mpacket directly from the RBUF element into DRAM memory.

   This four-step process repeats for each mpacket in the packet until done. For more details see Chapter 5.

5. The thread puts a handle to the reassembled packet onto a scratch-pad ring (or SRAM ring or queue) to be processed by another microengine.

The afternoon: packet processing

After the packet has been reassembled into DRAM memory, the microengines, or even the Intel XScale core, can do something with it. The packet processing typically consists of some level of packet classification, followed by packet modification.

1. A microengine thread checks for available packets on a scratchpad ring and finds one available. The thread gets the packet handle from the ring.

2. The packet classification stage begins reading various portions of the packet from DRAM, or RBUF elements, into the microengine's transfer registers. From there, the classification typically makes use of SRAM or scratchpad memory to store tables of moderate size that can be quickly searched. Additionally, the CAM and local memory can be used to cache the packet header or the search tables and the hash unit can be used to index the tables.

3. The packet is modified by overwriting the packet data already in DRAM memory.

   For more details about packet processing, see Chapters 6 through 8.

4. The handle of the modified packet is enqueued on an SRAM queue to be scheduled and transmitted.

The evening: packet transmission

To wrap up the packet's busy day, it must be transmitted out of the IXP2XXX processor. From a high-level perspective, the transmission process is just the reverse of the reception process. The important technical differences between the two processes are covered in later chapters.

1. A microengine thread notices the availability of a packet handle on the SRAM queue and dequeues it.

2. The thread computes the location of the next mpacket into the packet and places it in the next available TBUF element with a direct transfer from DRAM to the MSF.

3. The TBUF element control word is written to indicate the TBUF contains valid data.

   Like the receive process, the transmission process must repeat itself for each mpacket in the outgoing packet. The MSF detects the end of the packet through information contained in the control word supplied by the microengines. For more details, see Chapter 5.

4. Finally, once the MSF receives the EOP mpacket, the external media device transmits the packet, and the IXP2XXX processor is on to the next packet!

Summary

Each processor in the IXP2XXX family of processors has multiple processing units: the Intel XScale core and eight or sixteen microengines (IXP2400 and IXP2800, respectively). The large number of microengines enables highly-parallel packet processing to occur; a topic frequently visited throughout this book and key to the notion of 'extending the processing time of a packet.' The core can be programmed with common tools, standard languages, and can run standard operating systems. The microengines are special-purpose RISC processors with an instruction set tuned to bit, byte, and long-word manipulations of data.

Each microengine supports eight threads of execution. The context switch time between threads on a microengine is minimal because the hardware maintains an equal portion of the register pool for each thread. As you'll see in subsequent chapters, this feature is key to hiding memory latencies in your applications. In addition, the register set is partitioned into GPRs, transfer registers, and next-neighbor registers. Separate transfer registers allow the microengines to continue to compute with GPRs while memory and other functional units are accessed through transfer registers. Next-neighbor registers provide a high-speed communication channel between numerically adjacent microengines.

The IXP2XXX processor provides access to external SRAM memory, DRAM memory, and the external PCI bus through the SRAM, DRAM, and PCI functional units, respectively. The core and microengines can access external memory by issuing read and write commands to the SRAM and DRAM units. SRAM memory is smaller and has lower latency than DRAM memory. Additionally, the SRAM unit supports special commands, such atomic FIFOs, and atomic bit-test-and-set. The DRAM unit supports direct RBUF and TBUF data transfers. The PCI interface allows the core and microengines to initiate DMA transfers across the external PCI bus.

The SHaC houses scratchpad memory, a hashing unit, and system-wide CSRs.

The MSF provides an interface to the external data buses that carry the high-speed packet data from external devices to and from the IXP2XXX processor. The MSF segments packet data into chunks called mpackets. When receiving a packet, individual mpackets are moved from the external devices into RBUFs within the MSF. From there, the RBUF data can be moved into transfer registers in the microengines, or directly into DRAM memory. When transmitting packets, the micro-engines place mpackets into TBUFs and validate the TBUF. Subsequently, the MSFs transmit state machine moves the validated TBUF data to the external device.

For an in-depth discussion of IXA and the IXP2XXX hardware, check out the IXA network architecture book (Carlson 2003). Additionally, if you want to know more about the hardware as it relates to software, or if you just can't get enough information about the number of clocks it takes to flush the pipeline in an aborted class 3 conditional branch, then read the IXP2x00 network processor hardware reference manuals (Intel HRM 2002) available on the accompanying CD-ROM. The HRMs are a reference for all of the hardware details described in this book and a lot more, but are not necessary to understand the rest of this book.

IXP1200
Note

Here we summarize the major differences between the IXP12XX and IXP2XXX hardware:

- An Intel XScale core instead of a StrongARM core.
- Sixteen (or eight) microengines instead of six.
- Eight threads per microengine instead of four.
- More registers (GPRs and transfer), new indirect register access, and new next-neighbor registers.
- Local memory per microengine
- Generalized thread signals
- CRC unit per microengine, but no DRAM-based CRC unit
- CAM per microengine, but no SRAM CAM locks
- Scratchpad rings, SRAM rings, and SRAM queues, but no SRAM LIFOs
- MSF interface instead of FBI, supporting new media interfaces SPI-3, SPI-4, Utopia, and CSIX.
- Configurable RBUF and TBUF sizes (64, 128, 256 bytes) instead of 64-byte RFIFO and TFIFOs.
- New crypto unit on the IXP2850.

Chapter 3

Programming Models and Environment

So you now know a lot (perhaps more than you wanted to!) about the IXP2XXX hardware, but how do you program this hardware? First and foremost, you have to pick a programming model appropriate for your application. A programming model guides your decisions about how and why you use each of the various pieces of the IXP2XXX hardware. Selecting the appropriate programming model involves deciding how to make good use of the available hardware resources, whereas an inappropriate programming model can make development seem like running up hill into a head wind. The first part of this chapter discusses how to think about your application and the different programming models that have proven effective on the IXP2XXX processor.

Once you have selected a model, you probably don't want to start from scratch developing tools and libraries for basic access to the hardware and support for your model. Instead, you'll want to build your application using existing tools and libraries. Fortunately, a programming environment for working with the IXP2XXX processor, called the IXA SDK version 3.0, is available. This SDK includes tools, a framework supporting several effective IXP2XXX programming models, and libraries for developing code. We'll also cover the IXA SDK 3.0 in this chapter so you will have a general understanding of it and its application.

Building an Application: Understanding the IXP2XXX Programming Models

Consider the receive-process-transmit paradigm for network applications shown in Figure 3.1. This remarkably simple model is not only conceptually easy to grasp, but also represents a natural way to think about network software. Whether you are building a basic bridging application or a complete intrusion detection system, you can (and should) think about your application using this model as it helps put the pieces of the application into perspective. And, not surprisingly, this model applies to programming the IXP2XXX processor as well.

In the figure, the receive, process, and transmit tasks are shown running on the different IXP2XXX processors (microengines and the Intel Xscale core) with queues (or rings, see Chapter 10) between them. The queues pass packets, or, more accurately, packet handles, between these tasks. So, after the receive code reassembles an incoming packet, it places a handle to the packet onto its outgoing ring. The process task(s) then consume packet handles from this ring, do something interesting to the packet like filtering or address and protocol translation, and eventually place packet handles onto its outgoing ring. Finally, the transmit task consumes packets from its ring, segments the packets and instructs the hardware to transmit them.

This simple model is remarkably versatile. Once the basic receive and transmit drivers are written, you can build any network application by writing the appropriate packet processing code. For many applications, the receive and transmit drivers that come with Intel IXA SDK 3.0 are perfectly appropriate.

Of course, writing the packet processing code takes work. In particular, the questions of how to structure the packet processing code and map it onto the available processors, memory, and hardware accelerators have to be answered. And the answers to these questions help

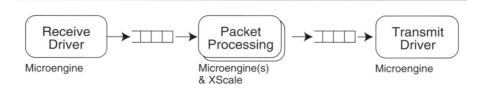

Figure 3.1 The Basic Structure of Receiving, Processing, and Transmitting Packets on the IXP2XXX processor

determine your programming model and depend on the characteristics of the application.

Mapping Code to Processing Resources

On the IXP2XXX processor, the first decision in your application design is the division of work between microengines and the Intel XScale core. Typically, the microengines handle all, or most, of the per-packet processing. The Intel XScale core typically handles infrequently-arriving packet types that require more complicated processing, such as control and configuration packets, or packets requiring lengthy processing like IP packets with options. It also corrects erroneous conditions, such as sending out ICMP destination unreachable packets, and provides configuration and management access for the entire application, including those functions executing on the microengines.

This final point is particularly important to remember. Very few network applications are useful that cannot be managed or configured. When thinking about functions mapped onto the microengines, don't forget to consider the corresponding management and configuration code necessary on the Intel XScale core.

Once you have decided on the partitioning between Intel XScale core and microengines, choosing how to utilize the microengines should come next. Depending on your background, you may see the microengines as a series of sequential processing functions or a pool of parallel processing functions as shown in Figure 3.2 (a) and (b), respectively.

In Figure 3.2 (a), the application is split into a series of sequential functions, which are then mapped onto different microengines. Packets pass through every function, and hence every microengine (possibly using next-neighbor registers on the IXP2XXX processor). Such a sequential model is good for applications that are fairly uniform in their treatment of packets, as each packet passes through the same functions. In addition, each function has complete command of the microengine resources (e.g., registers, CAM, local memory, etc.), which can prove advantageous in the function's design and implementation.

Alternatively, Figure 3.2 (b) shows a different model where all of the functions in the application are implemented on a single microengine, but multiple microengines execute this application code. Packets are distributed to any of the microengines to be processed and eventually transmitted. This "pool-of-microengines" approach is good for applications that both fit within the instruction store of a single microengine and are highly-parallel in nature. Co-locating functions on the same

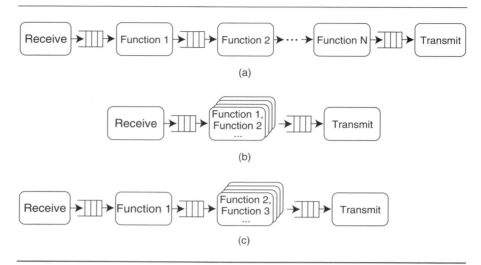

Figure 3.2 Different Usage Models of Packet Processing on the Microengines

microengine is advantageous when those functions need to share state or require synchronization.

However, realistically, your application won't fit either of these models exactly. Instead, most applications require a hybrid approach as shown in Figure 3.2 (c). For functions that require the full resources of a microengine and through which most, or many, packets pass, a sequential model works best. Similarly, for functions that are smaller and can be easily co-located, a pool-of-microengines should be used. Each of these approaches can be combined with rings of queues, such as those supported by the IXP2XXX hardware.

Mapping Data Structures to Memory Types

Once you have mapped your application to the various IXP2XXX processors, the next important design consideration is memory utilization. For each data structure, such as packet buffers, tables for packet processing operations, statistics, configuration and management structures, you must decide in which type of memory it should be stored. This decision should take into account any natural affinity of some data structures to a memory type, the sizes of the memory types, and finally the accessibility of the memory types to both the microengines and the Intel XScale core, as explained in the following list.

- *Natural affinity*: Often, the usage of the data structure identifies a natural affinity for one of the memory types. For example, nearly every application stores packet data in DRAM because RBUF and TBUF data can be transferred directly to and from DRAM memory. Additionally, statistics are typically not maintained in DRAM because both the SRAM and scratchpad memory controllers support atomic increment, decrement, add, and subtract operations that make maintenance of statistics a snap. Finally, don't forget about local memory! While relatively small, local memory is very fast, making it an excellent choice for state information passed between two functions on the same microengine, as well as the most frequently used entries in some larger data structure.

  Natural affinity of a data structure for a memory type may also come in the form of sizes of fields within the data structure. If you have a lot of 32-bit or smaller fields in a particular data structure, DRAM memory is less appropriate due to its 64-bit width. Optionally, you should consider padding data structures to fit the final choice of memory type to make address calculations easier and faster.

- *Memory sizes*: Once you map data structures with natural affinities to their appropriate memory types, consider the maximum size of any remaining data structures. Do you need to support one million flows? Then you certainly won't be able to store all of the per-flow data structure in local memory, and you probably won't be able to use scratchpad for the same reason. SRAM or DRAM would be better choices for storing such data structures.

- *Accessibility of memory*: Finally, be sure to consider interactions between microengines and the Intel XScale core. Data stored in local memory, for example, won't be easily available to the XScale core. Also, any fields in a data structure written by both the microengines and the Intel XScale core usually require some form of synchronization. Often, rearranging your data structures around the logical width of the memory type can eliminate the need for such synchronization.

Utilizing Hardware Accelerators

When determining the usage of the IXP2XXX hardware for your application, think about which of the hardware accelerators to use. What types of rings or queues are appropriate between the various functions? Will you use the hash, CRC, and CAM accelerators anywhere within the design?

Note	We have probably now generated more questions than answers regarding the choice of programming models. But don't worry, the rest of this book provides many examples of the different options available. Regardless of your choice of model, however, you do have a framework to support your development as explained in the next section.

Intel® IXA Portability Framework

The Intel IXA Portability Framework provides an excellent way to develop code on the IXP2XXX processor by eliminating the need to create common infrastructure code, like microengine and Intel XScale communications, and by defining modular building blocks for the microengines and Intel XScale core. The Intel IXA Portability Framework consists of libraries and infrastructure code for developing packet-processing code (microengine and Intel XScale core) and for interfacing this code to a control plane, as shown in Figure 3.3.

The following sections describe the components of the Intel IXA Portability Framework in detail.

Microblocks and Core Components

An important part of the Intel IXA Portability Framework is a modular building block architecture for developing both microengine and Intel XScale core code. The microengine building blocks are called microblocks, and the Intel XScale core building blocks are called core components.

Each building block represents a unit of packet-processing functionality. Examples include IPv4 unicast routing, Ethernet bridging, and network address translation (NAT). Intel provides some "driver" building blocks for receiving and transmitting packets and for queue management. Developers create and chain building blocks together, in both

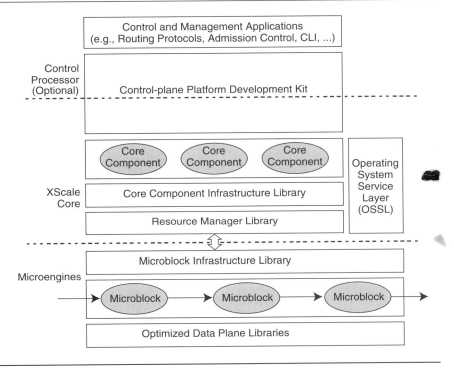

Figure 3.3 The IXA Portability Framework

sequential, "pooled" and hybrid manners, to form an application. For example, Figure 3.4 shows a simple NAT application built using building blocks. Notice the basic receive-process-and-transmit model, with three sequential process functions, as well as the use of both the Intel XScale core and the microengines. The Intel XScale core processes so-called exception packets and performs table management and configuration. Exception packets might be control-plane-related, such as routing update messages, or data-plane-related that require extra processing, such as an IP packet with options. In this scenario, microblocks and core components coordinate to enable the entire application to function.

The focus of this book is on programming the microengines, and to a lesser extent, programming the Intel Xscale core. So we'll dive into more details of microblocks and core components in subsequent chapters. But first, to complete the big picture, the control-plane interface needs a bit of explanation.

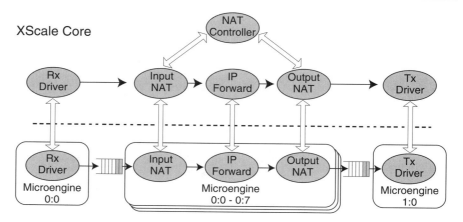

This figure shows a NAT application implemented using pairs of microblocks and core components. In this example, most of the packets are processed in the microengines, with occasional control packets or packets that need additional processing going to a core component. The core components can also contain additional communication mechanisms, as shown by the NAT controller.

Figure 3.4 A Sample NAT Application Built from Microblocks and Core Components

Control Plane Platform Development Kit

The Intel IXA Portability Framework includes the control-plane platform development kit (CP-PDK). The CP-PDK is a standards-compliant library for interfacing the data-plane code written for the IXP2XXX processor with a control-plane. In this context, control-plane code includes functionality like routing protocols and command-line interfaces for configuration and management. Data-plane code, as explain above, includes the actual packet processing (both within the microengines and on the Intel XScale core-components).

From a control-plane perspective, the CP-PDK implements APIs that are specified by the Network Processing Forum (NPF). For more details see the NPF web site (listed in References). From the data-plane perspective, the CP-PDK is tracking the on-going work on the Forwarding/Control Element Separation (ForCES) protocol by the Internet Engineering Task Force (IETF). For more details see the IETF web site (listed in References).

The CP-PDK eases the integration of the data plane and control plane in several ways by:

■ Providing a standard interface for the control-plane, enabling control-planes to be independent of the data-plane implementation.

■ Including pluggable libraries for the interface to the data-plane, enabling the data-plane to be independent of the control-plane implementation.

■ Providing physical separation of the control and data planes through a standard network protocol. Such separation enables computational resources to be kept separate so that control- and data-plane code can be developed and tested independently.

More information on the CP-PDK is available in the *Intel IXA Portability Framework Reference Manual* (Intel PFRM 2002).

Developing Microblocks

Microblocks are developed using "level 0" of the Intel IXA Portability Framework, which includes the data-plane libraries, the microblock infrastructure library, and the resource manager.

Optimized Microengine Data Plane Libraries

Working up from the bottom of Figure 3.3, the first part of level 0 is the microengine data plane libraries. Intel provides a set of software libraries for microengine assembly and microengine C developers.[1]

These libraries have two primary purposes:

■ To aid in portability. The interfaces into the microengine libraries were designed with portability in mind, so that code can be written for the IXP2XXX processor and still compile and run on successive generations of the microengines.

■ To help perform common programming tasks. For example, calculating the checksum of an IP header, an essential function of processing IP packets, can be done with a single library routine.

---

[1] The subsequent section in this chapter entitled The Tools provides an overview of both microengine assembly and microengine C. More information on these languages can be found in the *Development Tools User Guide* (Intel DTUG 2002).

The microengine libraries are categorized into several functional areas:

- Hardware abstraction, which is further subdivided into the following libraries:
  - Instruction Simplification, which provides simplified interfaces to microengine assembly instructions. Microengine C does not need this library.
  - Operating System Emulation, which provides services like mailboxes and critical sections, simplified memory accesses, and buffer manipulation.
  - Utilities, which provides simplified accesses to specialized hardware, such as hash tables, CRC, and threads.
- Protocol libraries, which help with standard network-packet-protocol processing like Ethernet field extraction and IP packet processing.

For the definitive reference to these libraries, refer to the *Intel IXA Portability Framework Reference Manual* (Intel PFRM 2002) on the accompanying CD-ROM.

Microblocks Infrastructure Library

The second part of level 0 is the microblock infrastructure library. This library provides routines for communication with the Intel XScale core as well as several mechanisms for organizing groups of microblocks into processing groups. In particular, the infrastructure supports both sequential processing using so-called context pipeline stages and pooled processing with both ordered and unordered thread execution models. We cover these different choices throughout the remainder of this book, but provide an overview here to help give you a taste for the fun still to come!

Context Pipeline Stages

A context pipeline stage performs one particular function and occupies one whole microengine. Thus, a context pipeline stage represents one function in the sequential model presented in Figure 3.2 (a). Threads in the context pipeline stage get packets to process from an incoming queue, and hand off completed packets to an outgoing queue. An illustration of a context pipeline stage is shown in Figure 3.5.

Context pipeline stages have some advantages because they run on only one microengine. Any state the pipeline stage must maintain can

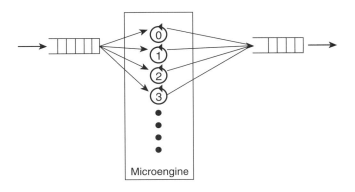

Figure 3.5 Context pipeline stage

be kept in registers or local memory, as long as none of it needs to be accessed from the Intel XScale core.

Context pipeline stages also have a couple of drawbacks. First, if the pipeline stage requires more time to execute than is needed to meet the packet arrival rate, nothing can be done short of extending the stage onto multiple microengines. If the pipeline stage expects or produces more than a few bytes of input or output, the queuing necessary between stages could be a large performance hit. Next-neighbor rings may help in this regard, but only if the data passed between stages is just a buffer handle, or other similar, small-sized data. Context pipeline stages are covered in Chapter 8.

Ordered and Unordered Thread Execution

When multiple microengines are used to collectively execute the same set of microblocks, as illustrated in the pooled model of Figure 3.2 (b), the threads in these microengines can either execute in an ordered or unordered fashion. The Intel IXA framework supports both models of execution.

Unordered thread execution means each thread retrieves a packet and processes it as quickly as possible. The processing is independent of the other threads in the pool. The advantages of unordered thread execution include its simplicity, and the independence of each thread allows for widely varying processing durations for different packet types. However, on the down-side, it is up to you to ensure packet ordering through the pool, if desired. We illustrate unordered thread execution in Chapter 7.

Ordered thread execution means each thread coordinates its execution with the other threads in the pool in a strictly ordered fashion. More specifically, the first thread in the pool dequeues a packet and begins processing. At some appropriate time (determined by the critical sections inherent in the application), this thread signals the next thread in the pool to dequeue a packet and begin processing. The process repeats for all of the threads in the pool.

The advantage of ordered thread execution is, of course, the automatic maintenance of packet ordering. Additionally, critical sections are also easily implemented through the use of signals. However, these benefits come at the cost of additional implementation complexity and the difficulty of dealing with non-uniform packet processing times. Ordered thread execution is covered in Chapter 9.

Combining multiple microblocks into a group in both ordered and unordered thread execution models involves writing a software loop, called a dispatch loop, which calls the microblocks one at a time. Dispatch loops are infinite loops—yes, you finally get rewarded for writing an infinite loop!—whose bodies contain calls to microblocks. For example, in Figure 3.2 (b) , the dispatch loop consists of calls to the microblocks for "function 1" through "function N", in the order appropriate for the final application.

An iteration of the dispatch loop represents the processing for a single packet. Thus, the first and last microblocks in a dispatch loop are special. The first microblock is called a *source* because it produces a packet for other so-called *transform* microblocks in the dispatch loops. The final microblock is called a *sink* because it disposes of the packet for each iteration of the dispatch loop. A packet can be disposed of by being dropped or queued to another processor for further processing, for example.

The information about the current packet in the dispatch loop iteration is stored in *dispatch-loop variables* so that the other microblocks can access the packet. While we cover many of these variables in this book, for a complete list of these variables, refer to the Intel IXA SDK 3.0 documentation.

An example of a dispatch loop is shown in the following pseudocode.

```
// An example dispatch loop
while (1) {
    dl_source(); // A microblock that gets a packet,
                 // e.g., dequeues from the RX ring.
```

```
classify();  // Another microblock to classify the
             // pkt

if (dl_next_block == BRIDGE) {
    ethernet_bridge(); // Perform L2 bridging
} else {
    ipv4_forward(); // Route the packet
}

dl_sink();   // Send the pkt, e.g. to the
             // transmit driver
}
```

In the example, the dl_source microblock retrieves a packet to be processed (probably by dequeing a packet from the receive driver). Next, the packet is classified by another microblock, which determines whether the packet is to be bridged or routed. Accordingly, one of two microblocks is called to perform the actual forwarding operation. Finally, the packet is sent to the next processing group, which, for example may transmit the packet.

The ordered and unordered thread execution models replicate dispatch loops similar to this one across any number of threads, including across multiple microengines. Packets are processed in parallel on the threads in the "pool."

Summarizing the Differences Between the Models

If the subtleties between context pipeline stages and ordered and unordered thread execution leaves you scratching your head, don't worry. The following summary lists the main differences between these models. In addition, the rest of the book goes into much more depth on all of these models.

- ■ Unordered thread execution:
    - — Each thread processes a single packet by performing multiple functions on that packet.
    - — Threads are independent of each other, so each thread runs as fast as it can.
    - — Synchronization between threads is your responsibility. You must assume that the pool of threads is running on more than one microengine, and thus synchronization must use memory or other globally-shared resources.
    - — This model is good for highly-variable packet-processing code because threads are independent of the timing of other threads.

■ Ordered thread execution:

— Each thread processes a single packet by performing multiple functions in order.

— Threads are dependent on each other. Each stage (e.g., a function) must only be executing on one thread at any given time.

— Synchronization between threads is handled by the infrastructure code using inter-thread signaling.

— This model is good for uniform packet-processing code that requires packet ordering and high-performance critical sections.

■ Context pipeline stages:

— A single stage that occupies exactly one microengine and processes one or more packets at a time.

— The code is written with the knowledge that it controls the entire set of resources of an entire microengine.

— Synchronization between threads in the microengine is your responsibility, but, typically, can be made very fast because all threads are known to be on the same microengine.

— This model is good for code that has a small amount, but high volume, of inter-thread communication.

Combining Different Models Together Within an Application

Combining one type of microblock model stage with another same-typed stage is pretty simple. Ordered and unordered thread execution stages can be connected with queues, or by simply adding microblocks into the dispatch loop. Context pipeline stages are connected using queues, perhaps even next-neighbor-register queues. Rarely does an application consist of just ordered thread execution stages, unordered thread execution stages, or context pipeline stages. So there must be some way of combining these different options.

Connecting different models is done with queues. Because ordered and unordered thread execution stages can exist on multiple microengines, next-neighbor registers cannot be used to connect these kinds of pipeline stages to any other types. So, the queues available in SRAM and/or scratchpad memory are the appropriate alternative.

Resource Manager

The final piece of the level 0 infrastructure is the resource manager. This library runs on the Intel XScale core and manages several aspects of the microengines and microblocks, including:

- Memory: DRAM, SRAM, scratchpad, and local memory can be allocated, freed, and initialized.

- Ring and queues: Both hardware rings and queues, as well as software-based rings and queues can be allocated and accessed.

- Microengines: Microengines can be started, stopped, and loaded with new code.

- Buffers: Packet buffers and buffer freelists can be created and accessed.

- Microblock communication: Both messages and packets can be moved between microblocks and the Intel Xscale core.

The resource manager is included in level 0 of the IXA Portability Framework and is the most basic library used to manage microengines and microblocks.

Drivers

Intel has developed certain functions, called drivers, that help developers code network applications on the IXP2XXX processor. These functions include receive and transmit operations, as well as a queue manager (discussed in Chapter 12).

Drivers represent functions that are closely coupled to the hardware. By relying on the Intel-provided drivers for these functions, application developers can insulate themselves from many of the hardware details.

The philosophy of this book is to cover programming in general, and while we primarily explore the IXP2XXX processor using packet-processing applications, we also explain some functions typically covered by drivers, specifically, receive, transmit, and the queue manager. While you can learn from the drivers explained in this book, for any production system, we encourage the use of the standard Intel drivers. Indeed, we use them whenever possible in our designs.

Developing Core Components

As a developer, you can choose to only use level 0 for developing microblocks and your IXP2XXX software. If you have a lot of existing legacy software, you may find this option particularly useful. However, in general, the level 1 part of the Intel IXA Portability Framework (i.e., core components) represents an easier way to develop Intel Xscale core code to compliment the microblocks running in the microengines.

Core components are developed by using level 1 of the Intel IXA Portability Framework. Level 1, which includes the core component infrastructure library, is layered on top of the level 0 infrastructure.

As discussed previously and shown in Figure 3.4, core components, like microblocks, represent a modular framework for developing packet processing applications. Core components execute on the Intel XScale core and are used for configuring and controlling microblocks, processing packets not handled by microblocks, and interfacing with any control-plane applications.

The core component infrastructure (CCI) library aids in the development of core components by:

■ Providing packet-communication channels to microblocks from core components and vice-versa. In addition, message passing between core components and microblocks is facilitated by the CCI.

■ Providing generic communications channels between core components.

■ Providing a flexible model for controlling the scheduling and execution of core components in the Intel XScale operating system threads.

To build a core component, you must supply four things:

■ An initialization routine. This routine might allocate memory to be shared with a microblock, or establish communications channels with other core components, the control plane, or the microblock.

■ A termination routine. This routine typically releases any resources owned by the core component.

■ One or more packet handler routines. Packet handlers might be provided to process exception packets—packets not handled by the microblock, or packets from the control plane or other core components. These packet handlers can be associated with communications channels so that all packets sent to the communications channel invoke the packet handler.

■ One or more message handler routines. These routines provide an analogous operation to the packet handler, except the content of the communications is not (necessarily) a packet and is instead an opaque message (e.g., for control and configuration).

In total, the CCI not only insulates programmers from details of the resource manager, it also encourages modularity through standardized communications mechanisms.

The Tools

In addition to the Intel IXA Portability Framework, the Intel IXA SDK 3.0 provides several tools for programming the IXP2XXX processor. These tools include a compiler for the microengine C language, an assembler for the microengine assembly language, as well as an integrated development environment (IDE) called the Developer's Workbench.

Microengine Assembly

This book has many examples of microengine assembly code. This section is a crash course in reading microengine assembly code, which is sufficient for reading this book and writing most microengine assembly code. If you need (or want!) more detail, read the *Programmer's Reference Manual* (Intel PRM 2002).

General Syntax and Semantics

Microengine assembly language instructions follow this basic format:

```
opcode[param1, param2, ...], opt1, opt2, ...
```

The opcode is like an opcode in any other architecture's assembly language. It describes the action being taken. For example, the alu opcode indicates that the arithmetic logic unit is being used to perform some computation.

Different opcodes have different parameter lists, and only nop and cam_clear have no parameter list at all. A common opcode is the alu opcode:

```
alu[dest_reg, a_operand, op, b_operand]
```

For the `alu` opcode, the `dest_reg` parameter is a register where the result of the computation is placed. The op parameter is a symbol that describes the computation performed. Examples are "+" for addition, and "B" for copying the b_operand into the `dest_reg`. The a_operand and b_operand parameters are the two numbers being used in the computation. They can be registers, immediate values, or "don't cares" (denoted by "--"). The "don't care" values are used for unary operations like "B". Many opcodes have restrictions on what operands can be used. For example, the `alu` opcode cannot work on two microengine global registers. See the *Programmer's Reference Manual* (Intel PRM 2002) for more complete information on these restrictions.

As an example, the following instruction adds 2 to var and puts the result in sum.

```
alu[sum, var, +, 2]
```

As illustrated by the generic instruction format above, some opcodes also have options. These options control the behavior of the instruction. The most common options are those used with the memory opcodes. An example is shown here:

```
sram[read, $xfer, addr, 0, 1], ctx_swap[sig_name]
```

This SRAM read takes one 32-bit value from the memory location `addr` and puts it in transfer register `$xfer`. The option on this instruction, `ctx_swap[sig_name]`, tells the microengine what to do while this memory reference is completing. In this case, this option instructs the microengine to swap out this thread and let other threads run until the memory read is complete (as indicated by the presence of the signal named `sig_name`).

Other memory options include `sig_done[sig_name]` and `defer[a]`. The `sig_done` option tells the microengine that the current thread should keep running and the SRAM unit should send the given signal to this thread when the access is completed. The thread must explicitly wait for this signal at some future point using the `ctx_arb[sig_name]` instruction. The `defer[a]` option is used with `ctx_swap` and tells the microengine to run thread a–a value between 1 and 2—more cycles before swapping out.

As you can see in the following example, these options can be coupled together.

```
sram[...], ctx_swap[sig_name], defer[1]
```

This instruction tells the hardware to execute the next instruction before swapping out and waiting for the SRAM access to complete.

Comments in the code can be in three different forms. The two comment forms acceptable in C++ (/* comment */ and // comment) are both treated as comments. Also, a comment can come after a semicolon (;) on a line. All text in between a semicolon and the end of the line is ignored by the compiler, similar to // in C++. Some comments are shown below:

```
alu[res, a, +, 1]   // A comment

alu[res, a, +, 1]   /* A comment */

alu[res, a, +, 1]   ; A comment
```

Branching

The IXP2XXX microengines offer several branching opcodes. Most of them follow this basic form:

```
br[label#]
```

The branch opcode shown here indicates an unconditional branch, but conditional variants exist as well. For example, br!=0 is an opcode that branches if the result of the last ALU instruction did not set the 0 condition code, and continues otherwise. The label defines where to branch, and they can be found in code in this form:

```
label#:
```

Registers

As described previously, four types of registers exist: general purpose, SRAM transfer, DRAM transfer, and next-neighbor. Within these types, three addressing modes exist: context-relative, absolute, and indexed. In microengine assembly, registers are represented symbolically. The symbol names for registers are mapped to physical registers during the assembly process.

Register names are strings of alphanumeric characters and underscores (_). They may not have a number as the first character. SRAM transfer registers have a single dollar sign ($) in front of them, DRAM transfer registers have two dollar signs ($$) in front of them, and next-neighbor registers have an n$ in front of them. Absolute registers add an "at" sign (@) in front, and indexed registers add an asterix (*) in front. Table 3.1 contains example register names.

Table 3.1 Example Register Naming Syntax

Register type	Context-relative name	Absolute name	Indexed name	Special Indexing
GPR	Gpr123_fab	@gpr123_fab	n/a	n/a
SRAM transfer	$_xfer	n/a	*$index	*$index++, *$index--
DRAM transfer	$$tmp	n/a	*$$index	*$$index++, *$$index--
Next-neighbor	n$reg	n/a	*n$index	*n$index++
Local memory	n/a	n/a	*l$index0, *l$index1	*l$index0++, *l$index0--, *l$index0[n] (n is between 0 and 15), -- same for *l$index1

Some of the indexed registers also support a post-increment and post-decrement, as well as an offset mode. The post-increment and post-decrement modes modify the appropriate index register after the instruction executes. Offset mode allows the given indexed registers to be accessed like an array. The offsets, however, must be compile-time constants.

Note

> When reading the assembly output of the microengine C compiler, some text is added to the front of register names. This text is the actual register name and is separated from the name with a colon. So the register name old_5_Ve1$0:a1 is actually GPR a1. This syntax can be confusing because the text in the front has dollar signs.

Signals

Although signals are numbered in the IXP2XXX hardware, the assembler can perform automatic assignment of these numbers. All you must do is declare and name signals using the .sig sig_name syntax. A signal name has the same format as a GPR name.

The assembler automatically allocates signal numbers to declared signal names. Better yet, the assembler even performs this allocation based on usage. So, if a signal name is used for an SRAM reference, a single signal number is allocated. If the same signal name is used for a DRAM reference, two consecutive signal numbers are allocated as required by the DRAM reference.

You can manually assign the signal number to a signal name using the .addr sig_name val syntax. Assigning a known value is necessary when sending inter-thread signals between microengines.

Microengine C

Microengine C is similar to the C language. It offers type safety, pointers to memory, and functions. Because the IXP2XXX microengines don't have hardware assistance for a stack, the C language does not provide recursive functions or function pointers. A stack could be implemented in software, but it would be terribly slow.

Like the previous section on microengine assembly, this section provides a brief overview of microengine C, but should not be considered a replacement of the *Microengine C Language Compiler Support Reference Manual* (Intel MicroC 2002) that comes with Intel IXA SDK 3.0.

General Syntax and Semantics

The expression syntax of microengine C is ANSI C, with the exceptions noted above about no support for function pointers and recursion. The built-in types are unsigned and signed char (8 bits), short (16 bits), int (32 bits), long (32 bits), long long (64 bits), as well as enum and pointers. Structures, including bit-fields, unions, and arrays are supported as well.

Depending on the optimization level of the compiler, functions are compiled into subroutines or in-lined. With no compiler optimization enabled, functions become subroutines implemented with the jump and rtn opcodes. When compiler optimizations are enabled, the compiler inlines small and infrequently called functions, which saves on execution time at the expense of greater code store.

You can control function inlining by adding the __inline and __forceinline modifiers to function definitions. The compiler ignores these modifiers when no optimizations are enabled. However, when compiler optimizations are enabled, the __forceinline modifier ensures the function is inlined and the __inline modifier provides a suggestion to the compiler that the function should be inlined.

Data Allocation

Because of the many exposed memory and register types in the IXP2XXX processor, variable declarations usually include an additional data allocation modifier. These __declspecs instruct the compiler on where to store the given variable. For example, __declspec(sram) int x would define a variable named x whose storage was in SRAM memory. Similar __declspecs exist for the other memory types: local_mem, sramN (for a particular SRAM bank), dram, scratch, rbuf, and tbuf.

Register allocation is also specified using __declspecs. For example:

```
__declspec(dram_write_reg) long long y
```

would define a variable named y whose storage was two DRAM write transfer registers. Other register __declspecs are: gp_reg, sram_read_reg, sram_write_reg, dram_read_reg, nn_local_reg, and nn_remote_reg.

If a variable has no such modifiers, the compiler attempts to allocate the variable to the most appropriate register type. Should that allocation fail, the compiler puts the variable in any memory region it chooses.

Finally, signals are also declared using two additional __declspecs: signal and signal_pair. To simplify the use of these __declspecs, the standard compiler header file, ixp.h, defines SIGNAL and SIGNAL_PAIR types to be single and double signals, respectively. However, unlike the assembler, the compiler forces you to understand the number of signals required for any instruction.

Intrinsics

Some of the unique features of IXP2XXX programming cannot be expressed in ANSI C. For example, asynchronous memory accesses, direct RBUF-to-DRAM data transfers, and waiting for signals are not of ANSI C expression syntax. Because these features are critical to effective microengine programming, the microengine C compiler exposes them through a library of intrinsics.

Intrinsics look like function calls in C, but the compiler treats them quite differently. When the compiler sees an intrinsic reference, it inserts well-known microengine assembly. For example, the following signature defines an intrinsic to atomically increment a scratchpad memory location:

```
void scratch_incr(
    volatile void __declspec(scratch) *address);
```

When referenced in a microengine C source file, the compiler inserts the following microengine assembly that corresponds to the atomic scratchpad increment operation:

```
scratch[incr, --, address, 0]
```

Many intrinsics are used and described throughout this book.

The Developer's Workbench

The integrated development environment provided in the IXA SDK 3.0 is the IXP2XXX Developer's Workbench. This development tool allows development and debugging of microengine assembly or microengine C code in a visual environment in Microsoft Windows*. The Developer's Workbench comes with a cycle-accurate simulator that is an excellent tool for prototyping and debugging software without hardware. In addition, the Developer's Workbench contains a syntax-highlighting editor for both microengine assembly and microengine C, as well as integration with the microengine assembler, microengine C compiler, and microengine linker. The Developer's Workbench also contains a source-level debugger for both microengine assembly and microengine C, allowing you to debug software running in the microengine simulator or on the hardware itself. This book makes extensive use of the Developer's Workbench, beginning with a getting-started guide in the next chapter.

Summary

The first, most important, and certainly hardest task when beginning development of an application on the IXP2XXX processor is the choice of programming model. Involved in this decision is how to map the application to the computational resources of the IXP2XXX processors including the memory hierarchy and hardware accelerators.

Once the choice of programming model is made, you can turn to the Intel IXA Portability Framework for support in implementing the application of choice. The Intel IXA Portability Framework includes microengine and core libraries, based on industry standards from the NPF and IETF where appropriate, as well as a building-block model (microblocks and core components) that decomposes network applications in a pipeline of computational stages. Each stage can be chained together to create a complete network-packet-processing application. The framework provides a model in which you can add new building blocks and have them interact with Intel's supplied building blocks.

The specific models for connecting microblocks together are context pipeline stages and ordered and unordered thread execution stages. Each of these models is covered in more detail in subsequent chapters.

The software tools provided in the Intel IXA SDK 3.0 include the microengine C compiler, microengine assembler, the Developer's Workbench IDE, and the Intel IXA Portability Framework.

The Developer's Workbench allows you to create, edit, simulate, and debug microengine code. The microengine C compiler and microengine assembler are integrated with the Developer's Workbench.

For further reading, the *IXP2x00 Programmer's Reference Manual* (Intel PRM 2002), available on the accompanying CD-ROM, is a great programming reference. Chapter 3 of the *IXP2x00 Programmer's Reference Manual* contains the complete instruction set for the microengines, and Chapter 5 details all of the register descriptions.

Chapter 4

"Hello World" for the Microengines

Learning to write code for the IXP2XXX microengines can be challenging, as learning to program on any new platform can be challenging. We'll take the typical approach to getting started by showing you a very simple IXP2XXX microengine program, similar in purpose to the "Hello World" programs written on other platforms. This chapter shows how a simple application is written using the IXP2XXX Workbench, an integrated development environment (IDE) for writing, building, and debugging microengine code. You could write microengine code without this IDE, using the command line tools alone, but the workbench is a great timesaving tool for developers. This chapter takes you through the process of installing the Workbench and the other tools needed to start writing code for the microengines. Then, we'll show you how to write a simple microengine program in microengine C and again in microengine assembly. Finally, we'll add some optimizations to the microengine assembly version to get some performance increases.

IXP1200 Note

If you are familiar with our IXP1200 Programming book, this chapter will look very similar to Chapter 3 from that book. The only material difference is the coverage of microengine assembly versions of the same "Hello World."

Note

> This chapter is not a complete reference for the syntax of microengine assembly or microengine C. The *Intel IXP2400/IXP2800 Network Processor Programmer's Reference Manual* (Intel PRM 2002) and *Intel IXP2400/IXP2800 Network Processors Microengine C Compiler Language Support Reference Manual* (Intel MCRM 2002), both in the "References" section of this book, are complete references.

Installing the Tools

The CD-ROM in the back cover of this book contains most of the tools you need to write, compile, and run the samples in this book. To install these tools, you need a PC running Windows NT 4.0, Windows 2000, or Windows XP.

The tools are part of Intel IXA SDK 3.0, which comes in three parts, all of which are on the CD-ROM in the back of the book. The first part, which is called the Intel IXA SDK Tools 3.0, contains the tools necessary for developing software for the IXP2XXX microengines. These tools include the Developer's Workbench, the microengine assembler, the microengine C compiler, and the simulator for the IXP2400 and IXP2800 processors. The second part is the Simulation Environment for the IXP2850 processor. You only need to install this if you want to simulate the cryptographic features of the IXP2850 processor. The third part is called the Intel IXA SDK Applications 3.0 and contains sample applications and libraries. The IXA SDK Applications 3.0 has some microengine library code that we use in our sample code, so if you want to run our sample code, you must install both the Intel IXA SDK Tools 3.0 and the Intel IXA SDK Applications 3.0.

To install the Intel IXA SDK Tools 3.0, follow these steps:

1. Insert the CD-ROM from the back of the book into the CD-ROM drive. A browser window should appear listing the CD-ROM'S contents.

2. To start the installation click the link entitled "Install Intel IXA SDK Tools 3.0".

3. As the installation proceeds, all of the default options are appropriate.

Note

> If the browser window does not appear, navigate the CD-ROM with Windows Explorer and open index.htm in a web browser.

To simulate code using the cryptographic features of the IXP2850 processor, you also need to install the Intel IXA SDK Tools 3.0 IXP2850 Simulation Environment. The cryptographic features of the IXP2850 processor are covered in Chapter 12. To install the IXP2850 Simulation Environment, follow these steps:

1. Insert the CD-ROM from the back of the book into the CD drive (if you haven't already done so). A browser window should appear listing the CD-ROM's contents.

2. To start the installation click the link entitled "Install the Intel IXA SDK Tools 3.0 IXP2850 Simulation Environment."

3. As the installation proceeds, all of the default options are appropriate.

To install the Intel IXA SDK Applications 3.0, follow these steps:

1. Insert the CD-ROM from the back of the book into the CD drive (if you haven't already done so). A browser window should appear listing the CD-ROM's contents.

2. To start the installation click the link entitled "Install Intel IXA Applications 3.0."

3. When the installation asks you for a directory in which to install the Intel IXA Applications 3.0, type "C:\IXA_SDK_3.0." All other default options are appropriate.

Note | The current version of the Intel IXA SDK Applications 3.0 has components for XScale core development that require the WindRiver Tornado[†] IDE and the BSPs for the IXP2XXX processor be installed first. If you don't have Tornado or the IXP2XXX BSPs installed, the Intel IXA SDK Applications 3.0 installation still installs some microengine libraries that are used throughout our sample code. But without Tornado or the IXP2XXX BSPs, the Applications installation does not allow you to compile core component code. Whether or not you have Tornado and the BSPs installed, follow the above steps to install the Intel IXA SDK Applications 3.0.

You are ready to write code for the IXP2XXX processor.

Setting up the Workspace

To run the Developer Workbench program:

■ Go to Start > Programs > IXA SDK 3.0 > DevWorkbench.

When the Workbench launches, you are greeted with a screen similar to those in other Integrated Development Environments (IDEs), like Microsoft[†] Visual Studio[†] or KDevelop.

As shown in Figure 4.1, the right-hand pane of the interface lists links to documentation. Later, you'll see lists of files and functions in this pane. The left-hand pane is for editing files, and the bottom pane is for compiler output and the output from other integrated utilities.

The Workbench uses projects to keep track of the program's source files and how to compile them. Additionally, the project keeps track of certain simulator and hardware debugging settings.

To create a project for your "hello world" program:

1. On the File menu, click New Project. The New Project dialog shown in Figure 4.2 displays.

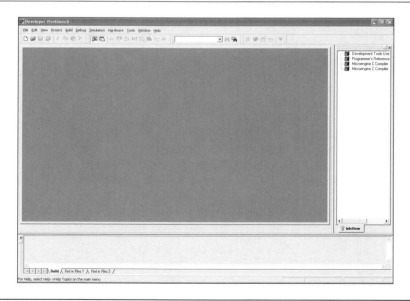

Figure 4.1 The Developer Workbench Main Window

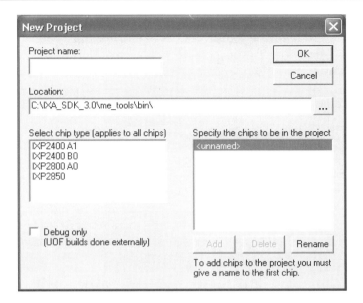

Figure 4.2 The New Project Dialog

2. In the Project Name box, type the project's name (something like hello_world works).

3. Change the project's location, if desired, by editing the Location box.

4. Select the chip type to be IXP2800 A0. The A0 denotes the silicon stepping of the chip.

5. Rename the chip by clicking the Rename button, entering a name for the chip, and clicking OK.

6. Click OK to accept the entries and close the dialog.

Writing the Program in Microengine C

What does a "hello world" program look like on the IXP2XXX microengines? Well, the microengines don't have a display device, so it certainly won't look much like a program written for a PC or other computer with a display. The "hello world" program executed on an IXP2XXX microengine reverses an array of 32-bit numbers in memory. That's about as exciting (or not exciting, as the case may be) as "hello world."

First, we'll show you how to write the program in microengine C. Later in this chapter, we'll show you how to write the same program in microengine assembly and do some optimizations with that version. The instructions in this section assume you have created a workspace and a project, as described above. If you haven't done so yet, do that now.

Compiling a Simple Source File

To create a source file:

1. On the File menu, click New.
2. For the kind of file to create select C Source File.
3. Click OK.
4. As with any C program, you need a `main` function. However, unlike most C programs, you also need to define an `exit` function.
5. Type the following:

```
void main () {
}

void exit (unsigned int arg) {
}
```

This code is enough to allow you to compile.

6. On the File menu, click Save As and save this file in the same directory as the rest of your project files under the name `hello_world.c`.
7. On the Project menu, click Insert Compiler Source Files.
8. Select `hello_world.c`.
9. Click Insert. Now your source file is part of the project. The file is also now listed under "Compiler Source Files" in the FileView pane on the right-hand side of the Workbench window.

To set up the build settings:

10. On the Build menu, click Settings, then click the General tab.
11. In the Compiler include directories box, add the `MicroengineC\ Include` directory. This directory is under the Intel IXA SDK root directory (typically `C:\IXA_SDK_3.0`) and has include files for functions that provide access to the IXP2XXX hardware. These low-level functions are called "intrinsics."

The Build Settings dialog should look like Figure 4.3.

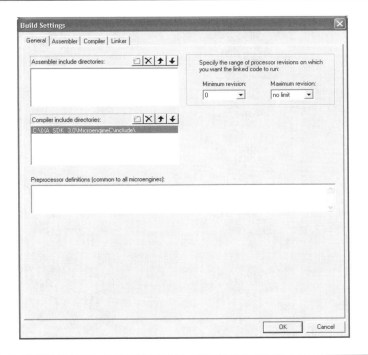

Figure 4.3 General Build Settings

Now set the Compiler settings.

1. Click the Compiler tab. The "Source files to compile" list shows you all of the microengine C files that are compiled when the Workbench builds your code. Microengine C files and microengine assembly files get compiled into intermediate files called .list files.

2. Click New .list file…

3. In the New dialog, type `hello_world_uc.list`.

4. Click Insert List File.

5. In the Insert List File dialog, click Choose source files… to add `hello_world.c` to the list of files to compile.

6. In the Contexts section of the dialog, change the Number field to 1. This setting ensures that your code only runs on one microengine thread. Multithreading is covered in subsequent chapters.

The settings should look similar to the dialog in Figure 4.4.

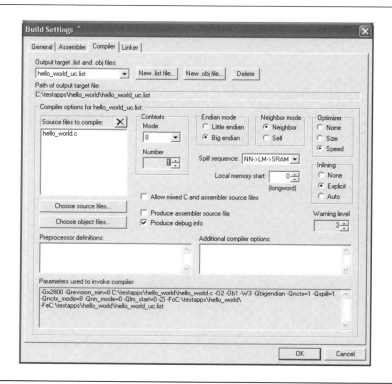

Figure 4.4 Compiler Settings for the Sample Program

Next, you need to set some linker settings.

1. In the Build Settings dialog, click the Linker tab. The linker takes a collection of .list files and turns them into a single .uof file. The .uof file also contains information telling the code loader which code belongs on which microengine. We'll run our program on just one microengine for now.

2. In the Microengine 0:0 box, select hello_world_uc.list.

The linker settings should look like Figure 4.5.

Note   The remaining settings are appropriate the way they are, but the memory segment settings are interesting to point out. The linker needs to know where to put variables that need to be stored in memory. The collection of boxes in the "Reserved memory segments for variables" allows you to tell the linker where to put these variables.

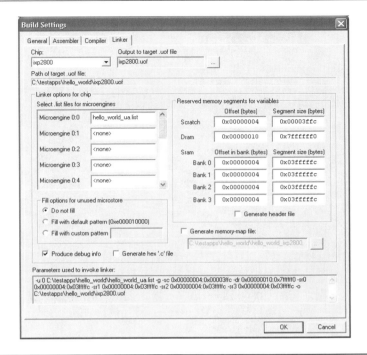

Figure 4.5 Linker Settings for the Sample Program

3. Click OK to close the dialog.

This is the exciting part! It is time to build the code!

On the Build menu, click Build, or press the F7 key. You will see messages indicating that your code has built successfully.

Adding Code to the Source File

Now add some more code expanding this very simple program so that it reverses an array in memory.

In the main function, declare two arrays—one for the original array and one for the soon-to-be-reversed array. Add the following lines to the main function:

```
_declspec(shared sram) int old_array[] =
    { 1, 2, 3, 4, 5, 6, 7, 8, 9, 10 };
_declspec(shared sram) int
    new_array[sizeof(old_array)/sizeof(int)];
```

You are now thinking "Whoa! That's not ANSI C!" It certainly isn't. Here are a couple of differences worth noting.

■ First, __declspec(shared sram) on lines 1 and 3 looks weird, doesn't it? The __declspec keyword allows you to tell the compiler what kind of variable you are declaring.

Note

> Because the IXP2XXX processor has four different memory types (SRAM, DRAM, scratchpad, and local memory), you must tell the compiler a memory type in which to put the data. The sram parameter of __declspec indicates that the compiler should put the data in SRAM. If you leave this modifier off the variable, the compiler does its best to put the variable in registers. If it can't be put in a register, the compiler chooses its own a memory type in which to put the data.

■ The shared modifier may be new to you as well. The shared modifier tells the compiler to avoid optimizations that might keep data from being written into memory. For example, consider the following function:

```
int foo() {
    __declspec(sram) int bar = 23;
    return bar;
}
```

The compiler might figure out that it would be pretty slow to write 23 into SRAM and then immediately read it again to put it in a register to return it. It could instead optimize this code to just assign 23 to the register using an immediate instruction. In your code, the shared modifier forces the compiler to actually put the data in SRAM. Having the data in SRAM might be important to you if you want another microengine or the XScale core to be able to read the data in SRAM.

The rest of the code looks just like ANSI C. Notice also that you put some data in the first array. This data will be reversed in your code. You even declared an array in which to put the reversed version of the array. Good job!

Now, you need to write some code to reverse the contents of the array. Being a good programmer, you'll see an opportunity for reuse here because who knows when you'll need to reverse an array again. So, put the following function prototype above the main function:

```
void reverse_array(volatile int* old,
                   volatile int* new,
                   int size);
```

The volatile keyword tells the compiler that modification of the variables or the memory they point to should be written immediately. Otherwise, the compiler might make optimizations preventing the modifications from being written immediately. While these optimizations would make the code run faster, they could also make it difficult to see the changed values from the Intel XScale core or in the simulator.

Implementation of this function can be done just the way you would do it in C. Here is our implementation:

reverse_array()

File: Chapter04\hello_world.c

```
94   void reverse_array(volatile int* old,
95                      volatile int* new,
96                      int size) {
97       int index = 0;
98
99       for (index = 0; index < size; index++) {
100          new[index] = old[size - index - 1];
101      }
102  }
```

You'll also have to call this function from your main function. Something like this:

```
reverse_array(old_array, new_array,
              sizeof(old_array)/sizeof(int));
```

If you don't feel like coding or typing, you can cheat. For this example, as well as the other examples in this book, we have put a Workbench project with our code on the CD-ROM. Go ahead and look, we won't tell.

Now that the code is all written, go ahead and compile it. If everything is correct, it should compile without a hitch.

Simulating the Microengine C Code

We'll bet you're so excited to run the code that you just can't hold it in! To keep you from exploding in front of your coworkers, let's do just that.

1. On the Debug menu, click Simulation.

2. Click the toolbar icon that looks like a bug. When you want to debug, click the bug. When you want to stop debugging, click the crossed out bug. The simulator should start.

If you are running the simulator for the first time, you won't notice much change. Open some debugging windows first.

1. On the View menu, click Debug Windows to see a list of available debugging windows.

2. Open the Data Watch, Memory Watch, and Thread Status windows. These windows can be undocked, docked, and moved around however you prefer.

Your screen should now look something like Figure 4.6.

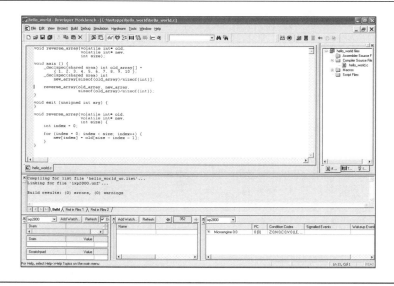

Figure 4.6 Initial Simulator Screen

- The Data Watch window lets you examine variables or CSRs.
- The Memory Watch window lets you examine memory locations.
- The Thread Status window shows the current status of the microengine threads, including the current program counter, condition codes, outstanding events, and events that the thread is waiting for.

Now, run your program and see how it works. Breakpoints are helpful here.

1. In the thread status window, click the plus sign next to Microengine 0:0.

2. Double-click thread 0 of microengine 0:0. A source file opens in the same area as the current source file. You'll see an arrow pointing into that source file showing where the current program counter is.

3. Scroll down to the reverse_array function and put the cursor on the line with the for statement.

4. On the toolbar click the white-hand icon. A breakpoint is inserted on this line.

5. On the toolbar directly above the source file listing window, you'll see a button with a picture of two files and two arrows. The icon for this button is shown in Figure 4.7. When you put your cursor over it, the tool tip should read "Toggle View." Click this button. Now the thread status window shows the disassembled microengine assembly. You can step or set breakpoints in this window as well. You don't need to do that now, however, so click Toggle View again to put the view back to the microengine C source.

6. Click the green light icon at the top of the screen to run the program. In pretty short order, the simulator will let you know that you hit your breakpoint. So far, so good!

7. Put your cursor over the "old" variable and right-click.

Figure 4.7 Toggle View Icon

8. On the pop-up menu, click "Set Data Watch for: old." Do the same for the "new" variable.

9. These variables should show up in the list in the data watch window. The data watch window should look like Figure 4.8.

To look in the array contents:

1. Click in the first column of the SRAM section of the Memory Watch window.

2. Type sram[, the address of the old array obtained from the data watch window, then]. For example, if the old array is 0x54, type sram[0x54] in the Memory Watch window and press Enter. The Workbench lets you know that the address has been modified to reflect long-word addressing. This is fine. The contents of this memory location should appear in the right hand column.

But this is an array, not a single integer! The Memory Watch window can show ranges of memory as well. Instead of entering one SRAM address in the memory description, enter the starting and ending addresses separated by a colon. So using the previous example, enter sram[0x54:0x7b] in the window. The result should look something like what is shown in Figure 4.9.

Your original array! Some of it may still be in the SRAM unit on its way to memory, so don't worry if it's not all displayed yet. Do the same for the new array. It should be all zeroes.

Now, see if your code actually works. Put another breakpoint at the end of the exit function and click the green light to continue running the simulator. Again, the simulator should let you know that it hit the breakpoint. Voila! The new array in the memory watch should have the

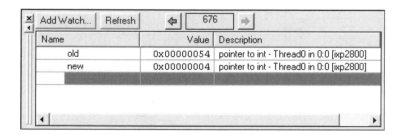

Figure 4.8 Data Watch Window Example

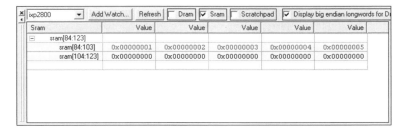

Figure 4.9 The Old Array in the Memory Watch

original array reversed. Some of the memory writes may not have completed, but you should see at least some of the new array, similar to that shown in Figure 4.10.

Congratulations! You are now a microengine C programmer.

Sram	Value	Value	Value	Value	Value
⊟ sram[84:123]					
sram[84:103]	0x00000001	0x00000002	0x00000003	0x00000004	0x00000005
sram[104:123]	0x00000006	0x00000007	0x00000008	0x00000009	0x0000000a
⊟ sram[4:43]					
sram[4:23]	0x0000000a	0x00000009	0x00000008	0x00000007	0x00000006
sram[24:43]	0x00000005	0x00000004	0x00000003	0x00000002	0x00000000

Figure 4.10 The New Array in the Memory Watch

Writing the Program in Microengine Assembly

Now that you have an idea of how microengine C works, let's look at microengine assembly. This section contains two versions of the assembly necessary to reverse an array in memory. The first one is the simple version, and the other is a faster, more advanced version.

The first step to writing the "hello world" program in microengine assembly is to create and compile a simple assembly file and include it in the project. The instructions in this section assume you have created a workspace and a project, as described previously. If you haven't done so yet, do that now.

Assembling a Simple Source File

These steps get you to the point of assembling a simple microengine assembly source file.

1. On the File menu, click New.

2. Select Source File for the kind of file to create.

3. Click OK.

   Unlike the simple microengine C program, the microengine assembly program has no standard entry point like main() or exit point like exit(). You just need to put a few nops in the file to compile it.

4. Type the following:

   ```
   nop
   nop
   nop
   ```

These three lines are enough to compile the code.

5. On the File menu, click Save As and save this file in the same directory as the rest of your project files under the name hello_world.uc.

6. On Project menu, click Insert Assembler Source Files.

7. Select hello_world.uc.

8. Click Insert. Now your source file is part of the project. The file is now listed under "Assembler Source Files" in the FileView pane on the right-hand side of the Workbench window.

To set up the build settings:

1. On Build menu, click Settings, then click the General tab.

2. In the Assembler include directories box, add the src\library\ dataplane_library\microcode\ directory. This directory is under the Intel IXA SDK root directory and has include files for some standard macros used in the code.

The Build Settings dialog now looks like Figure 4.11.

1. Click the Assembler tab.

2. Click the New button to create a new .list file.

3. In the New dialog, type hello_world_ua.list.

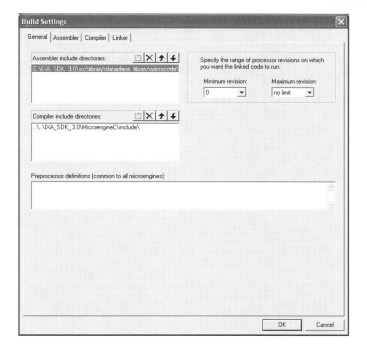

Figure 4.11 General Build Settings

4. Click Insert List File.

5. In the Root File field, select `hello_world.uc`. Because microengine assembly code does not have a "main" function, the code simply starts executing at the first line of code in the root file that is not in a macro definition.

The settings should look similar to the dialog in Figure 4.12.

Now that the assembler settings have been adjusted correctly, change the linker settings.

1. In the Build Settings dialog, click the Linker tab.

2. In the Microengine 0:0 box, select <none> instead of `hello_world_uc.list`.

3. In the Microengine 0:1 box, select `hello_world_ua.list`.

The linker settings should look like Figure 4.13.

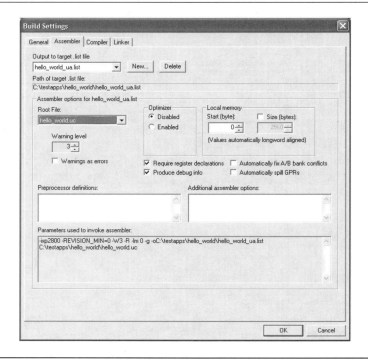

Figure 4.12 Assembler Settings for the Sample Program

4. Click OK to close the dialog.

As with the microengine C example, this code should build properly. In the Build menu, click Build, or press the F7 key. You will see messages indicating that your code has built successfully.

Adding Code to the Source File

Now write the code for reversing an array. First, write code to allocate space for the original and new arrays. In microengine C, this code was written with array declarations. In microengine assembly you do this with the .global_mem keyword. This keyword tells the linker to allocate space in a particular memory of a particular size.

IXP1200
Note
The addition of this keyword is a great improvement over the microengine assembly used on the IXP12XX. The IXP12XX assembler did not perform allocation of memory.

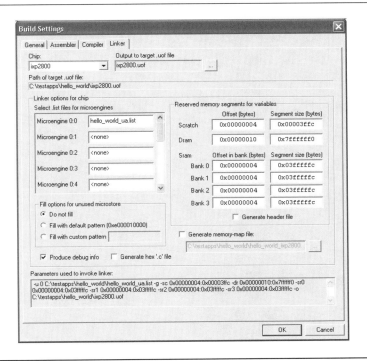

Figure 4.13 Linker Settings for the Sample Program

Add the following code to allocate space for your arrays:

```
// Allocate space for the initial array and the new array
.global_mem old_array    SRAM0 40
.global_mem new_array    SRAM0 40
```

Notice that the .global_mem keyword requires you to select which SRAM bank to use. Also notice that the sizes of the memory spaces are specified in bytes. To initialize the contents of the arrays, use the .init keyword, as in this code:

```
// Initialize the arrays
.init old_array      1 2 3 4 5 6 7 8 9 10
.init new_array      0 0 0 0 0 0 0 0 0 0
```

The lists of numbers in these directives are long-words that will be put into memory. Neither of these directives produces any actual code. The .global_mem directive allocates memory at link time from the memory spaces reserved for the linker in its settings dialog. The .init directive is passed on in binary form to the .uof file, and the memory is initialized when the microengine loader loads the code into the microengines.

For the part of the program that is analogous to main() in microengine C, use the following code:

hello_world

File: Chapter04\hello_world.uc

```
264   // This is the main part of the program
265   .begin
266      // Only do this on one thread
267      .if(ctx() == 0)
268         ctx_arb[voluntary]
269         // Call the reverse_array macro
270         start_simple_reverse#:
271         reverse_array_simple(old_array, new_array, 10)
272         end_simple_reverse#:
273         reverse_array_advanced(old_array, new_array_adv,
274                                        10)
275         end_advanced_reverse#:
276      .endif
277      ctx_arb[kill]
278   .end
279   nop
```

Let's look at what is going on in this code:

Line 265:

The .begin directive scopes all of the register and signal names. All of the names that occur between the .begin and the .end on line 278 are considered to be in the same scope.

Line 267:

The .if statement compiles in microengine assembly similar to a C if statement. In this case, the .if makes sure the code only runs on one context, context 0.

Line 271:

This line invokes a macro to reverse the array in memory. This macro implements a simple algorithm. Notice that the memory locations are the ones defined in the .global_mem directive. When this code is linked, the linker allocates space for these arrays and replaces these symbols with constants representing the array locations.

Line 273:

> This line invokes a faster, more complicated version of the same macro. Notice their interfaces are identical, so they can be used interchangeably. The next section describes this implementation in more detail.

The microengine assembly version of the code on the CD has macros, `reverse_array_simple` and `reverse_array_advanced`, which provide the same functionality as the `reverse_array` function in microengine C.

Assembly macros have a few properties that make them different from microengine C functions, however. First, macros are always inlined into the calling code, whereas functions can be either inlined or kept separate. Second, macro parameters are treated different from function parameters. Because these parameters are just inserted as strings into the macro code, the parameters could be registers, constants, signal names, or any number of things. If the parameters are registers, the macro could modify them as well. When writing microengine assembly macros, it is important to well-document the kinds of parameters that can be passed in and out and the side-effects of using the macro.

Let's look at the `reverse_array_simple` macro:

reverse_array_simple()

```
        File: Chapter04\hello_world.uc
48      #macro reverse_array_simple[in_old, in_new, in_size]
49      .begin
50          .reg entries_left current_old_entry
51          .reg current_new_entry
52          .reg $array_data
53
54          // Set up a count of remaining entries and SRAM
55          // pointers
56          move(entries_left, in_size)
57          // Set up a pointer to the current array entry in
58          // the old array
59          move(current_old_entry, in_old)
60
61          // Set up a pointer to the current array entry in
62          // the new array. This works out to be
63          // in_new + (in_size * 4) - 4, because the code
64          // starts at the back of the new array, and because
65          // it operates with 4-byte longwords.
```

Continues

```
66          move(current_new_entry, in_new)
67          add_shf_left(current_new_entry, current_new_entry,
68                       in_size, 2)
69          sub(current_new_entry, current_new_entry, 4)
70
71          // Now loop one longword at a time and copy the
72          // array
73          .while (entries_left != 0)
74              // Need a signal for SRAM accesses
75              .sig sram_sig
76              // Read the old array from SRAM
77              sram[read, $array_data, current_old_entry,
78                  0, 1], ctx_swap[sram_sig]
79
80              // Move the data from the read side of the
81              // transfer register to the write side
82              move($array_data, $array_data)
83
84              // Write the new array
85              sram[write, $array_data, current_new_entry,
86                  0, 1], ctx_swap[sram_sig]
87
88              // Update the counter and the pointers
89              sub(entries_left, entries_left, 1)
90              add(current_old_entry, current_old_entry, 4)
91              sub(current_new_entry, current_new_entry, 4)
92          .endw
93      .end
94  #endm
```

The first thing to notice is that this implementation is somewhat longer than the microengine C version. Much of the extra length is because microengine assembly does not include semantics for array indices in SRAM and algebraic formulae, like microengine C does. So we have to write the code for these manually. And because microengine assembly is probably less familiar to most people, we have added a few more comments than the equivalent microengine C code. A few specific parts of this macro are worth pointing out:

Lines 54-69:

Without the use of array indices, all access to memory is done through pointers. These lines initialize one register as a pointer to point to the first element of the old array and another register as a pointer to point to the last element of the new array. This code makes use of the Portability Macros move, add_shf_left, and sub. These macros usually assemble into one or two instructions and help to isolate the developer from changes in the instruction set that affect how ALU operations are written.

Line 73:

All structure is not lost in microengine assembly. In this line of code, we use a microengine assembly language feature that lets us construct a while loop, evaluating the contents of a register in each iteration of the loop. The assembler expands this loop construct into `alu` operations and conditional branches when it assembles this code.

Lines 74-78:

In microengine assembly, memory references are all explicit. Because the array we want to reverse is in SRAM, the code needs to issue a read request to the SRAM unit. This read request requires a signal, which is defined on line 75. The optional `ctx_swap` token at the end of the SRAM read request forces the context to be swapped out until the SRAM reference completes. The second parameter of the SRAM request specifies the transfer register into which the data is placed when the access completes. The third and fourth parameters are added together to get the address in SRAM from which the data is read. This address is a byte address, although the last two bits are ignored. The final parameter specifies the number of long-words that are read by this SRAM read. Notice that the units for memory addresses are bytes, while the units for memory access sizes are long-words. In the `reverse_array_simple` implementation, the array is reversed one long-word at a time. Later, in the `reverse_array_advanced` implementation, we'll show you how to read and write more than one long-word at a time to make the array reversing code run much faster.

Line 82:

At first glance, this line of code looks odd. Remember that transfer registers have a read side and a write side, and each side can contain different data. This line is necessary so that the data read from SRAM can later be written back to SRAM in the new array. As an alternative, the `read` and `write` sides of transfer registers can be declared separately, using the `read` and `write` keywords on `.reg` declarations.

IXP1200
Note

The ability to declare only the read or write transfer registers is an improvement of the assembly language over the assembly language used for the IXP12XX. The IXP12XX assembler allocated both a read and write transfer register for every declared transfer register.

Lines 85-86:

These lines issue an SRAM write access to write the data into the new array. The format of the write command is just like the format of the read command. This instance reuses the signal that was used for reading SRAM and also swaps the current context out until the access is complete.

Lines 89-91:

These lines update the loop counters that the code maintains in registers. These counters are either incremented or decremented by 4 because each iteration handles one long-word and SRAM is byte addressed.

This simple implementation doesn't look too different from the code the compiler creates for the microengine C implementation, so the performance is very similar. In the next section, you'll see how to use some of the features of microengine assembly to improve performance.

Optimizing the Microengine Assembly Implementation

Both of the implementations discussed so far are slower than they could be. These implementations reverse the array of long-words one at a time, but the SRAM unit allows the microengines to issue memory reads and writes with as many as 16 long-words at a time. The latency experienced when accessing memory can be broken down into two components. One component is relatively fixed with respect to the size of the memory access and includes queuing latency between the microengine and the memory controller. The other component scales with the size of the access and is influenced by the throughput of the memory itself. If our code were to read multiple long-word entries at a time, the first latency would have much less impact on the performance of the code because it would be incurred fewer times. So, instead of reading and writing one long-word array entry at a time, the optimized code reads and writes multiple long-words at a time.

Our optimized implementation has a loop that reads and writes 8 long-words at a time. Each iteration of the loop reads 8 long-words from SRAM, reverses these long-words in the transfer registers, and writes 8 long-words back to SRAM. If the arrays were all sized in multiples of 8, this operation would be simple. But this is not the case. In fact, our example arrays are 10 long-words. So the last iteration of the loop needs to reverse less than 8 long-words. Handling this special case for the last iteration is challenging. The microengine instruction set allows SRAM reads and writes to be even greater sizes than 8 long-words. We can make this code even faster by reading and writing up to 16 long-words at a time.

The first implementation we considered was to put the first read transfer register into the last write transfer register, the second read transfer register into the second-to-last write transfer register, and so on, regardless of how many registers were being reversed. See Figure 4.14 for an example.

This option requires that the SRAM write start at a different transfer register when the number of swapped registers changes. For example, in Figure 4.14, because four registers are being swapped, the SRAM write has to start with the fifth transfer register. Unfortunately, the SRAM instructions require that the starting transfer register be specified at compile time. So this option is not possible.

The next option we considered was to reverse the transfer registers such that the SRAM write always starts with the same transfer register. See Figure 4.15 for an example.

With this method, the SRAM write always starts at the first transfer register, avoiding the problem with the first option. When moving data from the read transfer registers to the write transfer registers, however, data from the first read transfer register does not always go into the last write transfer register. In the example in Figure 4.15, the data in the first read transfer register is written into the fourth write transfer register. Performing transfers like this is not a problem in the microengine instruction set because the ALU unit can perform indexed accesses to the transfer registers. Therefore, we chose this implementation option for our code. When we dissect the code, you'll see how this is done.

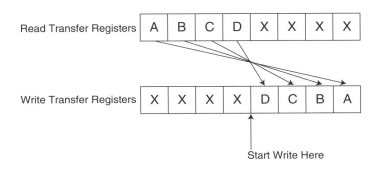

Figure 4.14 First Option for Reversing Transfer Registers

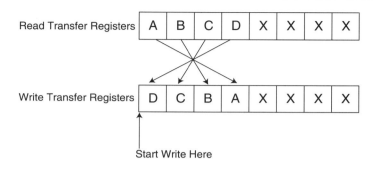

Read Transfer Registers | A | B | C | D | X | X | X | X

Write Transfer Registers | D | C | B | A | X | X | X | X

Start Write Here

Figure 4.15 Second Option for Reversing Transfer Registers

Although this optimized code is written in microengine assembly and not in microengine C, it does not mean that it could not be written in microengine C. However, to reverse multiple long-words at a time in microengine C, the code loses some of its elegance. The memory accesses have to be done with intrinsics instead of simple array accesses. It doesn't take too many such optimizations before the microengine C code starts looking a lot like microengine assembly.

The optimized microengine assembly code is implemented in the reverse_array_advanced macro here:

reverse_array_advanced()

```
        File: Chapter04\hello_world.uc
123     #macro reverse_array_advanced[in_old, in_new, in_size]
124     .begin
125         .reg entries_left current_old_entry current_new_entry
126
127         // We need an array of eight transfer registers to
128         // read and write eight longwords at a time
129         xbuf_alloc($array_data, 8, read_write)
130
131         // Set up a count of remaining entries and SRAM
132         // pointers
133         move(entries_left, in_size)
134         // Set up a pointer to the current array entry in
135         // the old array
136         move(current_old_entry, in_old)
137
138         // Set up a pointer to the current array entry in
```

Continues

```
139       // the new array. This works out to be
140       // in_new + (in_size * 4), because the code starts
141       // at the back of the new array, and because it
142       // operates with 4-byte longwords.
143       move(current_new_entry, in_new)
144       add_shf_left(current_new_entry, current_new_entry,
145                   in_size, 2)
146
147       // Now loop one longword at a time and copy the
148       // array
149       .reg entries_to_move    // The number of entries to
150                               // move on each iteration
151       .while (entries_left != 0)
152           // Need a signal for SRAM accesses
153           .sig sram_sig
154
155           // Figure out how many entries to move
156           .if (entries_left < 8)
157               move(entries_to_move, entries_left)
158           .else
159               immed[entries_to_move, 8]
160           .endif
161
162           // Figure out where to write the new data
163           sub_shf_left(current_new_entry,
164                       current_new_entry,
165                       entries_to_move, 2)
166
167           // Read the old array from SRAM. We use an
168           // indirect refernce to specify the number of
169           // entries to read
170           .reg sram_indirect
171           shf_left(sram_indirect, entries_to_move, 21)
172           sub_shf_left(sram_indirect, sram_indirect, 1, 21)
173           or_shf_left(sram_indirect, sram_indirect, 1, 25)
174           sram[read, $array_data[0], current_old_entry, 0,
175               max_8], ctx_swap[sram_sig], indirect_ref
176
177           // When we write the new array, we need to do so
178           // specifying the first transfer register with
179           // the data. So we need to use indexed transfer
180           // registers.
181           .reg xfer_index
182           shf_left(xfer_index, &$array_data[0], 2)
183           add_shf_left(xfer_index, xfer_index,
184                       entries_to_move, 2)
185           sub_shf_left(xfer_index, xfer_index, 1, 2)
```

Continues

```
186              local_csr_wr[T_INDEX, xfer_index]
187
188              // Move the data from the read side of the
189              // transfer registers to the write side
190              .reg xfers_to_move
191
192              // Assure the assembler that we know what we're
193              // doing
194              .set $array_data1 $array_data2 $array_data3
195              .set $array_data4 $array_data5 $array_data6
196              .set $array_data7
197
198              move(xfers_to_move, entries_to_move)
199              // The local_csr_wr above takes 3 cycles to take
200              // effect. The move above should take care of
201              // one cycle, the nops take care of the other
202              // two
203              nop
204              nop
205              move($array_data[0], *$index--)
206              sub(xfers_to_move, xfers_to_move, 1)
207              br=0[done_moving_xfers#]
208              move($array_data[1], *$index--)
209              sub(xfers_to_move, xfers_to_move, 1)
210              br=0[done_moving_xfers#]
211              move($array_data[2], *$index--)
212              sub(xfers_to_move, xfers_to_move, 1)
213              br=0[done_moving_xfers#]
214              move($array_data[3], *$index--)
215              sub(xfers_to_move, xfers_to_move, 1)
216              br=0[done_moving_xfers#]
217              move($array_data[4], *$index--)
218              sub(xfers_to_move, xfers_to_move, 1)
219              br=0[done_moving_xfers#]
220              move($array_data[5], *$index--)
221              sub(xfers_to_move, xfers_to_move, 1)
222              br=0[done_moving_xfers#]
223              move($array_data[6], *$index--)
224              sub(xfers_to_move, xfers_to_move, 1)
225              br=0[done_moving_xfers#]
226              move($array_data[7], *$index--)
227
228              done_moving_xfers#:
229
230              // Assure the assembler that we know what we're
231              // doing
232              .use $array_data0 $array_data1 $array_data2
```

Continues

```
233                 .use $array_data3 $array_data4 $array_data5
234                 .use $array_data6 $array_data7
235
236                 // Write the new array. Again we use an
237                 // indirect reference, which we have
238                 // conveniently saved in a register
239                 alu[--, --, B, sram_indirect]
240                 sram[write, $array_data[0], current_new_entry,
241                         0, max_8], ctx_swap[sram_sig], indirect_ref
242
243                 // Update the counter and the pointers
244                 sub(entries_left, entries_left, entries_to_move)
245                 add_shf_left(current_old_entry,
246                             current_old_entry,
247                             entries_to_move, 2)
248         .endw
249
250         xbuf_free($array_data)
251     .end
252     #endm
```

The first thing to notice is that this implementation has a lot more code!
Let's see what this code does:

Line 129:

This implementation reads and writes up to 8 long-words at a time. To
read this much data, we need to allocate eight transfer registers. The
xbuf_alloc macro does this. In this instance, it allocates 8 consecutive
SRAM transfer registers. Because the register set name in the macro is
$array_data, individual registers in this set can be referred to using zero-
based array indices. For example, $array_data[2] references the third
SRAM transfer register in the set.

Lines 131-145:

The initialization of loop registers in this implementation is very similar to
the initialization in the simple implementation. The only difference is that
the current_new_entry is set up to point to the memory location after the
last entry in the new array.

Lines 155-160

The entries_to_move register is set to the number of long-words that will
be moved on this iteration of the loop. The number of long-words is 8 for
all iterations but the last, where it is the same as the number of remaining
array elements.

Lines 162-165

> The current_new_entry pointer is set based on the entries_to_move register. This pointer points to the memory location where data will be written in this loop iteration.

Lines 167-175

> The simple version of the SRAM read instruction requires that the amount of data to be read be specified at compile time. Because our new implementation may read different amounts of data during different loop iterations, our read instruction gets a bit more complicated. The indirect_ref optional token on the SRAM read instruction tells the microengine to use the ALU output of the previous instruction to specify extra parameters to the instruction. In this case, we use it to specify the amount of data to read. The max_8 gives register usage information to the assembler. The assembler assumes that all 8 transfer registers are being written when this token is on a memory read. It needs to know this to perform optimizations and give register usage warnings to the developer.

Lines 177-228

> This code reverses the transfer registers as described previously. First, the T_INDEX CSR is set to point to the last read transfer register involved in the swap. Later in the code, the data is moved from read transfer registers to write transfer registers using the *$index-- token. This token references the SRAM transfer register indexed by T_INDEX, and then decrements T_INDEX, all at once. The moving of data from read transfer registers to write transfer registers would ideally be done in a loop. Unfortunately, that requires two transfer register indexes: one for the read transfer registers and one for the write transfer registers. Because the instruction set only has one transfer register index, we unroll the loop and add conditional branches to get the microengine to leave the code when all of the data has been reversed. Only one T_INDEX register exists per microengine, so it is very important that no context swaps happen in between setting and using this CSR, or else other threads could modify T_INDEX.

Lines 194-196

> The assembler tries to warn developers if uninitialized transfer registers are written to memory. In our case, we make it hard for the assembler to make this determination because we initialize only a subset of the write transfer registers, and then only write to SRAM the ones we have set. The .set statement assures the assembler that we know what we're doing and

suppresses any warnings. This information may also be used to dynamically allocate registers only when they are used. This code is placed where it is to prevent such allocations from happening incorrectly.

Lines 232-234

Because we are using indexed transfer register accesses to read from the SRAM read transfer registers, the assembler can't tell at compile time which registers are being read. The assembler normally uses this information to warn the developer if they fail to use a declared register. To avoid these warnings for our code, we added these `.use` statements to assure the assembler that these transfer registers are in fact being used.

Lines 239-241

This code performs a variable length SRAM write very similar to the SRAM read above.

This optimized implementation performs quite a bit better than the original version. In our example code, the ten entry SRAM array is reversed using only four memory accesses taking a total of 524 cycles, instead of twenty memory accesses and 1809 cycles needed in the original version. Of course, there is a code-store tradeoff. The original microengine assembly implementation compiles to 16 instructions, while the optimized implementation compiles to 57 instructions. Such tradeoffs are common when writing microengine code.

Simulating the Microengine Assembly Code

Running the microengine assembly code in the simulator is not too different from running the microengine C code in the simulator. The format in which the debugger shows assembled code is somewhat different, however. Following the steps from the "Simulating the Microengine C Code" section above, you should be able to open the window for thread 0:1, and it should look something like Figure 4.16.

This view shows small green arrows where the microengine assembly macros are. Right clicking a line with a macro brings up a menu with two options that help you see the contents of the macros. The two options are "Expand Macro One Level" and "Expand Macro Fully." The first option expands the macro in the window and leaves any sub-macros unexpanded. The second option expands the macro and all of its sub-macros, recursively. After expanding a macro, right clicking the line

```
global_mem old_array      sram0 40
global_mem new_array      sram0 40
global_mem new_array_adv  sram0 40
.init old_array       1 2 3 4 5 6 7 8 9 10
.init new_array       0 0 0 0 0 0 0 0 0 0
.init new_array_adv   0 0 0 0 0 0 0 0 0 0
.begin
    if(ctx() == 0)
    br!=ctx[0,1000_01#]
    ctx_arb[voluntary]
        start_simple_reverse#:
        reverse_array_simple(old_array, new_array, 10)
            1001_end#:
        end_simple_reverse#:
        reverse_array_advanced(old_array, new_array_adv, 10)
    .endif
        end_advanced_reverse#:
        1000_01#:
        1000_end#:
    ctx_arb[kill], any
    end
nop
```

Figure 4.16 Simulator Code View for Microengine Assembly Code

with the macro again brings up a menu with the option "Collapse Macro." This option collapses the macro in the code viewer. The two buttons shown in Figure 4.17 can also be used to expand and collapse macros. Clicking the button on the left expands all of the macros in the current view one level, whereas clicking the button on the right collapses all of the macros one level.

To see the microengine assembly code in action, expand the `reverse_array_simple` macro one level, and insert a breakpoint at the first `add_shf_left` macro. Now, run the simulator until the breakpoint is reached. Notice that when you hold your mouse over the `old_array` and `new_array` pointers, the simulator does not give you information about them. These values are constants, so the simulator does not tell you anything about them. Instead, hold your mouse over the `current_old_entry` and `current_new_entry` values and record their contents. The names of these variables get prefixed with a string that might make these register names look weird at first. Don't worry, this prefix identifies the scope in which the registers are declared, keeping the register names unique throughout the code.

At the point where you put the breakpoint, `current_old_entry` was initialized with the value of `old_array` and `current_new_entry` was initialized with the value of `new_array`. So, you have found the pointers to

Figure 4.17 Expand/Collapse Macro Buttons

the original and new arrays. Now you can add memory watches for the arrays in the same way you did for the microengine C code and watch the code reverse the arrays in memory. The SRAM completion signal is sent to the microengine a few cycles before the write is actually performed by the SRAM unit, so don't be surprised if the data watch takes a few cycles to update with new values.

Summary

The Workbench allows you to set up a workspace in which to write microengine C and microengine assembly programs for the IXP2XXX processor. Its features allow you to adjust the compile, assemble, and link settings in a user-friendly way, and it is indispensable for developing, simulating, and debugging code. Microengine C is a powerful language for writing microengine code. It is simpler to use than microengine assembly, but can result in slower code. Optimizing code can result in much better performance, but often comes at the expense of readability and code store size.

Chapter 5

Receive, Process, and Transmit Basics

While some packet-processing applications are more complicated than others, if you think about most network processor applications, the basic receive-process-transmit framework, as shown in Figure 3.1, most likely applies. Whether you are writing code for a switch that simply forwards packets, or you are building a content-aware load balancer that decrypts packet contents and performs string searches of URLs, your application receives, processes, and then transmits packets. The only difference lies in the complexity of the processing tasks.

Given this, a good place for you to start is with the most basic receive-processing-transmit application: counting packets. This approach shows you how to receive packets, get them to a place where they can be processed, and finally get them from there to the transmit task. Following this, you can extend the processing task to include bigger and better things than just counting packets.

To simplify the code in this chapter, all of the receive, process, and transmit functions execute in a single thread in their respective microengines. This way, synchronization methods on the microengines and complicated data structures and algorithms normally associated with a meaningful processing task are not needed. After all, this chapter contains the first serious piece of code in the book! Subsequent chapters deal with all of the issues avoided in this chapter.

Receiving Packets

A packet processing application without packets is fairly boring. So the first step to building an interesting application is to receive packets. Once a packet is received, it can be passed to the processing tasks where you can add all of your great code.

As described in Chapter 2, receiving packets on the IXP2XXX processor consists of reassembling mpackets. Each mpacket is marked, by the hardware, as a start-of-packet (SOP), end-of-packet (EOP), both, or neither. Because mpackets arrive in order, the absence or presence of SOP and EOP marks provides the microengines with enough information to reassemble mpackets back into packets. For SOP mpackets, the microengines allocate a new buffer and the SOP mpacket data is placed into the beginning of the buffer memory. Buffers and buffer allocation are discussed in Chapter 10. For now, you can think of buffers as continuous blocks of memory.

A new buffer is not needed for non-SOP mpackets. Rather, non-SOP mpackets are placed in the same buffer directly after the previous mpacket. Figure 5.1 shows the reassembly of mpackets into complete buffers. Each SOP mpacket is placed into a new buffer, and all subsequent mpackets up to, and including, the EOP mpacket are placed directly after each other.

So how much memory should you allocate for a given incoming packet? Surprisingly, typically you cannot know from the SOP mpacket alone. For packets whose total length is not contained within the first mpacket, the entire packet length is unknown until all of the mpackets have been received. However, the buffer must be allocated on reception of the first mpacket. The straightforward solution, and the one used in this book, is to allocate fixed-size buffers, each one large enough to contain the largest expected physical packet. A more complex solution, which can be found in the Intel IXA SDK 3.0 receive driver, would be to allocate multiple buffers for a single packet. During the reassembly process, when the current buffer is full, a new buffer is allocated and linked to the full buffer. This multiple-buffer-per-packet approach can result in better memory utilization, but comes at the cost of extra complexity and reassembly processing requirements.

Figure 5.2 shows a flowchart of the mpacket-reassembly logic for a single packet. As already described, for each mpacket a different action is taken based on the SOP and EOP marks. SOP mpackets cause a new buffer to be allocated and then are copied into the new buffer, whereas non-SOP mpackets are simply copied into the existing buffer.

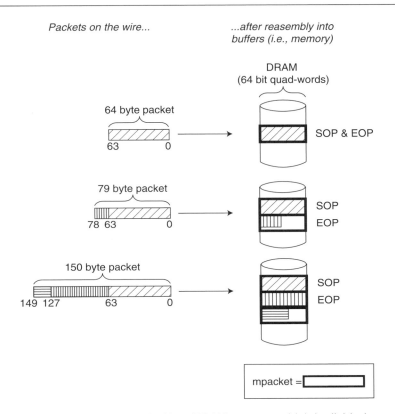

Mpackets are reassembled into DRAM memory, which is divided into buffers. The mpackets are placed contiguously in memory so that the buffer represents the packet data.

Figure 5.1 Reassembling 64-byte Mpackets Contiguously into Buffers, i.e., Memory

But how does the code know where to place the non-SOP mpackets? As the figure shows, the answer is through some kind of reassembly state information. This state information, as well as each of the steps in the reassembly flow, is detailed in the following examples.

Receiving One Mpacket

The first steps in the reassembly flow are to receive a single mpacket. Chapter 2 outlined the basic steps of receiving a single mpacket. Let's review these simple steps and at the same time write the corresponding code.

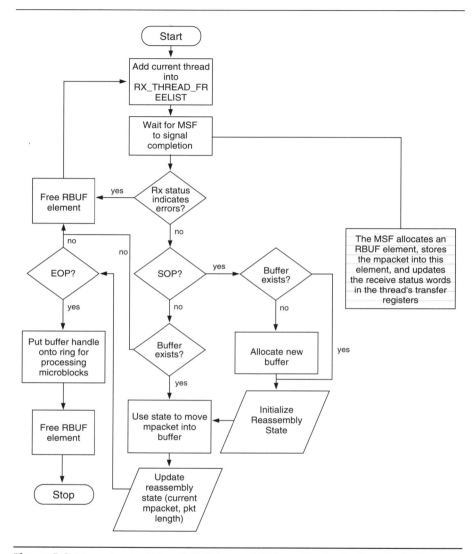

Figure 5.2 Flowchart of Mpacket Reassembly for a Single Packet (Including Errors)

To receive an mpacket, the microengines must:

1. Add the current thread into the receive thread freelist.
2. Wait for the MSF to signal the arrival of a new mpacket for the current thread.

It's that easy! Of course, in between these steps the MSF performs the hard work described in Chapter 2.

To add a thread into the receive thread freelist, the RX_THREAD_FREELIST_0 MSF CSR must be written. This CSR requires the following information, formatted as shown in Figure 5.3:

- The signal to send when the mpacket has been received.

- The transfer registers where the receive status should be written.

- The microengine and thread where the signal should be sent and where the transfer registers should be written.

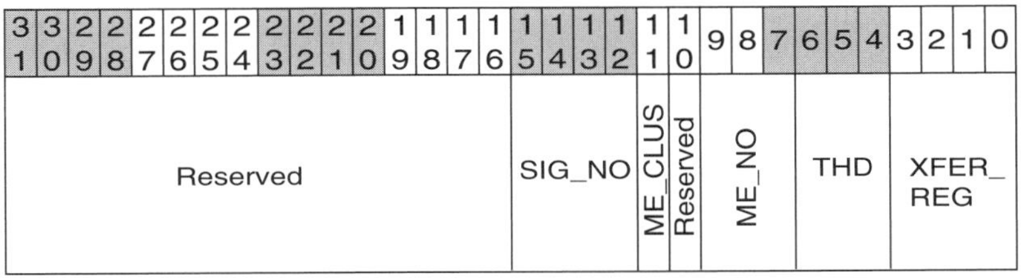

3 1	3 0	2 9	2 8	2 7	2 6	2 5	2 4	2 3	2 2	2 1	2 0	1 9	1 8	1 7	1 6	1 5	1 4	1 3	1 2	1 1	1 0	9	8	7	6	5	4	3	2	1	0
Reserved															SIG_NO				ME_CLUS	Reserved	ME_NO		THD			XFER_REG					

Figure 5.3 The Format of the RX_THREAD_FREELIST_0 CSR

The microengine assembly corresponding to receiving one mpacket is shown in the code below. The microengine C version of this code is also available on the accompanying CD-ROM.

_spi4_rx_get_mpacket()

File: Chapter05\spi4_rx.uc

```
146   #macro _spi4_rx_get_mpacket(out_rsw0, out_rsw1)
147   .begin
148       .sig rx_complete_sig
149       .reg rx_tfl rx_tfl_addr context
150
151       // Add the current thread into the thread freelist
152       .set_sig rx_complete_sig
153       // Add the wakeup signal when an mpacket arrives
154       shf_left(rx_tfl, &rx_complete_sig, 12)
155       // Add the microengine number to signal
156       alu_shf_left(rx_tfl, rx_tfl, OR, __UENGINE_ID, 7)
157       // Add the context to signal
158       local_csr_rd[ACTIVE_CTX_STS]
```

Continues

```
159        immed[context, 0]
160        alu[context, 0x7, and, context]
161        alu_shf_left(rx_tfl, rx_tfl, OR, context, 4)
162        // Add the transfer register address
163        // where the RSW words should be placed
164        alu_shf_left(rx_tfl, rx_tfl, OR, &out_rsw0, 0)
165
166        // Place the data into the upper 16 bits for
167        // the fast_wr operation
168        shf_left(rx_tfl, rx_tfl, 16)
169        immed32(rx_tfl_addr, MSF_RX_THREAD_FREELIST_0_ADDR)
170        msf[fast_wr, --, rx_tfl_addr, rx_tfl]
171
172        .set out_rsw0 out_rsw1
173        ctx_arb[rx_complete_sig] // wait for an mpacket
174    .end
175    #endm
```

Lines 146 – 149:

The `rx_get_mpacket` macro has two output parameters that correspond to the receive status associated with the received mpacket. These output parameters must be ordered SRAM read transfer registers. This routine instructs the MSF to write these transfer registers with information about the received mpacket, like the SOP and EOP markers.

The signal, `rx_complete_sig`, is part of the information placed on the receive thread freelist. The MSF sends this signal to the appropriate microengine after the mpacket has been received and the receive status has been written into the transfer registers discussed above.

Line 152:

The first line produces no instructions; rather it suppresses an assembler warning. The `.set_sig` directive, like the `.set` directive for registers, tells the assembler to assume that the given signal has been assigned a value. The assembler pairs instructions that generate signals with the instructions that wait for these signals. In this instance, the MSF is generating the signal and thus no instruction explicitly generates the signal. Without this directive, the assembler would assume the code that waits for this signal (line 173) was incorrect.

Line 154 – 164:

These lines of code form the value needed to write the RX_THREAD_FREELIST_0 MSF CSR. Specifically, these lines write the `rx_tfl` register with the signal, microengine, and thread numbers, according to the format of the receive thread freelist CSR, shown above in Figure 5.3.

In these lines, the syntax &rx_complete_sig and &out_rsw0 expand to constants corresponding to the signal number and transfer register number of the named variables, respectively.

Also, the three lines necessary to read the thread number (lines 158–160) require a bit of explanation. To read a microengine CSR, the local_csr_rd instruction is used with the name of the CSR to read. However, this instruction has no register argument where the value of the CSR should be placed! Instead, the next instruction must be an immed instruction with the destination register to be filled with the value of the CSR. So, after line 159, the context register contains the value of the ACTIVE_CTX_STS CSR. Line 160 extracts just the thread number from the CSR.

Lines 168 – 170:

These lines of code write the RX_THREAD_FREELIST_0 MSF CSR with the value formed in the previous lines. This write is accomplished with the msf[fast_wr, …] instruction.

The MSF is accessed as a single memory region. All aspects of the MSF—CSRs, RBUFs, TBUFs—are accessed by reading and writing the proper address in the MSF. So, to write the RX_THREAD_FREELIST_0 MSF CSR, the address of the CSR in the MSF memory map must first be found. Using the *Programmer's Reference Manual* (Intel 2002), we defined MSF_RX_THREAD_FREELIST_0_ADDR with this value, which is 0x30 for those who really like the details.

In addition to the correct address, the msf[fast_wr, --, arg1, arg2] instruction is given the value to write, with one peculiarity: the value is taken from the upper 16-bits of the logically OR'ed arguments (i.e., arg1 | arg2). Thus, the code must first shift the value up by 16-bits.

Lines 172 – 173:

Finally, these lines of code wait for the MSF to signal this thread that an mpacket has been received. Once this signal has been received, the value of the receive-status words for the mpacket are available in the SRAM transfer registers.

MSF Writes and fast_writes

An alternative to the msf[fast_wr, …] is the msf[write, …] instruction. For example, the lines 168 through 170 of the rx_get_mpacket macro could have been written with the msf[write, …] instruction as follows:

```
.begin
        .reg $rx_tfl_xfer
        .sig tfl_write_sig
        move($rx_tfl_xfer, rx_tfl)
        immed32(rx_tfl_addr,
                MSF_RX_THREAD_FREELIST_0_ADDR)
        msf[write, $rx_tfl_xfer, rx_tfl_addr, 0, 1],
                ctx_swap[tfl_write_sig]
.end
```

The difference between msf[fast_wr, …] and msf[write, …] is that the code does not have to wait for the former to complete before continuing execution. The code that uses msf[write, …], has to block the executing thread to wait for a signal indicating the write transfer register was read by the MSF.

So why would msf[write, …] ever be used? Well, msf[fast_wr, …] can only write 16-bits of data, and thus any MSF CSR that contains more than 16-bits of data must be written with msf[write, …].

Understanding RBUF Partitions

Why did the code in rx_get_mpacket write to RX_THREAD_FREELIST_0, instead of just RX_THREAD_FREELIST? Well the MSF hardware contains multiple receive thread freelists. The IXP2800 and IXP2850 have three such freelists, and the IXP2400 has four.

A thread can add itself to any receive thread freelist, at any time. And, so long as different wake-up signals and transfer registers are used for the receive status, a thread can simultaneously be on multiple receive thread freelists.

Each of these receive thread freelists behaves the same from the software's perspective. However, the receive thread freelist the MSF uses for incoming mpackets depends on both the processor as well as the hardware configuration.

In the IXP2800 and IXP2850, each of the three receive thread freelists is associated with an RBUF partition. An RBUF partition is simply a contiguous set of RBUF elements. Incoming mpackets are assigned to a RBUF partition based on interface (SPI-4 or CSIX) and type (CSIX control or CSIX data).

In the IXP2400, each of the four receive thread freelists is associated with either a channel—think 'port'—of the hardware, or type of data (CSIX control or CSIX data).

For more details on these hardware configurations, see (Carlson 2003). This chapter only deals with one port, one RBUF partition, and one receive thread freelist.

Reassembling Mpackets into Packets

Once a single mpacket is received, you can start assembling these mpackets into whole packets. As shown in Figure 5.2, this process involves checking the mpacket for errors, examining the SOP and EOP flags in the receive status words, and finally moving the mpacket into the appropriate location in DRAM.

To check for errors and the SOP and EOP flags, you must understand receive status words. The SPI-4 receive status word format is shown in Figure 5.4. This format helps you to understand the following code, which shows the spi4_rx() routine for reassembling mpackets into packets.

31	30	29	28	27	26	25	24	23	22	21	20	19	18	17	16	15	14	13	12	11	10	9	8	7	6	5	4	3	2	1	0
RPROT	Element							Byte Count								SOP	EOP	Err	Len Err	Par Err	Abort Err	Null	Type	ADR							

63	62	61	60	59	58	57	56	55	54	53	52	51	50	49	48	47	46	45	44	43	42	41	40	39	38	37	36	35	34	33	32
Reserved																Checksum															

Figure 5.4 The Format of the SPI-4 Receive Status Words

spi4_rx()

File: Chapter05\spi4_rx.uc

```
266     #macro spi4_rx()
267     .begin
268         .reg buf_length
269         .reg cur_mpacket_addr  // A pointer into dram where
270                                //   the next mpacket should be
271                                //   placed
272         .set cur_mpacket_addr
273         .reg rbuf_elem, elem_size
274                                // The RBUF element number
275                                //   and size of the current
276                                //   mpacket.
277
278         .reg $rsw0 $rsw1        // The receive status words
279         .xfer_order $rsw0 $rsw1
280
281         .sig buf_alloc_sig
282
283         immed32(dl_buf_handle, 0)
284         immed32(buf_length, 0)
285
286         .while(1)
287             // Get the next mpacket
288             _spi4_rx_get_mpacket($rsw0, $rsw1)
289             .use $rsw1 // Suppress an assembler warning
290
291             // Extract the RBUF element number and size
292             alu_shf_right(rbuf_elem,
293                         RSW_SPHY4_ELEMENT_MASK, AND,
294                          $rsw0, RSW_SPHY4_ELEMENT_BITPOS)
295             alu_shf_right(elem_size,
296                         RSW_SPHY4_BYTECOUNT_MASK,
297                         AND, $rsw0,
298                         RSW_SPHY4_BYTECOUNT_BITPOS)
299
300             // Check for errors in the packet
301             // These indicate that the current buffer,
302             // if any, should be discarded
303             .if (BIT($rsw0, RSW_SPHY4_ERRORS_BITPOS))
304                 .if (dl_buf_handle != 0)
305                     // Drop the packet
306                     dl_buf_drop(dl_buf_handle)
307                 .endif
308
```

Continues

```
309         _spi4_rx_free_rbuf(rbuf_elem)
310         immed32(dl_buf_handle, 0)
311         immed32(buf_length, 0)
312         .continue
313     .endif
314
315     // If this is the SOP, allocate a new buffer
316     .if (BIT($rsw0, RSW_SPHY4_SOP_BITPOS) == 1)
317         .if (dl_buf_handle == 0)
318             .begin
319                 .reg $buf_handle_xfer
320                 dl_buf_alloc($buf_handle_xfer,
321                             BUF_QARRAY_BASE,
322                             buf_alloc_sig,
323                             buf_alloc_sig)
324                 move(dl_buf_handle,
325                     $buf_handle_xfer)
326             .end
327             .if (dl_buf_handle == 0)
328                 // No more buffers
329                 _spi4_rx_free_rbuf(rbuf_elem)
330                 .continue
331             .endif
332         .endif
333         dl_buf_get_data(cur_mpacket_addr,
334                         dl_buf_handle)
335     .elif (dl_buf_handle == 0)
336         // An MOP or EOP mpacket was received
337         // without an SOP mpacket first
338         _spi4_rx_free_rbuf(rbuf_elem)
339         .continue
340     .endif
341
342     // Move the mpacket into DRAM
343     .begin
344         .sig rbuf_to_dram_sig
345
346         _spi4_rx_move_rbuf_to_dram(
347                 rbuf_elem,
348                 cur_mpacket_addr,
349                 elem_size,
350                 rbuf_to_dram_sig)
351
352         // Update the buffer length
353         add(buf_length, buf_length, elem_size)
354
355         // Wait for the mpacket to move into DRAM
```

Continues

```
356                      ctx_arb[rbuf_to_dram_sig]
357
358                      _spi4_rx_free_rbuf(rbuf_elem)
359
360                      // If this is the EOP mpacket then return
361                      .if (BIT($rsw0, RSW_SPHY4_EOP_BITPOS) == 1)
362                              .break
363                      .endif
364
365                      // Update the reassembly pointer
366                      add(cur_mpacket_addr, cur_mpacket_addr,
367                          elem_size)
368                 .end
369          .endw
370
371      dl_meta_set_offset(0)
372      dl_meta_set_buffer_size(buf_length)
373      immed32(dl_next_block, SPI4_RX_NEXT_BLOCK)
374  .end
375  #endm // rx_packet
```

Lines 303 – 313:

These lines check for any SPI-4[1] errors—abort, parity, or length—in the receive status. Notice only one bit is checked. Although each of the possible error conditions is also available in the receive status word, the MSF does a nice thing and logically ORs all of the errors in the receive status word into a single error bit. The actions taken on any error are the same:

■ Discard the current buffer, if it exists, using the buf_free macro[2]

■ Free the RBUF element using the _spi4_rx_free_rbuf macro

■ Clear out the reassembly state

To free an RBUF element, the `_spi4_rx_free_rbuf` macro writes the RBUF element number onto an RBUF element freelist in the MSF. As explained in Chapter 2, the MSF maintains a queue of RBUF elements that are available for storing incoming mpackets. After the microengines have received and finished using an mpacket, they must write the RBUF element back to this freelist. Otherwise, the MSF never again uses this RBUF element for new mpackets.

---

[1] Strictly speaking, SPI-4 Phase 2, but we refer to this interface simply as SPI-4 in this book.

[2] Buffers are covered in Chapter 10

Lines 316 – 340:

These lines of code first check the SOP bit in the receive status. If the SOP bit is set, a new buffer is allocated, and the reassembly state is initialized. If the SOP bit is not set, the code checks that a valid buffer handle exists. If not, a middle or end of packet (MOP or EOP) mpacket has been received without first receiving an SOP mpacket. In this situation, the only appropriate action is to return the RBUF element to the RBUF element freelist and wait for the next mpacket.

Actually, the code is not quite that simple. A few additional error checks and optimizations are performed that require further explanation.

First, if an SOP mpacket is received but a buffer is already allocated, for example, because the previous packet contained errors, then, conceptually the current buffer must be freed and a new one allocated. This situation would occur if the code never encountered an EOP mpacket for the previous packet. Instead of dropping the current buffer and reallocating another buffer, which would likely just be the same buffer, the current buffer is overwritten with the new packet.

Second, if the buffer allocation fails, the RBUF element number is returned to the RBUF element freelist. (You'll soon get tired of reading about freeing the RBUF element. Every path through the code must free the RBUF element or else the code would slowly leak RBUF elements, and, in turn, the receive process would stop. Not that we have ever done that.)

Lines 346 – 350:

This routine transfers the mpacket into DRAM memory at the given DRAM address. The details of this routine are explained after this example.

Lines 352, 366:

These two lines of code update the reassembly state. The first group updates the packet length. The second group updates the pointer to where the next mpacket should be placed in DRAM.

Lines 356 – 358:

After starting the transfer of the RBUF into DRAM, this code first waits for the signal indicating the transfer is complete. Next, the RBUF element is freed. The order of these operations is important. The RBUF element cannot be freed before the transfer of the current RBUF data into DRAM is complete because the MSF might then overwrite the current RBUF data with the data from a new mpacket.

Lines 361 – 363, 371 – 373:

When an EOP mpacket is encountered, the reassembly loop is stopped. However, before the routine returns, the dispatch loop metadata is updated. This process includes setting the variable dl_buf_handle (which we did throughout the routine), the offset from the start of the buffer to the first valid byte of the packet, the length of the packet, and the next microblock that should execute.

Actually, because we are writing a driver, we don't have to be so formal about following the dispatch loop and microblock model, however, using such infrastructure from the IXA SDK 3.0 just saves us time.

Moving Mpackets into Buffers

Looking at the flowchart in Figure 5.2, after an mpacket is received, the receive status is checked for errors, and after the buffer is found or allocated, the mpacket is transferred into the buffer. The following microengine assembly code shows the _spi4_rx_move_rbuf_to_dram routine which performs the task of transferring an mpacket into a buffer. This routine takes advantage of an instruction to directly transfer RBUF data into DRAM, as explained following the code.

_spi4_rx_move_rbuf_to_dram()

File: Chapter05\spi4_rx.uc

```
208   #macro _spi4_rx_move_rbuf_to_dram(in_rbuf_elem, in_dram_addr, \
209                           in_size, in_dram_sig)
210   .begin
211       .reg indir rbuf_addr qwords_to_xfer new_size
212
213       // Compute the RBUF address. This is the base RBUF
214       // address in the MSF plus the element number times
215       // 64. The multiplication by 64 comes from the fact
216       // that the element number given in the RSW is
217       // divided by 64
218       immed32(rbuf_addr, MSF_RBUF_BASE_ADDR)
219       alu_shf_left(rbuf_addr, rbuf_addr, +,
220                   in_rbuf_elem, 6)
221
222       // Override the rbuf addr
223       shf_left(indir, 1, 4)
224       alu_shf_left(indir, indir, OR, rbuf_addr, 5)
225       // Override the transfer size
226       alu_shf_left(indir, indir, OR, 1, 25)
```

Continues

```
227        add(new_size, in_size, 7)
228        alu_shf_right(qwords_to_xfer, 0xff, AND, new_size, 3)
229        sub(qwords_to_xfer, qwords_to_xfer, 1)
230        alu_shf_left(indir, indir, OR, qwords_to_xfer, 21)
231        dram[rbuf_rd, --, in_dram_addr, 0, max_16],
232            indirect_ref,
233            sig_done[in_dram_sig]
234        .use indir // Suppress an assembler warning
235    .end
236    #endm
```

Lines 218 – 224:

The dram[rbuf_rd, …] instruction requires an indirect token to specify several parameters of the RBUF-to-DRAM transfer. This token is built up successively into the register indir.

The first piece of information placed into this indirect token is the RBUF element address from which to transfer. This address is composed of the RBUF base address—remember all of the MSF is memory mapped, even RBUFs!—plus the RBUF element number.

Except it isn't quite that simple, the RBUF element number provided by the receive status is in units of 64 bytes.[3] The indirect token requires a byte address, so the RBUF element number is multiplied by 64 before adding it to the base address and placing it in the indir register.

Lines 225 – 230:

Instead of specifying the number of bytes to transfer, the indirect token specifies the number of quad-words to transfer, minus one. The quad-word transfer size is based on the native transfer size of DRAM. The subtraction by one is because it does not make sense to transfer zero quad-words, so a zero value is used to represent one quad-word, which leads to two quad-words being represented with a one, and so on.

Lines 231 – 234:

Finally, the actual dram[rbuf_rd, …] instruction is issued. The address into which to transfer the data, in_dram_addr, is the given byte address into DRAM. The indir value built up in the previous lines of code specifies the RBUF element and size of the transfer.

The instruction is told to generate the signal passed into the routine. The calling routine must eventually catch this signal to ensure that the transfer has completed.

---

[3] The RBUF addressing on the IXP2800 and IXP2850 works in this manner. However, as we describe in Chapter 13, the RBUF and TBUF address on the IXP2400 depends on the size of the RBUF or TBUF, respectively.

These lines of code do not handle 256-byte RBUFs. The maximum transfer size of the `dram_rbuf_read_ind` intrinsic is 16 quad-words (i.e., 128 bytes). Had we wanted to support 256-byte RBUFs, this code would need to call `dram_rbuf_read_ind` twice. Each would transfer 128 bytes of data.

Putting the Receive Task Together

Now that we have a packet reassembled, the final step is to put each received packet on a ring for the processing task. After all, almost as boring as not receiving packets is receiving packets and then not doing anything with them.

The following code shows the main processing loop—a dispatch loop—for the receive task's microengine. Chapter 10 covers the details of initializing and accessing rings and queues.

spi4_rx_dl()

```
File: Chapter05\dispatch_loop\spi4_rx_dl.uc
51          .while(1)
52              // Reassemble a packet
53              spi4_rx()
54
55              // Enqueue the packet on the rx to processing
56              dl_sink()
57          .endw
```

Lines 51 – 57:

These lines are easy to understand. The `spi4_rx` routine is called to receive a packet. When this routine returns, the `dl_buf_handle` and dispatch loop metadata represent a received packet.

The `dl_sink` routine enqueues the current packet onto a ring for the processing task. We cover rings and queues in Chapter 10.

■ Processing Packets

Now things start getting more exciting. We have completed the first step in our receive-process-transmit pipeline, so you have the code that receives packets and puts them on a ring. So, go ahead and dream about all the possible processing you want to do on these packets. We dreamed and came up with: counting packets.

The basic steps of our packet processing task are:

1. Get the next packet from the receive-to-processing packet ring.

2. Increment the packet counter in scratchpad memory.

3. Put the packet onto the processing-to-transmit ring.

The following microengine assembly code illustrates these steps, with an explanation following the code.

count_dl()

```
        File: Chapter05\dispatch_loop\count_dl.uc
55                .while(1)
56                    // Dequeue a packet from the rx task
57                    dl_source()
58
59                    .if (dl_buf_handle == 0)
60                        .continue
61                    .endif
62
63                    // Increment the counters
64                    count()
65
66                    // Enqueue the packet on the processing to tx
67                    // scratch ring
68                    dl_sink()
69                .endw
```

Lines 57 – 60:

The dl_source routine pulls packets from the ring between the receive driver and this microengine. After this routine returns, the dl_buf_handle variable and dispatch-loop metadata represent the next packet to process.

However, realize that the dl_source routine can (and should!) return periodically regardless of the availability of a packet. This behavior enables other microblocks in the dispatch loop to execute, which can prove to be particularly important for some applications that execute even in the absence of packet stimulus (see Chapter 11 for more details). In this simple example, the count microblock does not need to run unless a packet is available so this dispatch loop continues to execute dl_source until a valid packet is returned.

Line 68:

Once the count microblock has finished with the packet, the dl_sink routine places the packet onto a ring to the transmit driver. Notice that this instance of dl_sink is distinct from (although named identically to) the dl_sink routine in the receive driver. This naming is possible because the two pieces of code execute on different microengines.

The implementation of the count microblock is shown in the following example.

count()

File: Chapter05\count.uc

```
78   #macro count()
79   .begin
80       .reg $buf_length_xfer buf_length
81       .reg addr
82       .sig counter_sig
83
84       move(addr, g_pkt_count)
85       scratch[incr, --, addr, 0]
86
87       dl_meta_get_buffer_size(buf_length)
88       move($buf_length_xfer, buf_length)
89       move(addr, g_byte_count)
90       scratch[add, $buf_length_xfer, addr, 0],
91           ctx_swap[counter_sig]
92
93       immed32(dl_next_block, COUNT_NEXT_BLOCK)
94   .end
95   #endm
```

Lines 84 – 85:

Once a packet is retrieved from the ring, the packet counter in scratchpad memory is atomically incremented. This task is accomplished with a single instruction, which does not require a signal to be generated or caught.

Lines 87 – 91:

In addition, we atomically add the length of the packet to a byte counter also maintained in scratchpad memory. To do this, we first extract the packet length from the dispatch loop metadata using the dl_meta_get_ buffer_size macro that is supplied with the Intel IXA SDK 3.0. Then, we use the atomic addition feature of the scratchpad memory, which is explained in more detail in Chapter 7.

Transmitting Packets

Armed with code to receive and count packets, all that is left to complete the framework is to write the transmit driver. And just think, once you understand this last task, you can expand on the processing task and build any application you want!

The transmit driver reverses the reassembly done in the receive driver by breaking packets into one or more mpackets. The size of each mpacket is determined by the size of each TBUF, which can be configured as 64, 128, or 256 bytes.

Transmitting One Mpacket

From the microengine's perspective, the process of sending an individual mpacket has four steps:

1. Select a TBUF element in which to write data.

2. Wait for that TBUF element to be clear of valid data.

3. Transfer the mpacket into the TBUF element from DRAM, or possibly microengine transfer registers.

4. Write and validate the control words of the TBUF element with the SOP, EOP, and port information.

IXP1200 Note

You probably noticed, and welcomed, the lack of any transmit ready bits in these steps. On the IXP2XXX processor, the MSF takes care of dealing with the 'transmit readiness' of physical devices. The microengines only need to make sure the TBUF element being written does not contain valid data. However, the lack of ready bits does not mean you can completely avoid the issues of flow control and head-of-line blocking on the outgoing interface, because both of these problems can still occur on the IXP2XXX processor (like any other device transmitting data!). We discuss these issues more in Chapter 12.

To illustrate these steps, let's look at one 64-byte mpacket as it is moved from DRAM to a TBUF.

Selecting a TBUF Element

The first step of selecting a TBUF element in which to write an mpacket depends, to a great extent, on the ports supported by the device. For example, the code either allocates TBUF elements to particular ports, or even to microengines if more than one microengine is transmitting packets. For this chapter and this example, we'll blissfully ignore these complications and deal with only one port and one thread. Thus, all TBUFs are for use by the single transmit thread for the single port and are allocated in round-robin order.

Waiting for the TBUF Element

The second step, waiting for the TBUF to be clear of valid data, is the most complicated step and involves a global view of the TSM hardware. So let's skip this step for now and return to it last. For now, assume by some miracle, that the microengine code chooses to work on TBUF element 5, which does not contain valid data, as shown in Figure 5.5.

Moving DRAM Data to a TBUF

The third step is for the microengines to put data into the TBUF element by initiating a transfer from its SRAM transfer registers or by initiating a transfer from DRAM directly into the TBUF element. Figure 5.5 shows data from DRAM being transferred directly into the TBUF element from DRAM.

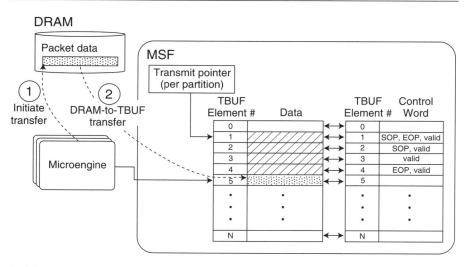

In this diagram, the microengine has completed a direct transfer of the packet data from DRAM to TBUF element 5.

Figure 5.5 Transferring Data from DRAM to a TBUF Element

The code to perform this transfer is shown below in the microengine assembly macro _spi4_tx_move_dram_to_tbuf.

_spi4_tx_move_dram_to_tbuf()

File: Chapter05\spi4_tx.uc

```
106   #macro _spi4_tx_move_dram_to_tbuf(\
107       in_tbuf_elem, \
108       in_dram_addr, \
109       in_size, \
110       in_dram_sig)
111   .begin
112       .reg indir tbuf_addr qwords_to_xfer new_size
113
114       // Compute the TBUF address. This is the base TBUF
115       // address in the MSF plus the element number times
116       // 64.
117       immed32(tbuf_addr, MSF_TBUF_BASE_ADDR)
118       alu_shf_left(tbuf_addr, tbuf_addr, OR,
119                    in_tbuf_elem, 6)
120       // Override the tbuf address
121       alu[indir, --, B, 1, <<4]
122       alu[indir, indir, OR, tbuf_addr, <<5]
123       // Override the transfer size
124       alu_shf_left(indir, indir, OR, 1, 25)
125       add(new_size, in_size, 7)
126       alu_shf_right(qwords_to_xfer, 0xff, AND, new_size, 3)
127       sub(qwords_to_xfer, qwords_to_xfer, 1)
128       alu_shf_left(indir, indir, OR, qwords_to_xfer, 21)
129       dram[tbuf_wr, --, in_dram_addr, 0, 8],
130           indirect_ref,
131           sig_done[in_dram_sig]
132       .use indir // Suppress an assembler warning
133   .end
134   #endm
```

Lines 117 – 128:

In a series of steps nearly identical to those used to move data from an RBUF into DRAM, these lines of code transfer data from DRAM into a TBUF. The same tricks necessary for the RBUF-to-DRAM transfer are used. Namely, the TBUF element number is converted into an MSF address, and the size of the transfer is converted from bytes into quad-words, minus one.

Lines 129 – 131:

> Finally, the `dram[tbuf_wr, …]` instruction is used in place of the `dram[rbuf_rd, …]` instruction.

Writing the Transmit Control Words

The fourth step to transmitting a single mpacket is to write to the control words associated with the TBUF element. These control words contain information for the transmit state machine about the port on which to send the data, the amount of data to send, and whether or not the data is the first, middle, or last mpacket of a larger packet, as shown in Figure 5.6.

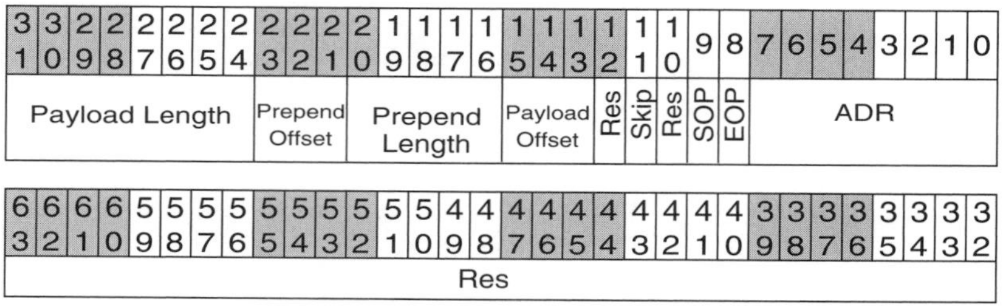

3 3 2 2 2 2 2 2 2 2 2 2 1 1 1 1 1 1 1 1 1 1										
1 0 9 8 7 6 5 4 3 2 1 0 9 8 7 6 5 4 3 2 1 0		9 8 7 6 5 4 3 2 1 0								
Payload Length	Prepend Offset	Prepend Length	Payload Offset	Res	Skip	Res	SOP	EOP	ADR	

6 6 6 6 5 5 5 5 5 5 5 5 5 5 4 4 4 4 4 4 4 4 4 4 3 3 3 3 3 3 3 3
3 2 1 0 9 8 7 6 5 4 3 2 1 0 9 8 7 6 5 4 3 2 1 0 9 8 7 6 5 4 3 2
Res

Figure 5.6 The Format of the SPI-4 Transmit Control Words

Writing to the transmit control words associated with a TBUF element automatically validates the element, as shown in Figure 5.7.

The following code shows how to write the transmit control words for a TBUF element associated with a SPI-4 port.

_spi4_tx_validate_tbuf()

File:Chapter05\spi4_tx.uc

```
158    #macro _spi4_tx_validate_tbuf(\
159        in_tbuf_elem, \
160        in_sop, \
161        in_eop, \
162        in_size)
163    .begin
164        .reg $tbuf_control_xfer $reserved tbuf_control
```

Continues

```
165         .xfer_order $tbuf_control_xfer $reserved
166         .reg tbuf_addr
167         .sig msf_sig
168
169         // Set the mpacket length
170         shf_left(tbuf_control, in_size, 24)
171         // Set SOP and EOP
172         alu_shf_left(tbuf_control, tbuf_control, OR,
173                     in_sop, 9)
174         alu_shf_left(tbuf_control, tbuf_control, OR,
175                     in_eop, 8)
176
177         immed32(tbuf_addr, MSF_TBUF_CONTROL_BASE_ADDR)
178         alu_shf_left(tbuf_addr, tbuf_addr, OR,
179                     in_tbuf_elem, 3)
180
181         move($tbuf_control_xfer, tbuf_control)
182         immed32($reserved, 0)
183         msf[write, $tbuf_control_xfer, tbuf_addr, 0, 2],
184             ctx_swap[msf_sig]
185     .end
186     #endm
```

Lines 170 – 175:

This routine first formats the transmit control words. The format of these two control words for the SPI-4 interface can be found in the *Programmer's Reference Manual* (Intel 2002) and is shown in Figure 5.6. The only fields that must be filled in are the mpacket length and the SOP and EOP bits.

Lines 177 – 183:

Of course, before the transmit control words are written into the MSF, the MSF address corresponding to the TBUF control words must be known. This address is computed by adding the base address of all transmit control words and the TBUF element number multiplied by eight. This multiplication is necessary to convert the TBUF element number into a byte offset since the two words per TBUF element are stored in eight bytes.

Once the transmit control words have been written, the MSF automatically validates the TBUF element, and the microengine code is finished with that mpacket. Transmitting the mpacket is now up to the TSM hardware. It processes the TBUF elements in order and advances the transmit pointer when it completes one. When it advances the transmit

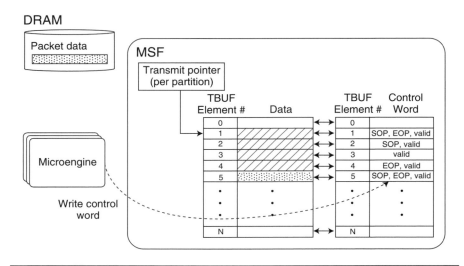

Figure 5.7 Microengine Validating the TBUF Element by Writing the Control Words Associated with the TBUF

pointer to element 5, the state machine sends the data in the TBUF element to the physical interface and it also marks the TBUF element as invalid, as shown in Figure 5.8.

Waiting for the TBUF Element: Revisited

A single mpacket has now been successfully transmitted by transferring it from DRAM into a TBUF and then writing the transmit control words for that TBUF. However, a crucial step was skipped, namely ensuring the TBUF did not contain valid data before writing it. This step is necessary to ensure that the transmit microblock does not overwrite previous mpackets before the TSM has had a chance to transmit them.

The solution to this problem is to read the current value of the transmit pointer and ensure that it has already passed beyond the TBUF element currently being written. A naïve implementation would read the value of the transmit pointer before every TBUF element was written.

A more efficient solution would be to only read this pointer once and then fill all of the TBUF elements possible before reading the pointer again. With this solution, reading the transmit pointer is done much less frequently, which means lower latencies for the transmit driver.

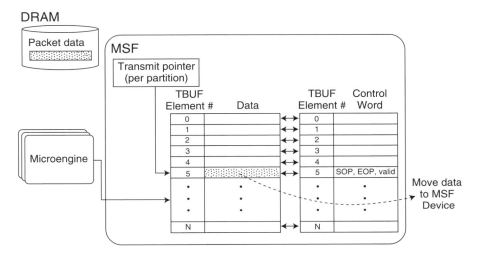

Once the transmit state machine moves its pointer to a valid TBUF element, it copies the data to the MSF device as indicated in the control word. The hardware also invalidates the TBUF element.

Figure 5.8 The Transmit State Machine Copying Data to the MSF device

Thus, the code which checks that the TBUF element does not contain valid data and the code that segments entire packets into mpackets must be written together. As shown in Figure 5.9, the segmentation tasks can be combined with the solution to checking that TBUF elements contain no valid data before writing them.

In each iteration of this loop, the next TBUF element is selected by adding one to the current TBUF element.

The first operation in the loop checks to see whether the code should write into this next TBUF element, which is accomplished by maintaining a count of the number of TBUF elements "in-flight" in a microengine register. The number of TBUFs in-flight corresponds to the number of TBUF elements the microengines have written data into since the last time the transmit pointer was read.

When the number of in-flight TBUF elements equals the total number of TBUF elements, the transmit microblock must assume that all of the TBUF elements are used, i.e., contain valid data. While the TSM has most likely advanced the transmit pointer, the microcode cannot assume so.

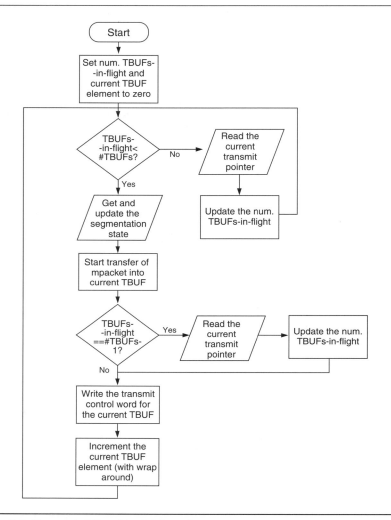

Figure 5.9 Transmit Microblock Flowchart

Rather, when the number of in-flight TBUF elements reaches this threshold, the microengines must read the current transmit pointer and update the actual number of TBUF elements in-flight.

Once the number of in-flight TBUF elements is less than the total number of TBUF elements, the transmit algorithm can proceed to retrieve the segmentation state. The segmentation state is a set of global registers that indicates where the packet being transmitted is in the transmission process. If the code transmitted packets on multiple ports, this algorithm would need segmentation state registers for each port.

The next mpacket, obtained from the segmentation state, is placed into the next TBUF element and the TBUF element's control words are written. When the current number of TBUF elements in-flight is one less than the maximum number of TBUFs, an optimization is made. Specifically, during the latency associated with transferring the mpacket into the TBUF element, the number of TBUFs in-flight is updated by reading the current transmit pointer. This optimization enables the code to hide the latency associated with reading the transmit pointer in nearly all situations.

The following code shows how the loop portion of this algorithm is implemented in microengine assembly. The algorithms for updating the number of in-flight TBUF elements and for maintaining the segmentation state are shown in the following sections.

spi4_tx()

```
        File: Chapter05\spi4_tx.uc
356   #macro spi4_tx()
357   .begin
358        // State used during the transmission to ensure
359        // the TBUFs are used in order and without
360        // overruning the hardware
361        .reg next_tbuf_elem    // The index of the next tbuf
362                               // element to be used
363        .reg last_tx_seq       // The value of the last read
364                               // to the tx_sequence number
365        .reg tbufs_in_flight   // The number of TBUFs
366                               // currently being transmitted.
367
368
369        // State associated with the current mpacket
370        .reg sop eop
371        .reg mpkt_addr mpkt_length
372        .sig dram_to_tbuf_sig
373
374        // Initialize the transmit state
375        immed32(next_tbuf_elem, 0)
376        immed32(tbufs_in_flight, 0)
377        immed32(last_tx_seq, 0)
378
379        // Setting the global EOP = 1 will force a
380        // dequeue
```

Continues

```
381         immed32(tx_eop, 1)
382
383     // Suppress assembler warnings
384     .set tx_cur_mpacket_addr tx_remaining_length
385     .set tx_cur_buf_handle tx_sop
386
387     .while(1)
388         // Check that the TBUF is available for use
389         .while (tbufs_in_flight == NUM_TBUFS)
390             // We are out of TBUFs, wait for the
391             // sequence number to increase
392             _spi4_tx_update_tbufs_in_flight(
393                 tbufs_in_flight,
394                 last_tx_seq)
395         .endw
396
397         // Get the state (next mpacket) for the
398         // current TBUF element.
399     .   _spi4_tx_get_and_update_state(
400                 dl_buf_handle,
401                 mpkt_addr,
402                 mpkt_length,
403                 sop, eop,
404                 next_tbuf_elem)
405
406         // Move the next portion of the packet into
407         // the next tbuf
408         _spi4_tx_move_dram_to_tbuf(
409             next_tbuf_elem,
410             mpkt_addr,
411             mpkt_length,
412             dram_to_tbuf_sig)
413
414         // As an optimization, if we have only one
415         // more TBUF available (after this one), then
416         // read and update the tbufs in fight during
417         // the transfer from DRAM to TBUF
418         .if (tbufs_in_flight == (NUM_TBUFS - 1))
419             _spi4_tx_update_tbufs_in_flight(
420                 tbufs_in_flight,
421                  last_tx_seq)
422         .endif
423
424         // Wait for the TBUF to be filled
425         ctx_arb[dram_to_tbuf_sig]
426
427         // Write the TBUF control word to validate
428         // the entry
```

Continues

```
429               _spi4_tx_validate_tbuf(
430                   next_tbuf_elem,
431                   sop,
432                   eop,
433                   mpkt_length)
434
435               // Update the global transmit state
436               add(next_tbuf_elem, next_tbuf_elem,
437                   (TBUF_ELEM_SIZE / 64))
438               alu_op(next_tbuf_elem, next_tbuf_elem,
439                     AND, 0x7f)
440
441               add(tbufs_in_flight, tbufs_in_flight, 1)
442
443               .if (eop)
444                   // Free the buffer
445                   dl_buf_drop(dl_buf_handle)
446               .endif
447           .endw
448       .end
449   #endm
```

Lines 389 – 395:

These lines of code wait for the current TBUF element to be clear of any valid data. Most of the time the number of TBUF elements in-flight is less than the number of TBUF elements and so this code executes only the .while statement (i.e., a single branch instruction).

When the number of in-flight TBUF elements equals the number of TBUF elements, the routine _spi4_tx_update_tbufs_in_flight is used to read the current transmit pointer. This routine is shown in the next section.

Lines 399 – 404:

These lines of code retrieve the current segmentation state from the global registers using a routine shown in the next section. This state has a pointer to the next mpacket to transmit, as well as SOP and EOP information for the mpacket.

Lines 418 – 425:

These lines of code implement the performance optimization discussed previously. This code updates the number of in-flight TBUF elements when the current number of in-flight TBUF elements is one less than the maximum. This update helps performance because, most likely, the TSM has advanced the transmit pointer and so this routine decreases the number of in-flight TBUF elements by more than one. This decrease, in turn, means the next iteration through the loop does not need to read the transmit pointer.

The advantage of reading the transmit pointer at this point in the code is that this occurs during the time when the current mpacket is being moved from DRAM to a TBUF element. Thus, the latency associated with reading the transmit pointer is hidden.

Lines 436 – 441:

These lines of code update the current TBUF element and the number of TBUF elements in-flight. The only trick with updating the current TBUF element is that the number must wrap around. That is, once this number reaches the total number of TBUF elements (128), it should restart at zero. Finally, the number of in-flight TBUFs is incremented.

Lines 443 – 446:

These lines of code free the buffer when the packet is completely transmitted. If we, hypothetically, forgot to add these lines, the code would eventually run out of buffers and stop receiving packets. Hypothetically speaking, of course.

The following code shows how the transmit pointer is read and the number of in-flight TBUF elements is updated.

_spi4_tx_update_tbufs_in_flight()

File: Chapter05\spi4_tx.uc

```
217  #macro _spi4_tx_update_tbufs_in_flight(\
218      io_tbufs_in_flight, \
219      io_last_tx_seq)
220  .begin
221      .reg $cur_tx_seq_xfer cur_tx_seq addr tbufs_used
222      .sig msf_sig
223
224      // First read the current sequence number
225      immed32(addr, MSF_TX_SEQUENCE_0_ADDR)
226      msf[read, $cur_tx_seq_xfer, addr, 0, 1],
227          ctx_swap[msf_sig]
228      alu_op(cur_tx_seq, 0xff, AND, $cur_tx_seq_xfer)
229
230      // Compute how many TBUFs have been consumed
231      // since the last read. Account for wrap
232      .if (io_last_tx_seq <= cur_tx_seq)
233          sub(tbufs_used, cur_tx_seq, io_last_tx_seq)
```

Continues

```
234        .else
235            sub(tbufs_used, io_last_tx_seq, cur_tx_seq)
236        .endif
237
238        // Subtract the tbufs_used from the current
239        // number of tbufs in flight
240        sub(io_tbufs_in_flight, io_tbufs_in_flight,
241            tbufs_used)
242
243        // Save the sequence number
244        move(io_last_tx_seq, cur_tx_seq)
245    .end
246 #endm
```

Lines 225 – 228:

The first step is to read the current transmit pointer. Unfortunately, the transmit pointer is not directly available from the hardware. Instead, a counter is read that indicates the number of times the current transmit pointer has been incremented.

What is the difference? Well, the transmit pointer rolls over after it reaches the end of the TBUF elements, which, for 64-byte TBUF elements is 128. This counter rolls over after it reaches 256. Weird, yes, but no big deal because accounting for this difference is easy, as shown in the next lines of code.

To read this counter, simply locate the correct MSF address and read the value.

Lines 232 – 236:

These lines compute how many TBUF elements have been transmitted since the last time the transmit pointer was read by subtracting the current transmit counter value from the previous value, and accounting for the case where these counters roll over.

Lines 240 – 244:

The number of transmitted TBUF elements is used to update the number of in-flight TBUF elements. For each TBUF element transmitted, one fewer TBUF element is in-flight.

Finally, the current transmit counter value is saved into a register so that the next time this routine is called, the process can successfully repeat itself.

The following code shows how the segmentation state is read and updated.

_spi4_tx_get_and_update_state()

File: Chapter05\spi4_tx.uc

```
283    #macro _spi4_tx_get_and_update_state(\
284        out_buf_handle, \
285        out_mpkt_addr, \
286        out_mpkt_length, \
287        out_sop, \
288        out_eop, \
289        in_next_tbuf_elem)
290    .begin
291        // If EOP is true, get a new packet
292        .if (tx_eop)
293            .while (1)
294            .begin
295                // Dequeue a packet from the processing task
296                dl_source();
297
298                // Check for an empty queue
299                .if (dl_buf_handle != 0)
300                    immed32(tx_sop, 1)
301                    move(tx_cur_buf_handle, dl_buf_handle)
302                    dl_buf_get_data(tx_cur_mpacket_addr,
303                                      dl_buf_handle)
304                    dl_meta_get_buffer_size(
305                                      tx_remaining_length)
306                    .break
307                .endif
308            .end
309            .endw
310        .endif
311
312        move(out_mpkt_addr, tx_cur_mpacket_addr)
313        move(out_buf_handle, tx_cur_buf_handle)
314        move(out_sop, tx_sop)
315
316        // Update the global state for the next call to
317        // this macro. Check for EOP
318        .if (tx_remaining_length <= TBUF_ELEM_SIZE)
319            immed32(tx_eop, 1)
320            move(out_mpkt_length, tx_remaining_length)
321        .else
322            immed32(tx_eop, 0)
323            move(out_mpkt_length, TBUF_ELEM_SIZE)
324        .endif
325
```

Continues

```
326          add(tx_cur_mpacket_addr, tx_cur_mpacket_addr,
327              TBUF_ELEM_SIZE)
328          sub(tx_remaining_length, tx_remaining_length,
329              TBUF_ELEM_SIZE)
330
331          immed32(tx_sop, 0)
332          move(out_eop, tx_eop)
333      .end
334      #endm
```

Lines 292 – 310:

You might be surprised to find code in this routine that gets a packet from the processing task (dl_source). Nevertheless, this code is correct. After a packet was been completely segmented and transmitted, the next segmentation state should correspond to the next packet.

Here the EOP state flag is used to determine whether the previous packet has been completely transmitted. If so, the code gets the next packet from the packet-processing ring.

After a packet has been retrieved, the segmentation state is initialized to indicate the start of packet, to contain a pointer to the beginning of the packet, and to contain the total length of the packet.

Lines 312 – 314:

These lines of code copy the global segmentation state into the output parameters of the routine. While not strictly necessary for our simple single-port example, if multiple ports were needed, these lines could select from the proper per-port global segmentation state.

Lines 318 – 324:

These lines check for EOP by examining how many bytes of the packet remain to be transmitted. If this length is less than or equal to the size of a TBUF element, this mpacket is the EOP mpacket.

Lines 326 – 332:

The remaining steps are to update the global segmentation state to point to the next mpacket and to subtract the length of an mpacket from the total length.

The SOP flag is cleared because the next time this routine is called either a new packet should be retrieved, or the next non-SOP mpacket should be sent. Strictly speaking, the SOP flag only needs to be cleared if it was set. However, adding in a branch instruction to check for this condition actually slows down the code.

Setting Up the Packet Simulator

Now let's run the code!

All of the code samples in this chapter are available on the accompanying CD-ROM. The Chapter05 directory contains the project called rx_count_tx.dwp. When you open this project and begin debugging, the simulator's packet generator is probably unfamiliar, so we cover it in a bit of detail next.

Simulating the code would be fairly boring if the simulator did not generate packets for the receive driver to reassemble. While we have already configured the simulator project on the CD-ROM to inject packets on a single SPI-4 port, we should explain how to do this configuration so you can do the same yourself.

Four steps are needed to configure packet input and output in the simulator:

1. Enable packet generation and transmission in the simulator.
2. Add one or more MSF devices to the IXP2XXX processor.
3. Create one or more streams of packets.
4. Assign the packet stream(s) to the MSF device(s).

Each of these steps is accomplished with a different dialog box in the Developer's Workbench.

Enabling Packets in the Simulator

Before doing anything with MSF devices, packet streams, or the like, first check the Enable Packet Simulation in the Simulation menu of the Developer's Workbench. This option instructs the Workbench to initialize and include the appropriate packet generation libraries. Without enabling this, the rest of your hard work to create packets and media devices will be for not.

Adding an MSF Device

Figure 5.10 shows the MSF Devices and Ports dialog (on the Simulation menu, click Devices and Bus Connections), which is used to accomplish the second step. Two SPI-4 devices have been added, one for receiving packets and one for transmitting packets.

Each device has a single port, which can be defined when the device is created. The rate, buffering capabilities, and receive and transmit thresholds can be configured for each port.

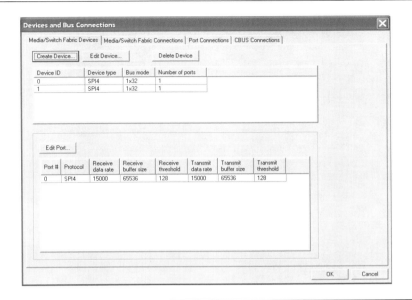

Figure 5.10 The MSF Device Simulator's Devices and Bus Connections Dialog

The receive threshold indicates the amount of data the device buffers before indicating to the IXP2XXX MSF that an mpacket is available. For optimal performance, this threshold should be set to the size of the RBUF elements.

The transmit threshold indicates the amount of data the device buffers before beginning to transmit the packet. The smaller the value the better as a smaller value enables the device to be transmitting the beginning of the packet at the same time the transmit microblock is writing the next mpackets into TBUF elements. The only caveat is that the smaller the threshold, the faster the transmit code needs to run. If the transmit microblock does not provide the next mpacket to the device before the device has completed transmitting the data in its internal buffers, then an underflow occurs. The result of an underflow is an invalid transmitted packet.

By adding these devices, the simulator includes a simulation of the devices that generate the correct MSF bus signals, including packet data transfers.

Creating Packet Streams

Simply adding devices to the simulator does not mean these devices inject any packet data. Instead, a set of streams that the devices use needs to be configured to simulate packet data arriving at the device. To add streams, on the Simulation menu, click Data Streams. In the Data Streams dialog, one or more streams of packets can be created, as shown in Figure 5.11.

Each stream contains a single type of packet. The Developer's Workbench contains templates for several packet types including IP packets encapsulated in Packet Over SONET (POS), IP packets encapsulated in Ethernet, and ATM AAL5 packets.

Within each stream, one or more packets can be defined by clicking the Edit Stream button. The data in each packet can be edited through a dialog box specific to the type of packet in the stream.

In our example, a single stream was created with a single packet. The packet contained an IP packet encapsulated in a POS packet.

Assigning Packet Streams to Devices

To complete the simulator's setup, the packet steams created must be assigned to particular ports. To assign data streams to ports on devices,

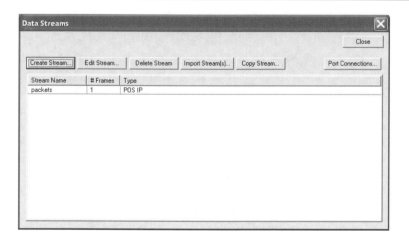

Figure 5.11 The Simulator's Data Streams Dialog

on the Simulation menu, click Data Streams and then click Port Connections. In the MSF Devices and Bus Connections dialog, data streams can be assigned to ports, as shown in Figure 5.12.

Notice, we only assign streams to the ports on which we want to receive packets. It does not make sense to inject packets into the port used for transmitting packets.

So how do you determine what packets are transmitted? Have the simulator log packets transmitted out a port! Under the Simulation menu, click Packet Simulation Options. As shown in Figure 5.13, under the Logging tab of the Packet Simulation Options dialog box, the Enable Logging box is checked and a file into which to log has been specified. After the simulation runs for a while, this file can be examined to see what packets were transmitted.

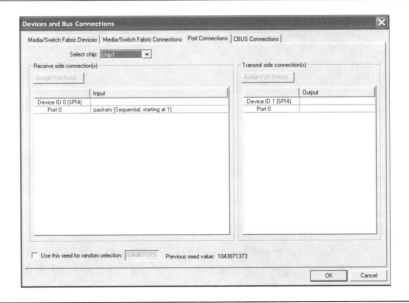

Figure 5.12 The Simulator's Port I/O Assignment Dialog

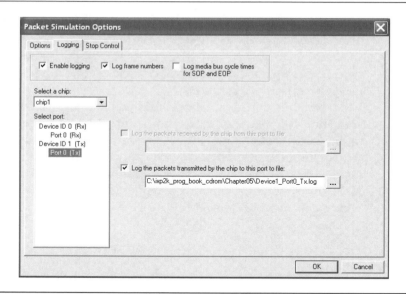

Figure 5.13 Enabling Logging in the Packet Simulator

Should You Reinvent the Receive and Transmit Wheel?

You might be wondering whether every application requires unique receive and transmit code, or whether this code can be written once and used with any application. While some developers may want to enhance the receive and transmit tasks to suit a particular system or application design, most people do not need to write receive and transmit tasks.

Instead, the Intel IXA SDK 3.0 supplied by Intel provides tested receive and transmit code for the development boards supported by Intel. This code is more full-featured than the code in this chapter. It can deal with packets that span multiple buffers. It uses all of the threads and resources available on the assigned microengines and has been performance tuned. Our recommendation, and indeed what we do, is to use the receive and transmit code from the Intel IXA SDK 3.0 and only change it if our application or hardware requires it.

If you find it necessary to write your own receive and transmit code or modify the receive and transmit code supplied with the Intel IXA SDK 3.0, this chapter, along with the multithreading techniques of subsequent chapters, give you the necessary information.

Summary

The basic framework for network applications is receive, process, and then transmit packets.

Receiving packets involves reassembling mpackets into buffers. Buffers represent a contiguous block of memory where the packet is stored. The reassembly task involves moving mpackets in RBUF elements to DRAM and keeping track of the start, end, and length of the final packet.

Our packet-processing task is a simple packet counter. While this task is overly simplistic, we expand on this task in subsequent chapters.

Transmitting packets involves segmenting packets into mpackets and then moving mpackets into TBUF elements. The segmentation task involves keeping track of the start, end, and length of the current packet as well as understanding the transmit state machine to ensure TBUF elements are used only when appropriate.

Chapter **6**

Packet Processing in a Single Thread

Instead of just counting packets as the application in Chapter 5 did, the application described in this chapter does some more complicated tasks. The application takes IP packets encapsulated in Ethernet II frames, and performs IPv4 five-tuple classification and Random Early Detection (RED) congestion avoidance on them before forwarding the packets out. The example code for this application is much simpler than what you would write in a production system, but will give you an idea of how packet processing works on the IXP2XXX processor. The example application also gives an opportunity to explain some of the cool hardware features available on the IXP2XXX processor that help you process packets, including the hash unit, CRC unit, unaligned access instructions, indexed registers, local memory, multiplication instruction, and random number generator.

Performing these functions involves writing both microblocks on the microengines and core component code on the Intel XScale core. This chapter focuses on the microblocks because they are probably less familiar to most readers. However, this chapter has a section at the end that describes how the core component code is written as well.

The microblocks in this chapter are written to process packets on only one thread. This simplifies the code somewhat, allowing us to focus on some of the features of the IXP2XXX processor that help us process packets. Processing packets on a single thread is, of course, not as fast as processing them on multiple threads. In later chapters, we'll make the code multi-threaded, increasing the performance.

The Application

The flow of packets in the application is shown in Figure 6.1. The packet-processing code takes packets from the scratch ring on which the receive code places packets. The code then processes the packets. When processing is complete, the packets are put on one of the SRAM rings from which the transmit code reads. In between these steps, the Ethernet header of the packet is validated and removed, the packet is classified based on the fields in the IP header, a new Ethernet header is added, and RED congestion avoidance is done. Each of the blocks in this figure is implemented as a microblock. Writing microblocks implies that the code is written without knowledge of the other microblocks, which allows microblocks to be reused across different applications with different microblocks. So for example, the IPv4 five-tuple classification microblock is used to process packets that arrived as Ethernet frames, but it doesn't care about the encapsulation in which the packet arrived. The classification microblock could also be used to process packets that arrive in other encapsulations, such as Packet-Over-SONET.

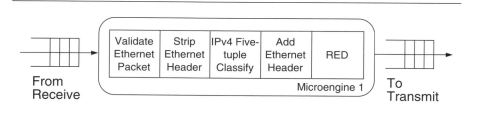

Figure 6.1 The Sample Application Data Flow

The code in this chapter is implemented as Intel IXA SDK 3.0 microblocks using dispatch loops as described in Chapter 3. We have also implemented a core component for the microblock that adds the Ethernet header to the packet. A later section of this chapter describes the design and implementation aspects of this core component.

But enough of the big picture, you need the details! Here is an excerpt from the microengine C version of the dispatch loop for this application:

main()

File: Chapter06\dispatch_loop\process_dl.c

```
55      while (1)
56      {
57          // Dequeue a packet from the rx task
58          dl_source();
59          if (dlBufHandle.value == 0)
60          {
61              continue;
62          }
63
64          // Verify that this packet is an acceptable
65          // Ethernet packet and that it is locally
66          // addressed.
67          ethernet_validate();
68          if (dlNextBlock != ETHERNET_VALIDATE_LOCAL)
69          {
70              goto drop;
71          }
72
73          // At this point we know we have an Ethernet II
74          // packet. Before we send it to the IPv4
75          // classifier, we have to make sure that it is
76          // an IP packet. Then, since the classifier is
77          // L2 agnostic, we have to move the packet data
78          // pointer past the Ethernet header.
79          ethernet_strip_header();
80          if (dlNextBlock != ETHERNET_PROTO_IP)
81          {
82              goto drop;
83          }
84          eth_proto = dlNextBlock;
85
86          // Now that we have a packet, send it the IPv4
87          // 5-tuple classifier. The classifier will
88          // assign an output ring, and a next hop IP
89          // address.
90          ipv4_five_tuple_class();
91          if (dlNextBlock == IX_DROP)
92          {
93              goto drop;
94          }
95
96          // Before we transmit the packet, we have to add
```

Continues

```
97              // the Ethernet header back on. We do this
98              // based on the next hop IP address retrieved
99              // from the classifier.
100             ethernet_add_header(eth_proto);
101             if (dlNextBlock == IX_DROP)
102             {
103                 goto drop;
104             }
105
106             // Now that the output ring is assigned, send it
107             // to the RED buffer manager to either enqueue
108             // or drop
109             red();
110             if (dlNextBlock == IX_DROP)
111             {
112                 goto drop;
113             }
114
115             // Once we get here, the packet is put on the
116             // ring to go to transmit.
117             dl_sink();
118             continue;
119
120     drop:
121             Dl_BufDrop(dlBufHandle);
122         }
```

Lines 58 and 117:

> You might recognize a few things from reading Chapter 5. The dl_source and dl_sink drivers are used here to dequeue and enqueue packets just as they are in the transmit and receive code.

Lines 68, 80, 91, 101, and 110:

> In a microengine dispatch loop written using Intel IXA SDK 3.0, some per-packet state is kept in global variables. This state is used by the dispatch loop code and microblock code to process the packets and is called "packet metadata." This state includes the buffer handle for the buffer in which the packet is contained, the size of the buffer, and the input and output ports of the packet. One piece of packet metadata that is used by this dispatch loop is the "next-block" value. This value is modified by microblocks to tell the dispatch loop which microblock to execute next. In microengine C dispatch loops, the next-block value is stored in the variable named dlNextBlock, and in microengine assembly dispatch loops, this value is stored in the general-purpose register named dl_next_block. For example, on line 68 of the preceding code, the dispatch loop checks

the value of dlNextBlock. If this value is set to ETHERNET_VALIDATE_LOCAL after the ethernet_validate microblock, the processing of the packet continues. If not, the packet is dropped.

Most microblocks have a finite number of output targets, each with a defined next-block value. The ethernet_validate microblock is this way. It has five targets, denoted using the next-block values of ETHERNET_VALIDATE_INVALID, ETHERNET_VALIDATE_LOCAL, ETHERNET_VALIDATE_MULTICAST, ETHERNET_VALIDATE_BROADCAST, and ETHERNET_VALIDATE_OTHER. The ethernet_strip_header is a bit different. The next-block value set by this microblock is the standard Ethernet protocol number of the encapsulated packet, and the dispatch loop code makes decisions based on this value. It decides what protocols it can process (in this case, just IP) and drops the others.

Now that you know how to combine microblocks together, you'll see how the microblocks themselves are built.

Ethernet Processing

Three of the microblocks in Figure 6.1 are used to either process or generate Ethernet headers. The microblocks are called ethernet_validate, ethernet_strip_header, and ethernet_add_header. The ethernet_validate microblock ensures that the packet is a valid Ethernet II frame and has different targets for multicast, broadcast, locally-addressed, and other packets that are not multicast, broadcast, or locally-addressed. The ethernet_strip_header microblock removes the Ethernet header so that code that processes higher-layer packets—in this case the IPv4 five-tuple classifier—can process the packets encapsulated by the Ethernet frame. The ethernet_add_header microblock does the opposite, adding Ethernet encapsulation around the IP frame. It determines the Ethernet destination MAC address from the next-hop ID determined by the classifier.

In our design we split up the ethernet_validate and ethernet_strip_header microblocks in an attempt to maximize reuse. We might get better performance by combining the two. But, for example, if we were to write an Ethernet bridge, we would find the combination of the two microblocks to be more work than needed, whereas ethernet_validate by itself might suffice.

The code for ethernet_validate is very straightforward. The packet is validated by checking the actual length to ensure it is greater than or equal to the minimum length and less than or equal to the maximum length of an Ethernet II frame. This microblock also tells the dispatch loop if the frame is locally addressed, multicast, or broadcast. To determine the type of frame, it looks at the destination MAC address in the Ethernet header.

The implementation of the ethernet_strip_header microblock is also straightforward. This microblock first gets the Ethernet protocol number from the packet by parsing the packet header. Then, it removes the Ethernet header. Each packet comes with metadata registers that specify the length of the packet and the offset within the buffer at which the packet begins. The ethernet_strip_header microblock adjusts these two metadata values to remove the header.

So how does this microblock "parse the header?" Examining headers in packets is done differently in microengine C than it is in microengine assembly. In microengine C, the ability to use structures makes it easier. A structure can be defined for most headers. For example, the following structure is used in our code to examine the Ethernet header:

```
typedef __declspec(packed) struct _ethernet_header
{
        unsigned int destination_addr_hi32;
        unsigned int destination_addr_lo16 : 16;
        unsigned int source_addr_hi16      : 16;
        unsigned int source_addr_lo32;
        short protocol;
} ethernet_header;
```

With the structure defined, it is very easy to retrieve fields from Ethernet headers.

Microengine assembly does not have support for structures, so the code needed to extract fields from headers needs to be written manually. Here is the microengine assembly code used to extract the destination MAC address:

```
dram[read, $eth_header0, eth_header_start, 0, 1],
    ctx_swap[dram_sig]
alu[d_mac_hi32, --, B, $eth_header0]
alu[d_mac_lo16, --, B, $eth_header1, >>16]
```

To determine whether or not the packet is locally addressed, the destination MAC address of the packet is compared to the device's MAC address. Some MAC devices external to the IXP2XXX processor may do this in hardware, but for fun, let's assume the hardware we are using does not. This address is stored in SRAM and is initialized by the XScale core component. In a production system, the design may involve the ability to assign one or more MAC addresses to each interface. If this is the case, determining if a packet is locally addressed is more complicated.

The final Ethernet packet-processing microblock, `ethernet_add_header`, is a bit more complicated than the others. The `ethernet_add_header` microblock needs to determine the Ethernet source address and destination address for the outgoing packet. The source address is just the device's Ethernet address. In our sample application, this address is stored in SRAM and is the same address used earlier to determine if the packet is locally addressed. To determine the destination MAC address, the microblock uses a "next-hop ID" that is converted into a destination MAC address. The IPv4 five-tuple classifier microblock sets a packet metadata value called the next-hop ID, which identifies the machine to which the current packet should be forwarded. The `ethernet_add_header` microblock maps this next-hop ID into a destination MAC address. Because the number of next-hop IDs is small, this mapping is done with a simple array, using the next-hop ID as the array index.

The XScale core component associated with the `ethernet_add_header` microblock maintains the next-hop-ID-to-DMAC array in SRAM. If the `ethernet_add_header` microblock processes a packet and the table does not have an entry for the packet's destination IP address, the microblock could use a protocol, such as the Address Resolution Protocol (ARP), to resolve the IP address to the proper MAC address. But implementing ARP may take more code store than we can spare. Plus, the majority of packets that go through the device will likely have a destination IP address that is already in the table, so ARP rarely has to be done. These factors lead us to implement ARP on the Intel XScale core component.

With that design decision, the microblock is implemented to send any packets with destination IP addresses that are not in the table to the Intel XScale core for further processing. The microblock portion of this is shown in the code below, while the core component code for handling packets from the microengines is described later in this chapter.

The following microengine assembly code looks up the next-hop ID in the SRAM array:

ethernet_add_header()

File: Chapter06\ethernet.uc

```
319    // Look up the next hop id in the ARP table, using
320    // the ID as an index
321    .reg array_index
322    dl_meta_get_nexthop_id(array_index)
```

Continues

```
323        shf_left(array_index, array_index,
324               ARP_TABLE_ENTRY_SIZE_SHIFT)
325
326        // Get the array contents
327        .reg dest_mac_addr_hi32 dest_mac_addr_lo16 valid
328        .reg table_entry_ptr
329        .sig sram_sig
330        xbuf_alloc($table_entry, ARP_TABLE_ENTRY_SIZE_LW,
331               read)
332
333        immed32(table_entry_ptr, ETHERNET_DATA)
334        add(table_entry_ptr, table_entry_ptr,
335           ETHERNET_ARP_TABLE_OFFSET)
336        sram_read($table_entry[0], table_entry_ptr,
337               array_index, ARP_TABLE_ENTRY_SIZE_LW,
338               sram_sig, sram_sig, ___)
339
340        // Check to see if the entry is valid
341        xbuf_extract(valid, $table_entry,
342               ARP_TABLE_VALID)
```

Line 322:

The next-hop ID is stored in a packet metadata register that is accessed using the dl_meta_get_nexthop_id macro, supplied by the Intel IXA SDK 3.0 libraries.

Lines 323 – 324:

To turn this index into a byte offset, this code simply shifts the next-hop ID left a few places. For this to work, the number of bytes in each array entry must be a power of two.

Lines 334 – 338:

Here the code adds the offset that it just computed to the base address of the table, and reads the table entry into registers.

■ IPv4 Five-tuple Classification

Our sample application performs IPv4 five-tuple exact-match classification on the IP packets extracted from the Ethernet packets. The microblock that implements this classification takes the packet and modifies two pieces of packet metadata based on the contents of the packet: the flow ID, which in our application also identifies the ring number on which to put the packet after the packet has been processed, and a next-hop ID identifying the next hop to which the packet should be forwarded. This classifier is more useful as a programming example than it would be in the real world for a couple of reasons. First, this classifier forwards packets to next hops based on an exact match of the five-tuple, which is not normally how packets are forwarded. Second, this classifier ignores some aspects of IP packets that probably should not be ignored in a production environment, such as the handling of packets with IP options and ICMP packets. These aspects make the classifier a simple example for the purposes of this book. A more complicated, "industrial-strength" classifier can be found in the Intel IXA SDK 3.0 reference designs.

The IPv4 five-tuple consists of five fields in the packet: IP source and destination addresses, IP protocol number, and the next-layer source and destination ports. The IP protocol number should not be confused with the Ethernet protocol number. The Ethernet protocol number defines the type of packet inside the Ethernet packet, while the IP protocol number defines the type of packet inside the IP packet. The next layer source and destination ports are header fields for the two protocols most commonly placed inside IP packets: TCP and UDP. Our classifier drops packets that are not one of these two protocols. Luckily, the TCP source and destination ports exist at the same byte offsets in the TCP header as the UDP source and destination ports exist in the UDP header. So we can write one piece of code to access both the TCP and UDP versions of the source and destination port fields.

To perform IPv4 five-tuple classification, the microblock needs to extract the five-tuple and search for a matching five-tuple somewhere in its lookup table. Extracting the five-tuple may appear fairly straightforward, but is complicated by the issue of alignment. For maximum reusability, the microblock should be able to handle any alignment of the IP packet within memory, but the memory in which the packet is stored, DRAM, only allows 8-byte aligned accesses. Also, the design of the lookup table can greatly effect the ease and speed of the search task. So finding the right data structure for the lookup table is critical.

Unaligned Access

One of our design goals complicates the implementation of the IPv4 five-tuple classifier microblock. We said in the beginning that the microblock should work regardless of the encapsulation in which the IP packet arrived. Without knowledge of this encapsulation, the code also lacks knowledge of the byte offset at which the IP header begins. Because DRAM memory accesses all happen on 8-byte boundaries, this complicates the code somewhat. For example, if the IP packet arrived in an Ethernet packet, the IP header begins 14 bytes into the buffer, assuming the Ethernet header starts at byte 0. Figure 6.2 shows this scenario.

Thankfully, microengine C and microengine assembly provide ways to perform unaligned memory accesses in a way that does not sacrifice much performance. In microengine C, the unaligned accesses are done using the intrinsics that start with "ua_". Intrinsics exist for signed and unsigned values of 8, 16, 32, and 64 bits. For example, the following intrinsic is used to extract unaligned, signed 32-bit data from memory:

```
int ua_get_s32(void* ptr, unsigned int offset)
```

These intrinsics take an aligned pointer and an integer byte offset as parameters. The alignment of the pointer depends on the type of memory being accessed. Remember, all of the memory types are aligned on 4-byte boundaries, except DRAM, which is aligned on 8-byte boundaries.

In microengine assembly, byte-alignment instructions help to provide unaligned access to memory. The byte-alignment instructions work on big-endian or little-endian data in any type of registers. These instructions take unaligned data as input and return aligned data as output. The number of bytes of alignment shift must be set beforehand in the BYTE_INDEX microengine CSR. The following sample code takes eight bytes of

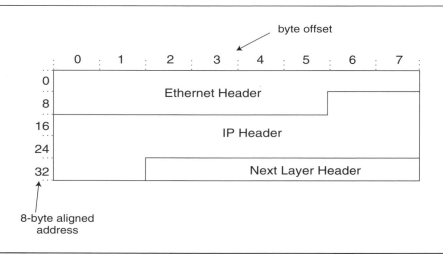

Figure 6.2 Unaligned IP Header in an Ethernet Packet

big-endian data from SRAM byte address 0x2001 and aligns it in two general-purpose registers.

```
sram[read, $xfer0, zero_reg, 0x2000, 3], ctx_swap[my_sig]
local_csr_wr[BYTE_INDEX, 1]
byte_align_be[--, $xfer0]
byte_align_be[reg0, $xfer1]
byte_align_be[reg1, $xfer2]
```

The sram instruction retrieves the data from memory. Notice that the instruction specifies that three long-words be read, even though we only need two. The code does this because the two long-words we need are spread over three long-words of SRAM. The next instruction sets the byte alignment to one byte because the SRAM address in which we are interested is one byte away from four-byte alignment. The next three instructions take the three long-words that contain the data we want and put the aligned data in the destination registers. Notice that the first of the three byte_align_be instructions has no output register. Knowledge of the internals of this instruction's implementation helps to explain this. Figure 6.3 shows the operation of the instruction. The diagram shows that the microengine has an internal register in which it stores a temporary value. The output register gets the first bytes of the temporary value and the last bytes of the input register. Since the temporary value is undefined when we start this, the first output is useless.

IXP1200 ***Note***	The IXP12XX processor does not have byte-alignment instructions, so any re- alignment must be done with ALU instructions.

As we mentioned before, microengine C code does not need to worry about the byte alignment CSRs and instructions. Microengine C has intrinsics that do this work.

Indexed Transfer Register Access

Using unaligned access instructions alone is great when you know which register has the first byte of useful data. Because the sample application is reading the IP header from DRAM, which is eight-byte aligned, the IP header could be up to seven bytes out of alignment. So, not knowing the alignment in advance, the first byte of the IP header will be in one of two different registers.

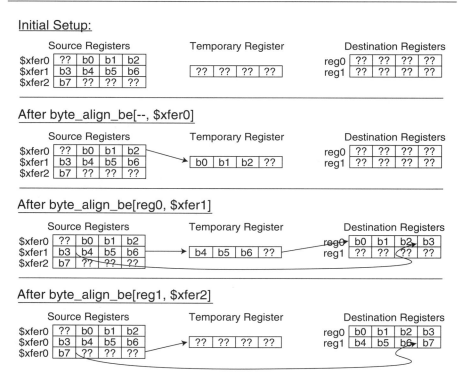

Initial Setup:

After byte_align_be[--, $xfer0]

After byte_align_be[reg0, $xfer1]

After byte_align_be[reg1, $xfer2]

In this diagram, the temporary register is internal to the microengine and cannot be accessed directly using microengine code. Only one temporary register exists for each microengine.

Figure 6.3 Unaligned Access Instructions

To resolve this, the microengines provide indexed access to microengine transfer registers. When the code sets the T_INDEX microengine-local CSR, it can then access the transfer registers in an indexed mode. In microengine assembly, this is done by using the *$index keyword and the *$$index keyword for SRAM transfer registers and DRAM transfer registers respectively. If you want to access multiple ordered transfer registers, you can use the post-increment or post-decrement features of indexed transfer register access. For example, using *$index++ in an instruction accesses the indexed transfer register and increments T_INDEX in one step.

IXP1200
Note

> The IXP12XX processor does not have indexed register access. To access a
> register in an array, when the exact register is not known at compile-time, the
> code must use branch instructions.

Indexed transfer register usage and byte-alignment instructions are often used at the same time to allow the code to treat transfer registers as an array of bytes. When you need to do both of these things at the same time, the code can set the T_INDEX_BYTE_INDEX register, which is a one-step way to set both the T_INDEX and BYTE_INDEX at the same time.

Our sample application needs to use both at the same time because we do not know the starting register of the IP header or the starting byte of the IP header within that register. The following code uses unaligned access and indexed transfer registers to move the IP header from being unaligned in a series of registers to being aligned in a series of registers:

read_unaligned_header()

File: Chapter06\ipv4_five_tuple_class.uc

```
111        // Use the byte alignment instructions and
112        // indexed transfer register access to re-align
113        // the header in an xbuf
114        .reg sub_align
115
116        // We need to include the context number in the
117        // transfer register index
118        local_csr_rd[ACTIVE_CTX_STS]
119        immed[sub_align, 0]
120        and_shf_left(sub_align, sub_align, 0x7, 0)
121        add_shf_left(sub_align, &in_header[0], sub_align, 4)
122
123        // Now add in the passed-in alignment
124        add_shf_left(sub_align, align, sub_align, 2)
125        local_csr_wr[T_INDEX_BYTE_INDEX, sub_align]
126        nop
127        nop
128        nop
129        byte_align_be[--, *$$index++]
130        byte_align_be[out_header[0], *$$index++]
131        byte_align_be[out_header[1], *$$index++]
132        byte_align_be[out_header[2], *$$index++]
133        byte_align_be[out_header[3], *$$index++]
```

Continues

```
134        byte_align_be[out_header[4], *$$index++]
135        byte_align_be[out_header[5], *$$index++]
136        byte_align_be[out_header[6], *$$index++]
137        byte_align_be[out_header[7], 0]
```

Lines 116 – 124:

> The index of the first transfer register that might hold the IP header is computed in these lines of code. The ampersand (&) operator in line 121 gets the register number of the first register that might hold the IP header. This register number is relative to the current context, and the absolute register number is needed. So the code retrieves current context number and uses it to turn the context-relative register number into an absolute register number. The T_INDEX_BYTE_INDEX register takes this register number in bits two through eight, so we shift the register number left two bits. We add the alignment to this value, leaving the byte address in bits zero and one of the register, and possibly adding one to the register number field.

Lines 125 – 128:

> These lines write the sub_align value to the T_INDEX_BYTE_INDEX register and wait the required three cycles for the write to take effect.

Line 129:

> Here the code starts the process of realigning the data by moving the first bytes into the microengine's internal temporary register. The *$$index++ notation references the register indexed by T_INDEX and increments T_INDEX after the data has been read.

Lines 130 – 137:

> The code in these lines moves the rest of the data through the realignment hardware, putting the results in the array of output registers and incrementing the T_INDEX CSR at each step.

Hash Tables

When an application receives a packet, often one or more table look-ups, based on the contents of the packet, are used to know how to process the packet. For example, the sample application we are building in this chapter uses an IP five-tuple to determine how to process IP packets. The code has to look for the correct next hop ID and flow ID in some sort of table. The design of the table and algorithm used to perform this lookup has a huge impact on the performance and resource requirements of the system.

A linked-list of five-tuples is easy to search, but is typically slow, especially when you need to support a large number of five-tuple instances in the lookup table. For as faster alternative, you could use an array indexed by the five-tuple. But, since the five-tuple is 104 bits long, using it as an array index would not work because the array would have to have $20*10^{30}$ entries! Although a table that size would make RAM manufacturers happy, it is not practical. The same is true for any other table-lookup key with more than a trivial number of bits.

Here's where hash tables become important. For those of you that may have forgotten, here is a refresher on hash tables. A hash table is like the array approach described above, but first a hash function is used to map a large lookup key to a smaller value that makes for a better table index. Of course, mapping a huge set of lookup keys to a much smaller set of table indexes implies that multiple lookup keys map to a single table index. When two keys map to the same index, the result is called a "collision", and any hash table lookup design must handle such collisions properly.

To resolve collisions, our hash tables are constructed as an array of linked lists as shown in Figure 6.4. Each entry in the linked list contains

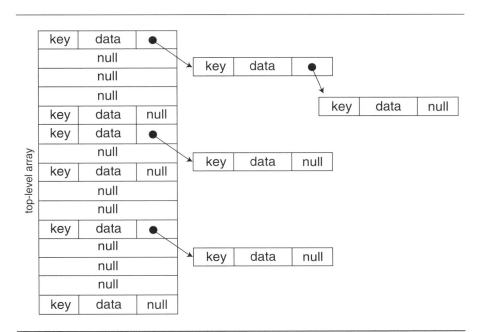

Figure 6.4 A Simple Hash Table Data Structure

the full lookup key and the table data we want to acquire. To perform a lookup, the array is indexed by the table index generated from mapping the lookup key to a smaller value. Then, the linked list at that array index is searched for the correct key. Optimizations to this algorithm exist, but this one is simple enough for illustration purposes and still has reasonable performance.

In the IPv4 five-tuple classifier microblock, the code treats the five-tuple as the key, and the next-hop ID and flow ID as the data. The code maps the five-tuple to a eight-bit quantity that is used as an array index. The array entry is then treated like a linked list. The five-tuple is compared to the five-tuples in the list entries until one matches or until there are no more linked list entries. If one matches, the table lookup was successful and the table data is read. Otherwise, the table lookup fails.

Having a lot of collisions makes a hash table inefficient since the first lookup is $O(1)$ and the linked list search is $O(n)$ in its most basic form. So it is important that the mapping of lookup keys to table indices produce as few collisions as possible. A naïve implementation of this mapping for the classifier microblock would mask off the lower few bits of the five-tuple and use this as the table index. But statistical patterns abound in the fields of the IP five-tuple, so collisions would be common. For example, what if an operator decided to use only even host numbers? In this case, half of the table space could be wasted.

Good hash functions are usually difficult to implement in software, so the IXP2XXX microengines have access to two different hardware hashing mechanisms. The CRC unit in the microengines and hash hardware unit in the SHaC help to remove patterns from lookup keys. They produce results with a uniform statistical distribution, regardless of the input, reducing the number of collisions experienced from processing packets. Each bit of the output value is independently one or zero with equal probability. So, to generate good hash-table inputs, the lookup key can be run through either of these hardware units, and the result can be used to index into the top-level array. Using either of these hash functions certainly produces fewer hash collisions than simply masking off bits of the key.

Both hardware hash approaches have advantages and disadvantages that you must consider when deciding how to generate hash table indexes. In the sample code on the CD in this book, we have implemented the IPv4 five-tuple classifier using both of these methods, and the following sections describe both of these approaches.

The Hash Unit

The hash functionality within the IXP2XXX SHaC unit is accessed by the same hardware queues that service other SHaC accesses. The hash unit can perform 48-bit, 64-bit, or 128-bit hashes with up to three hashes per instruction.

In microengine assembly, hash instructions are used to perform hashes, while in microengine C, intrinsics are used to perform hashes. The microengine assembly instructions and microengine C intrinsics are of the form hash_n, where n is the number of bits to hash. Both have an input parameter to specify the number of hashes to perform, between one and three.

The data returned by the hash is the same size as the data provided to the intrinsic. So hash_48 returns a 48-bit hash, hash_64 returns a 64-bit hash, and hash_128 returns a 128-bit hash. This is where you are supposed to get suspicious. We told you a 48-bit quantity is too big to be a table index. Don't worry, a 48-bit quantity is too big, but the hash function creates a normal statistical distribution in the lower bits of the hash result as well as the whole result. So it is acceptable to mask off the low-order bits of the hash result to fit whatever table size you want. For example, if you have room for a 1024 entry hash table, you can mask off the low-order 10 bits of the hash result and use them as your table index.

In some designs, having extra bits in the hash result is useful. In an application environment with a large number of collisions, the performance of the hash table lookups can sometimes be increased by using multiple hash tables. In these designs, the code simultaneously indexes into these hash tables using different sets of bits from the hash result. In some environments, this implementation results in better packet throughput and delay compared to one performing a single hash table lookup per packet.

Here is the microengine C code we use in the IPv4 five-tuple classifier to hash the five-tuple using the hash unit in the SHaC:

```
hash_input = five_tuple;
hash_128(&hash_input, &hash_result, 1, sig_done,
         &hash_signal);
wait_for_all(&hash_signal);
```

In this code, hash_input is an array of SRAM write transfer registers, hash_result is an array of SRAM read transfer registers, and five_tuple is an array of GPRs containing the five-tuple hash input. As you can see, performing hashes with the hash unit is not much different from any other hardware access. The input is provided in write transfer registers, the output is provided in read transfer registers, and a signal is generated when the operation is complete.

The CRC Unit

The CRC unit implements two standards-based CRC algorithms often used by network protocols to detect when packets have been corrupted in transit on a network. Its use in this capacity is covered in detail in Chapter 12. Both of the CRC algorithms implemented by the CRC unit can also be used to perform hashes of lookup keys as part of a hash table lookup.

IXP1200 Note

The IXP1240 and IXP1250 can do CRC calculations only as part of a DRAM access, so using CRC as part of a hash table lookup algorithm may not be possible on these processors.

One advantage of using the CRC unit over the hash unit is that each microengine has its own CRC unit. Sending requests to the CRC unit, therefore, does not require a bus transaction or hardware queuing. So, performing hashes with the CRC unit is much faster and consumes fewer resources than performing hashes with the hash unit in the SHaC. The drawback to using the CRC unit is that the result is either 16 or 32 bits, so performing lookups in multiple hash tables as described above may not be an option when using the CRC unit.

The CRC unit takes 32-bits of data input from local memory, general-purpose registers, or read transfer registers and performs a computation based on the input data and the contents of a microengine-local CSR called CRC_REMAINDER. The results of this computation are placed back in the CRC_REMAINDER CSR. Before hashing begins, the CRC_REMAINDER must be initialized to some well known value. To hash data larger than 32 bits, the data should be fed to the CRC unit 32 bits at a time. Reading the CRC_REMAINDER register will fetch the result.

Each microengine has only one CRC_REMAINDER register and one CRC unit, so it is important that only one thread attempts to perform a hash at any one time. A good way to ensure this is to simply avoid context swaps while performing the hash. Because the microengine threading is not pre-emptive, as long as the code does not explicitly give up the context while performing CRC, it is safe. The following microengine assembly code uses the CRC unit to perform a hash:

ipv4_five_tuple_class()

File: Chapter06\ipv4_five_tuple_class.uc

```
243        // Set up the CRC remainder
244        .reg remainder
245        immed32(remainder, 0x42424242)
246        local_csr_wr[CRC_REMAINDER, remainder]
247        // There is a three cycle delay before local CSR
248        // writes take effect
249        nop
250        nop
251        nop
252        // Run the hash key through the CRC unit.
253        // This preprocessor loop emits code for each
254        // register in the five_tuple xbuf
255        #define_eval LOOP (HASH_KEY_SIZE_LW-1)
256        #while (LOOP >= 0)
257        crc_be[crc_ccitt, --, five_tuple[LOOP]]
258        // There is a one cycle delay before another CRC
259        // can be done
260        nop
261        #define_eval LOOP (LOOP-1)
262        #endloop
263        #undef LOOP
264
265        // Get the result
266        // There is a five cycle delay before we can do this
267        // but we have already taken care of one
268        nop
269        nop
270        nop
271        nop
272        local_csr_rd[CRC_REMAINDER]
273        immed[remainder, 0]
```

Lines 243 – 251:

These lines of code set up the CRC_REMAINDER microengine local CSR with a well-known value. The nops are necessary because it takes three cycles before local CSR writes take effect. The assembler will attempt to put unrelated instructions in place of the nops to minimize their performance impact.

Lines 252 – 263:

> The five-tuple input is stored in an array of general purpose registers. This preprocessor loop results in a series of `crc_be` instructions, one for each of the input registers. A `nop` is also used after each `crc_be` instruction because the CRC unit requires one cycle in between `crc_be` instructions.

Lines 265 – 273:

> The CRC unit requires five-cycles between the last `crc_be` instruction and the retrieval of the CRC_REMAINDER. Because one `nop` was emitted from the pre-processor loop above, we only need four more here. Then, `local_csr_rd` is used to retrieve the CRC_REMAINDER, which is the hash result.

Hash Table Modification

When designing a data structure for the IXP2XXX processor, it is important to keep synchronization in mind. For hash tables, the design must consider that modification of the hash table may be happening in the Intel XScale core at the same time lookups in the hash table are happening in the microengines. Take care to make sure these concurrent operations do not affect one another. In many cases, the fact that the SRAM controller performs 32-bit writes atomically from the Intel XScale core can help avoid the need for synchronization. For example, in the simple hash table shown in Figure 6.4, adding an entry into a linked list can be done by setting up the entry key and data and later adding a pointer to the new entry in the last linked-list entry. Updating the pointer can be done without any extra synchronization because it happens atomically as long as it is 32-bit aligned.

Unfortunately, deleting the head of the linked list, for example, cannot be done atomically if the key is larger than 32 bits. In this scenario, no single SRAM write can invalidate the entry, and multiple SRAM writes would make the data structure invalid for a period of time. To resolve this, we can modify the design of the hash table to have 32-bit pointers in the top-level array instead of actual hash-table entries. This eliminates the need for extra synchronization. This data structure is shown in Figure 6.5.

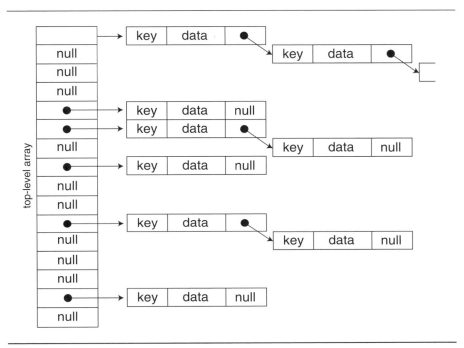

Figure 6.5 Modified Hash Table

Random Early Detect (RED) Congestion Avoidance

Before the sample application enqueues packets for the transmit code, it performs RED on the queue. RED is a congestion-avoidance algorithm invented by Sally Floyd and Van Jacobson while at the University of California. It allows packet-processing devices in TCP/IP networks to maintain high utilization of output links without inducing large queuing latencies in the network.

In our device, we are only supporting two ports, so congestion is very unlikely. So, the inclusion of RED in our application is somewhat gratuitous. But, many other devices that can be built with IXP2XXX processors may need congestion avoidance, and implementing RED exposes some exciting features of the IXP2XXX processor, so we included it in our application anyway.

The RED algorithm is fairly simple. When a packet arrives at the system, the RED algorithm decides to either drop the packet or forward it. This decision is based on minimum and maximum thresholds, defined by the user, for a particular queue. If the number of packets in the queue is less than the minimum threshold, the packet is forwarded. If the number of packets in the queue is greater than the maximum threshold, it is dropped. If the number of packets in the queue is between the minimum and maximum thresholds, there is a random probability that the packet will be dropped. This probability increases linearly between the minimum threshold and the maximum threshold. Figure 6.6 shows the probability of a packet being dropped as a function of the number of packets in the queue.

TCP/IP traffic can be fairly bursty. So instead of using the instantaneous number of packets in the queue to determine the probability of dropping a packet, RED uses the average number of packets in the queue. Specifically, RED uses the exponential weighted moving average (EWMA) of the number of packets in the queue.

We could spend pages and pages describing the RED algorithm, its motivations and optimizations, but plenty of other resources are available, including "Random Early Detection Gateways for Congestion Avoidance" (Floyd and Jacobsen 1993), listed in the "References." We will tell you (and show you next) that implementing RED exercises

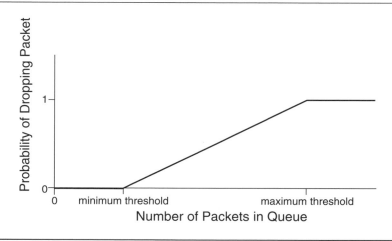

Figure 6.6 Probability of Dropping a Packet

some interesting features of the IXP2XXX processor, including local memory, multiplication, and random-number generation.

Local Memory

Our implementation of RED allows the user to configure different RED parameters for each queue. These parameters, and other queue state variables needed by the RED algorithm, need to be accessed for every enqueued packet. In our implementation, the per-queue data structure is 92 bytes long. Because we are using 16 queues to move packets around, we only need a total of 1472 bytes (16 queues * 92 bytes per queue). Also, we are doing RED on only one microengine. These two facts make storing this data structure perfect for local memory.

In case you have forgotten from Chapter 2, each microengine on the IXP2XXX processor comes with 2560 bytes of local memory. Local memory is accessed only in indexed mode, similar to the indexed transfer register mode discussed above. The code sets a microengine-local CSR called either ACTIVE_LM_ADDR_0 or ACTIVE_LM_ADDR_1. The code can then reference local memory at either index by using the *l$index0 or *l$index1 symbols. These symbols can be used in post-increment or post-decrement mode just like the indexed transfer registers. They can also be used in an offset mode. Using the symbol *l$index0[x] accesses the local memory location x long-words from ACTIVE_LM_ADDR_0. In the sample code, the following line of code sets the ACTIVE_LM_ADDR_0 local CSR to point to the beginning of the RED parameters:

```
local_csr_wr[ACTIVE_LM_ADDR_0, queue_data_index]
```

Later, this code is used to perform a computation using a particular RED parameter:

```
sub_shf_right(q_minus_avg, queue_length,
              *l$index0[RED_AVERAGE_LENGTH_INDEX],
              AVG_TO_ACTUAL_SHIFT_RIGHT)
```

If you write code to access local memory in microengine C, you don't need to know any of this. The compiler generates the correct CSR modifications and symbol usage. To access local memory in microengine C, use the __declspec(local_mem) keyword when declaring a variable. This variable is then stored in local memory and the compiler handles the rest. In the RED code, a pointer to the queue data structure for the queue being considered is declared using the following code:

```
__declspec(local_mem) queue_info* queue;
```

To access data in this region of local memory, the pointer is initialized and used like any other pointer. The following code accesses the queue's current average length:

```
queue->average_length
```

IXP1200 Note

> The IXP12XX processor does not have local memory. The fastest memory it can access—besides registers—is scratchpad memory.

Local memory is a great resource for storing small amounts of data that only need to be modified by one microengine. Because local memory is inside each microengine, it is not very effective at storing information that needs to be modified by multiple microengines since code would have to be written to keep the local memories of the microengines up-to-date. But, having local memory in the microengine allows for much faster access times than are available with any other memory on the IXP2XXX processor.

Multiplication

At one point in the RED algorithm, a new average queue length needs to be computed using EWMA. This computation involves multiplying the difference between the current queue length and the average queue length by the EWMA parameter. Looking closely at the ALU instructions, you'll find that no multiply opcode exists.

Instead, the IXP2XXX processor provides a different instruction to perform integer multiplication. This instruction can multiply 24-bit integers by 8-bit integers, 16-bit integers by 16-bit integers, or 32-bit integers by 32-bit integers. Regardless of the size of the multiplicand or multiplier, multiplication happens in multiple steps using the same instruction. The first step uses a "start" option, the middle steps use "step" options, and the last step(s) use one or two "last" options. As an example, the following microengine assembly code could be used by the example to multiply the 32-bit EWMA parameter by the difference between the current queue length and the average queue length:

```
mul_step[ewma_param, q_minus_avg], 32x32_start
mul_step[ewma_param, q_minus_avg], 32x32_step1
mul_step[ewma_param, q_minus_avg], 32x32_step2
mul_step[ewma_param, q_minus_avg], 32x32_step3
mul_step[ewma_param, q_minus_avg], 32x32_step4
mul_step[low_result, --], 32x32_last
mul_step[high_result, --], 32x32_last2
```

The first instruction starts the multiplication. The next four steps continue the process. Multiplying different integer sizes takes different numbers of steps. The final two instructions get the low-order 32 bits and high-order 32 bits of the result. Multiplying two 32-bit integers requires two instructions to get the results because the other types of multiplication only produce 32-bit results. The other multiplication types need only one instruction to get the results because these results can be at most 32 bits.

IXP1200
Note

The IXP12XX processor does not have multiplication. On the IXP12XX processor, some multiplication can be done through table lookups. Any others have to be done on the StrongARM core.

Thankfully, Intel IXA SDK 3.0 provides a microengine assembly macro to perform multiplication if you don't want to write it yourself. The actual code used in the sample application to perform the necessary multiplication is:

```
multiply32(*l$index0[RED_AVERAGE_LENGTH_INDEX],
          temp, *l$index1, OP_SIZE_16x16)
```

In this case, we are using the fact that the operands are both 16 bits or less to perform the multiplication quicker.

Doing multiplication in microengine C is much simpler. I'll bet you've already guessed it. The following microengine C code multiplies the same integers as the above microengine assembly code:

```
result = ewma_param * q_minus_avg;
```

The microengine C compiler generates assembly code similar to the microengine assembly above.

Random Number Generation

When the average queue length is between the minimum threshold and the maximum threshold, the RED implementation computes a probability that the given packet should be dropped. To actually decide if a particular packet should be dropped, the algorithm compares this probability to a pseudo-random number. The IXP2XXX processor has a pseudo-random number generator on each microengine that generates 32-bit pseudo-random numbers. The pseudo-random number generator can be initialized with a seed value to produce repeatable results. The sequence of numbers generated repeats only after being used 2^{32} times.

To acquire a pseudo-random number in microengine assembly, the code reads a microengine-local CSR creatively called PSEUDO_RANDOM_NUMBER. The following code shows how this is done:

```
local_csr_rd[PSEUDO_RANDOM_NUMBER]
immed[random, 0]
```

The microengine C code below does the same thing:

```
random = local_csr_rd(local_csr_pseudo_random_number);
```

IXP1200
Note

> The IXP12XX processor does not have a pseudo-random number generator. Rather, random number generation must be done with table lookups, which repeat faster than the pseudo-random number generator in the IXP2XXX processor and take longer to access.

Core Components

All of the microblocks described in this chapter need some configuration and control from the Intel XScale core. In general, anything with a lookup table in memory needs the core to maintain these in-memory data structures. For example, the IPv4 five-tuple classifier needs some Intel XScale core code to maintain its lookup table. This code would allow users to update the table though a command-line interface, over the network, or through some other facility. When using the Intel IXA SDK 3.0, this code is typically implemented as a "core component." The Intel IXA SDK 3.0 provides a framework for implementing core components.

A single core component can service multiple microblocks, although doing so can sometimes limit the reusability of both the microblocks and the core component. For example, if you built a core component to support both the RED microblock and the IPv4 five-tuple classifier microblock, it would become difficult to deliver those two microblocks separately. In the case of our application, however, ethernet_add_header and ethernet_validate share some of the same in-memory data structures. So we implement one ethernet core component to service them both. This is not likely a problem for reuse because applications that receive Ethernet packets almost always send them as well.

The Intel IXA SDK 3.0 core component infrastructure has facilities for allocating memory, patching load-time constants, and passing messages and packets. This infrastructure allows messages and packets to be passed between core components and microblocks, or between multiple core components. You'll see how this all works in this section.

In the application built in this chapter, the `ethernet_validate`, `ipv4_five_tuple_class`, `ethernet_add_header`, and red microblocks need core components to manage memory, handle a small amount of packets, and provide a software interface to other Intel XScale core application code. The `ethernet_strip_header` microblock, however, has no in-memory lookup table, so a core component is not necessary for it. In this section, you'll see how the core component for `ethernet_add_header` and `ethernet_validate` is implemented.

Core Component Initialization and Shutdown

At the very least, core components must implement two C functions: an initialization function and a shutdown function. When an application instantiates a core component, it passes pointers to these two functions to the Intel IXA SDK 3.0 execution environment. The signature for these functions must follow this specification:

```
typedef ix_error (*ix_cc_init)( ix_cc_handle hCC,
                                void** ppContext );

typedef ix_error (*ix_cc_fini)( ix_cc_handle hCC,
                                void* arg_pContext );
```

When the framework calls either of these functions, it passes the core component handle as the first parameter. This handle is used in many of the other calls into the core component infrastructure. The other parameter in the initialization function is an opaque context pointer. This output parameter allows the framework to maintain some state for the core component. For example, when the core component for the Ethernet microblocks is initialized, it allocates a memory structure that contains all of the information the core component needs to operate. It then sets the context variable to point to this memory. The framework passes this context variable in all subsequent calls to the core component. This allows the core component to find the state information for which it allocated memory when it was initialized. The following code shows how our sample core component allocated memory for state and sets the context variable appropriately.

ethernet_cc_init()

```
       File: init.cc
57         // Allocate memory for Context
58         eth_context = (ethernet_context*)
```

Continues

```
59                    ix_ossl_malloc(sizeof(ethernet_context));
60       if (eth_context == NULL)
61       {
62           return IX_ERROR_WARNING(IX_CC_ERROR_OOM,
63             ("Failed to allocate memory for context"));
64       }
65       *context = eth_context;
```

The shutdown function is called when the core component is being shut down, which usually only occurs when the device is being shut down. The shutdown function releases any resources allocated by the core component during initialization or at any other time in its operation.

Managing Memory

Managing memory that is used only by the core component is accomplished with standard mechanisms, such as `malloc` and `free`. However, when some memory needs to be accessed by the microengines, the Resource Manager must be used to manage this memory. The Resource Manager manages memory that is not available to the standard C library memory allocator, such as SRAM and scratchpad memory. Also, the Resource Manager ensures that any DRAM it uses can be used by the microengines, which may or may not be true for all of the memory accessible to the Intel XScale core.

To allocate memory from the Intel XScale core using the Resource Manager, use the `ix_rm_mem_alloc` function. The signature of this function is:

```
IX_EXPORT_FUNCTION
ix_error ix_rm_mem_alloc(
                        ix_memory_type arg_MemType,
                        ix_uint32 arg_MemChannel,
                        ix_uint32 arg_Size,
                        void** arg_pMemoryAddr
                    );
```

This looks a little different from `malloc`, doesn't it? Don't worry, it's not that scary. First, instead of returning the memory address, this function returns an error code, in case the memory allocation fails. The memory address is instead returned in the memory pointed to by `arg_pMemory-Addr`. The `arg_Size` parameter is the size, in bytes, of the requested memory region. The `arg_MemType` and `arg_MemChannel` parameters allow you to select a memory type and channel for the region of memory. For example, if you want to allocate memory from channel 0 of SRAM, these parameters let you do so.

Selecting a memory channel in which to store a lookup table may have some performance implications to your application. If all of an application's SRAM accesses occur on the same channel, the channel may be a performance bottleneck for the application. Thus, it is usually advisable to spread SRAM tables across memories on multiple channels, either by putting different tables in memories on different channels or by spreading individual tables across memories on multiple channels. To get information about your board's current memory configuration, use the `ix_rm_mem_info` function. This function gives you information about the available memory channels. For the `ethernet core` component, we use this function to just pick the first SRAM channel with enough free space to hold the core component's data.

The pointer returned by `ix_rm_mem_alloc` is a pointer that can be directly dereferenced by the Intel XScale core. All of the various memories, except for microengine local memory, are mapped into the address space of the Intel XScale core. Remember, however, that in the microengines, different instructions are used to access different memory types. So the addresses the microengines use may be different than the addresses the Intel XScale core uses. For example, the microengines can access SRAM at address 0x0000abcd and DRAM at address 0x0000abcd because the accesses are disambiguated by the instructions used to initiate the accesses. So, if you want to give an address returned by `ix_rm_mem_alloc` to the microengines, it must first be converted into an address that the microengines can use. The `ix_rm_get_phys_offset` function does this. Not only does it tell you the correct address to use from the microengines, but also the memory type and channel as well, if you need them.

Now that you know how to manage memory in a core component, you are ready to see how it is used in the `ethernet core` component. The microblocks require a top-level data structure that contains the device's local Ethernet address and an array for mapping next hop IDs to destination MAC addresses. In the initialization function of the `ethernet core` component, the following code is used to allocate memory for the data structure and get an address for this data structure that is appropriate for the microengines:

ethernet_cc_init()

```
File: init.cc

72      // Find a SRAM channel in which to allocate memory
73      // for the control block
```

Continues

```
74           bool channel_found = false;
75           for (channel = 0; channel < 4; channel++)
76           {
77               ix_memory_info mem_info = { 0 };
78               err = ix_rm_mem_info(IX_MEMORY_TYPE_SRAM,
79                                    channel,
80                                    &mem_info);
81               if (err != IX_SUCCESS)
82               {
83                   err = IX_ERROR_WARNING(IX_CC_ERROR_OOM,
84                       ("Failed to allocate memory for "
85                       "control block"));
86                   goto control_block_alloc_failed;
87               }
88               if (mem_info.m_FreeSize >=
89                   sizeof(ethernet_control_block))
90               {
91                   channel_found = true;
92                   break;
93               }
94           }
95           if (!channel_found)
96           {
97               err = IX_ERROR_WARNING(IX_CC_ERROR_OOM,
98                   ("Failed to allocate memory for "
99                   "control block"));
100              goto control_block_alloc_failed;
101          }
102
103          // Allocate memory for the control block that will
104          // be shared between the core component and the
105          // microblocks
106          err = ix_rm_mem_alloc(
107                      IX_MEMORY_TYPE_SRAM,
108                      channel,
109                      sizeof(ethernet_control_block),
110                      (void**)&eth_context->control_block);
111          if (err != IX_SUCCESS)
112          {
113              err = IX_ERROR_WARNING(IX_CC_ERROR_OOM,
114                ("Failed to allocate memory for "
115                "control block"));
116              goto control_block_alloc_failed;
117          }
118
119          ix_ossl_memset(eth_context->control_block, 0,
120                  sizeof(*(eth_context->control_block)));
121
```

Continues

```
122        // Get the physical offset of the control block
123        // so we can give it to the microblock
124        err = ix_rm_get_phys_offset(
125                    eth_context->control_block,
126                    NULL, NULL, NULL,
127                    &control_block_phys);
128        if (err != IX_SUCCESS)
129        {
130            err = IX_ERROR_WARNING(IX_CC_ERROR_OOM,
131              ("Failed to allocate memory for "
132              "control block"));
133            goto get_phys_offset_failed;
134        }
```

Lines 72 – 101:

This code implements a loop that uses `ix_rm_mem_info` to find a memory channel with enough SRAM to hold the data structure needed to communicate between the core component and the microblock.

Lines 103 – 117:

This section of code uses `ix_rm_mem_alloc` to allocate memory in the channel we selected previously.

Lines 122 – 134:

Here, `ix_rm_get_phys_offset` is used to turn the core-addressable pointer into an address that the microengines can use in their instruction set. The `NULL` parameters are for output parameters that we don't need, including the memory type, channel, and channel offset.

When the core component is shut down, the memory allocated using the Resource Manager needs to be freed. This code is used to free the memory, where eth_context is obtained from the context handle as shown above:

```
    // Free memory for control block
    ix_rm_mem_free(eth_context->control_block);
```

Patching Load-time Constants

When the core component gets an address for the data structure, it needs to communicate this information to the microengine code. This is a perfect job for a load time variable.

Microengine C and microengine assembly allow for the declaration and use of a special type of constant called a "load-time constant", also known as an "imported variable." The values of these constants are not known at the time the microengine code is compiled, but rather are determined at the time the code is loaded in the microengines. Once load-time constants are set, they cannot be changed without stopping and reloading the microengines.

Load-time constants are perfect for patching memory locations that are determined when the core component is initialized. For example, in the `ethernet` core component, the address of the data structure is kept in a load-time constant because it is not determined until the core component is initialized, and it does not change throughout the course of the device's operation. The Resource Manager `ix_rm_ueng_patch_symbols` function patches load time variables. The signature of this function looks like this:

```
IX_EXPORT_FUNCTION
ix_error ix_rm_ueng_patch_symbols(
                ix_uint32 arg_MENumber,
                ix_uint32 arg_SymbolsNumber,
                const ix_imported_symbol arg_aSymbols[]
                            );
```

This function takes a microengine number, an array of structures containing symbol/value pairs, and an integer indicating the size of the array.

The following line of code declares a load time constant, or "imported variable," in microengine assembly code:

```
.import_var ETHERNET_DATA
```

This line of code does the same in microengine C:

```
int ETHERNET_DATA =
                LoadTimeConstant("ETHERNET_DATA");
```

When writing microengine code, imported variables can pretty much be used in code just like constants in microengine assembly and microengine C. The only subtle difference is that the assembler cannot tell the number of bits in the constant because the constant is not known ahead of time. So the assembler may force you to treat the constant as a 32-bit constant in your code.

For the `ethernet_add_header` and `ethernet_validate` microblocks, the symbol used for the memory address of the data structure is `ETHERNET_DATA`. Because the simulator does not manipulate load time variables, a `#define` is used so that the code functions properly on the simulator as well as on hardware. When using the simulator, the `ETHERNET_DATA` symbol is defined on the compiler/assembler command line.

In the ethernet core component, the ETHERNET_DATA symbol is patched using the following code:

ethernet_cc_init()

```
File: init.cc
136        // Now, patch the control block symbol for all
137        // of the microengines on which Ethernet
138        // microblocks will run
139        for (i = 0; i < sizeof(me_numbers); i++)
140        {
141            ix_imported_symbol symbol;
142            symbol.m_Value = (ix_uint32)control_block_phys;
143            symbol.m_Name  = ETHERNET_SYMBOL_NAME;
144
145            err = ix_rm_ueng_patch_symbols(i, 1, &symbol);
146            if (err != IX_SUCCESS)
147            {
148                goto patch_symbol_failed;
149            }
150        }
```

Handling Configuration Messages

Most core components need to take input from or give output to other Intel XScale core code. For example, the ethernet core component manages a data structure that stores the device's local Ethernet address. Somehow, something external to the core component must be able to set this address to the correct value. With IXA SDK 3.0, core components communicate with the outside world through configuration messages.

IXP1200
Note

If you are familiar with IXA SDK 2.0, configuration messages replaced the RPC mechanism and IDL compiler that are available with IXA SDK 2.0.

Core components have functions that are called when the core component framework receives a message destined for the core component. These functions have the following signature:

```
typedef ix_error (* ix_msg_handler) (
                    ix_buffer_handle arg_hDataToken,
                    ix_uint32 arg_UserData,
                    void* arg_pComponentContext );
```

The `arg_pComponentContext` parameter is the context value returned when the core component was initialized. The `arg_hDataToken` points to a buffer of memory. The contents of the memory and the value in the `arg_UserData` parameter are set by the code sending the message. It is up to you as the core component developer, to properly specify the format of this memory and integer parameter.

During initialization, the core component registers its message handlers with the core component infrastructure using the `ix_cci_cc_add_message_handler` function. This function associates the message handling function with a unique numerical identifier. When another piece of core code sends messages to the core component, it must use the identifier.

For the `ethernet` core component, we have implemented three message handlers, `set_local_ethernet_addr`, `add_arp_entry`, and `remove_arp_entry`. These message handlers set the local Ethernet address of the device, add ARP entries to the hash table, and delete ARP entries from the hash table, respectively. Here is the code for `set_local_ethernet_addr`:

---

set_local_ethernet_addr()

```
     File: messages.cc
92   ix_error set_local_ethernet_addr(ix_buffer_handle data,
93                                     ix_uint32 user_data,
94                                     void* context)
95   {
96       set_local_ethernet_addr_msg* message = NULL;
97
98       // Get the message structure out of the passed-in
99       // buffer
100      ix_cc_msup_extract_msg(data, (void**)&message,
101                             &context);
102
103      // Set the local Ethernet address
104      _set_local_ethernet_addr(context,
105                               message->eth_address);
106
107      return IX_SUCCESS;
108  }
```

Line 96:

We have defined a message structure for this message and called it `set_local_ethernet_addr_msg`. When messages arrive at this routine, it is assumed that the messages are in this format.

Lines 98 – 101:

> This function call extracts the message data pointer from the `ix_buffer_handle`, putting the pointer in our `message` variable.

Lines 103 – 105:

> An internal function actually does the work of setting the local Ethernet address. The implementation of this internal function is shown here:

> File: messages.cc

```
128   void _set_local_ethernet_addr(void* context,
129                                 char eth_addr[6])
130   {
131       ethernet_context* eth_context =
132                       (ethernet_context*)context;
133
134       // Set the local Ethernet address
135       memcpy(
136           &eth_context->control_block->device_addr_hi32,
137           eth_addr,
138           sizeof(eth_addr));
139   }
```

Lines 131 – 132:

> The context pointer passed to this function is the same one we gave to the framework in our initialization function. So here we just cast this value to a pointer to the data structure holding the local Ethernet address.

Lines 134 – 138:

> Here, the Ethernet address passed by the sender of the message is copied into the same location the microengines are now using to find the device's local Ethernet address. Because the Intel XScale core does memory writes in 32-bit quantities, the local Ethernet address will be invalid for a short period of time. This condition can be resolved by giving the microengines access to a pointer to the local Ethernet address, instead of the address itself. Then when the address is set, the core component can allocate new memory for the new address and adjust the pointer.

> In the initialization function for the `ethernet` core component, the following code registers this message handler with the Resource Manager:

```
err = ix_cci_cc_add_message_handler(
            cc_handle,
            ETHERNET_SET_LOCAL_ETHERNET_ADDR,
            set_local_ethernet_addr,
            IX_INPUT_TYPE_MULTI_SRC);
```

Handling Packets

Many core components need to handle packets as well as configuration messages. For example, the operating system's network stack may want to send packets out of the device. Without a direct way to send packets to the microengine, these packets are sent to a core component to be sent to the correct microblock. Also, some microblocks send packets to their core components for further processing. For example, the ethernet_add_header microblock sends to the ethernet core component the packets for which it cannot find a MAC address matching the packet's next hop ID. This allows the core component to implement the ARP protocol to discover this MAC address.

Handling packets in a core component is not much different than handling messages. The signature of the handler function is exactly the same, and ix_cci_cc_add_packet_handler is called to register the handler, instead of ix_cci_cc_add_message_handler.

When the microblock wants to send packets to its core component, it sets the next block value to the unique packet handler identifier. The microblock can also set a 32-bit exception code. This code is passed to the packet handler with the packet itself.

For the ethernet_add_header microblock, the following microengine C code sends packets to the ethernet core component:

```
// If the entry is not valid, drop this packet.
if (!table_entry.valid)
{
    dl_set_exception(ETHERNET_EXCEPTION_ID ,0);
    dlNextBlock = IX_EXCEPTION;
    return;
}
```

The dl_set_exception function takes the block ID of the core component and a value that is sent to the core component so it knows why the packet was sent to it. The ethernet_add_header microblock only sends packets to its core component if it needs to perform ARP, so we hard-code the second parameter of dl_set_exception to 0 for this microblock. Normally, the dl_sink driver takes packets that have a next-block value of IX_EXCEPTION and sends them to the core. Because we left the implementation of ARP to you, our dl_sink driver drops them.

Core components can also send packets to microblocks using ix_cci_send_packet. This function is used to send packets to other core components as well.

More Core Component Topics

The core component infrastructure does other interesting things that we don't show in our sample application. For example, it allows core components to be mapped to different processes with different task scheduling algorithms. It also allows you to set up periodic or timed messages that are sent to core components. See the *Intel® Internet Exchange Architecture (IXA) Portability Framework Developer's Manual* (Intel PFRM 2002) for more information.

Summary

In this chapter we used a sample data-plane application as a vehicle for showing you how such applications are written on the IXP2XXX processor. Up to this point, we have ignored threading issues in the microengines and focused on other hardware functions available to optimize common network processing tasks. Specifically, we showed the use of the hash unit, unaligned access instructions, indexed registers, local memory, multiplication instruction, and random number generator. We focused on many of the interesting code sections in our sample application, the rest of which can be found on the CD in the back of this book. You also learned about how the Intel XScale core code, and in particular core components, is built and how it interacts with the microengines through the framework provided with Intel IXA SDK 3.0.

Chapter 7

Unordered Thread Execution

At this point, we have created a complete packet-processing application, but it's pretty slow. With the sample microengine assembly from Chapter 6, the microengine that processes packets is actually executing instructions for less than 10% of the time. The rest of the time is spent waiting for memory references, queue operations, and hashes. With the techniques described in this chapter, and the sample code on the CD, you can raise that utilization and increase packet throughput.

In this chapter, you'll learn how to make the packet-processing code run on multiple threads and multiple microengines. You get some performance benefit from these changes, but because you are still running with single-threaded receive code and single-threaded transmit code, the performance will not yet be as good as you might hope for. The higher performance will come in Chapter 11, when you add multithreaded receive and transmit code to this multi-threaded packet-processing code.

Two programming models exist for running the same series of packet-processing components on multiple threads. These programming models are called "ordered thread execution" and "unordered thread execution." This chapter shows the unordered thread execution model of programming. In some previous Intel literature, the unordered thread execution model is called "Pool of Threads." The models are exactly alike. In Chapter 3, we described the basics of both of these programming models. After reading this chapter and Chapter 9, you should understand these two models well enough to decide which model works best for your application.

Multiple Threads

The code in Chapter 6 under-utilizes the processing power of the IXP2XXX microengines, and the solution to this problem is to use the hardware threads of the IXP2XXX microengines. These hardware threads allow the code to switch contexts when the current context is waiting for an I/O reference. So, running our packet-processing code on multiple threads does much to address the utilization problem.

The sample code in Chapter 6 also has 13 unused microengines. Once you make the code run properly on multiple threads of a single microengine, it is not much more difficult to make it run properly on multiple microengines. All of these microengines give you a lot more computing power allowing packets to be processed much faster.

Making the processing code run on multiple threads involves a different set of steps for microengine assembly than for microengine C. In the sample microengine assembly code for Chapter 6, the packet-processing code in the `process.uc` file is surrounded with a `.if` statement like this:

```
.if (ctx() == 0)
    <packet-processing code here>
.endif
```

This keeps the code running in only one context. To get the code to run in multiple contexts on a microengine, simply remove this `.if` and its associated `.endif`.

For the microengine C code, changing some compiler settings makes the code use all of the contexts on a microengine. In the Compiler tab of the Build Settings dialog, adjust the "Context mode" and the "Number of contexts" to "8". Figure 7.1 shows this.

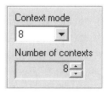

Figure 7.1 Compiler Settings for Multithreaded Microengine C Code

It's easy to run it on more microengines. In the Linker tab of the Build Settings dialog, just add the same .list file to multiple microengines. In the Workbench, the Linker settings should look similar to Figure 7.2.

Software developers familiar with other platforms know that multi-threaded programming is not as simple as running single-threaded code on multiple threads. The first problem to deal with is synchronization. Our packet-processing code accesses shared data structures, so you need to make sure parallelizing the code does not introduce the possibility of corrupting these data structures. The second problem you have to deal with is a characteristic of many network applications: packet ordering. Many network applications require that packets within a flow come out of a device in the same order they arrive, and many micro-blocks internally need to process packets in the order they are received at the device. Keeping packets in order is easy with single-threaded code because it is impossible for packets to be reordered. When the code is run on multiple threads, however, you must ensure that threads finish processing packets in the same order the threads begin working on the packets. The rest of this chapter shows how the problems of synchronization and packet ordering are addressed in the unordered thread execution model of programming.

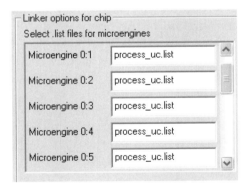

Figure 7.2 Linker Settings for Running Code on Multiple Microengines

Keeping Packet Order

When processing packets in a network device, packet ordering is an issue in two ways. First, many devices require that packets within a single flow exit the device in the same order in which they arrive. We call this requirement "end-to-end packet order." The other way ordering becomes an issue is for particular packet-processing blocks that must process packets within a single flow in a particular order. For example, when doing IP header decompression, the ability to decompress a packet's header depends on having already decompressed the packets that have arrived before it in the same flow. Thus, a block performing IP header decompression must process packets in the order they are received within a particular flow. This ordering is called "partial packet order." In both end-to-end and partial packet ordering, the semantics of the "flow" depends on the application. For example, an IPv4 router may define a flow as the packets traveling from one unique IP address to another unique IP address, whereas an IP header decompression function might define a flow based on the context identified in the compression header of the packet.

The issue of packet ordering did not arise in the Chapter 6 design because the receive, processing, and transmit microengines are each handling packets on one thread in strict order. However, when the processing code is run on multiple threads, it processes multiple packets at once, so packet ordering is no longer guaranteed. Unless the amount of time needed to process a packet is constant, packets could be reordered. In our sample code from Chapter 6, cases can be found where two packets could take vastly different amounts of time to process. For example, a hash table lookup could take two memory reads if the correct entry is found in the first level of the hash table, or it could take many more memory reads if the code has to follow the linked list in the hash table. Even for cases where two packets follow the same code path, the processing time is not necessarily the same. Memory access times and throughputs are not constant, and the activities of other threads on the microengine could affect the amount of time it takes to process the packets. So, the code could reorder any of the incoming packets, breaking both end-to-end packet order and partial packet order requirements, as shown in Figure 7.3.

Although end-to-end and partial packet ordering are somewhat different from a requirements standpoint, usually the methods used for fulfilling both of these requirements are similar. For example, end-to-end packet order can be achieved in our example application by making sure that the final packet enqueue in the processing microengines happens in the order the packets are received. Enqueuing packets in order is no different that treating the enqueue code as a block of code that

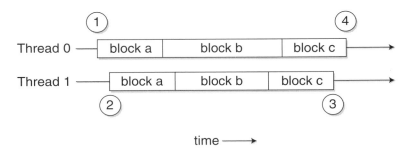

At time 1 in this diagram, Thread 0 dequeues a packet from a queue
containing packets in the correct order. The packet is then processed
using "block a." At time 2, Thread 1 dequeues the next packet. Assume
the packets are in the same flow. The time it takes to process the first
packet in block b is longer than the time it takes to process the second
packet in block b. Therefore, the second packet is enqueued (at time 3)
before the first packet (at time 4). Thus, the packets will come out of the
device out of order, breaking end-to-end packet order. Also notice that
block c processes the second packet before the first packet. If block c
requires partial packet ordering, it would not occur.

Figure 7.3 Example Timeline Showing Packets Being Reordered

requires partial packet ordering. In fact, achieving end-to-end packet
ordering can almost always be done by imposing partial-packet-ordering
requirements on a few blocks of code.

Many solutions have been developed to allow microblocks to process
packets in order. All of these solutions fall into one of two categories:
blocking and non-blocking. A blocking solution causes threads to "take
turns" entering microblocks that require packet ordering. A non-blocking
solution typically involves buffering packets that arrive at microblocks
out of order. Blocking solutions usually involve simpler algorithms that
use fewer resources, but in some cases they cause threads to waste a lot
of time waiting for their turn. Non-blocking solutions usually involve
more complicated algorithms, but allow threads to keep busy even
when packets arrive out of order.

It would be impossible to cover all of the various packet ordering
solutions in this chapter. Instead, we show an example of a blocking
packet-ordering algorithm and a non-blocking packet-ordering algorithm. These solutions achieve end-to-end packet order in our design.

Non-blocking Packet-ordering Algorithm

Remember that our sample design processes packets in three stages: receive, process, and transmit. Our solution to maintaining end-to-end packet order is to allow packets to get out of order in the process stage and enforce ordering on the enqueue block just before transmitting the packets. So long as the receive and transmit drivers do not reorder packets (which they don't!), this approach ensures end-to-end packet ordering. We only enforce ordering within flows, as identified by the flow ID assigned by the IPv4 five-tuple classifier.

The non-blocking reordering algorithm for our sample application has three basic steps that occur at different points in the processing code: flow-determination, sequence number assignment, and packet reordering.

Flow Determination

So what is a flow? To this point we have used the term without defining it. The term "flow" is used in many contexts in the networking field outside the area of packet ordering. For the purpose of packet ordering, we define a flow as a set of packets which require end-to-end packet ordering. That's pretty vague, isn't it? The real answer depends on the application. Some applications may require ordering for all packets, some may require ordering for all packets with unique input and output ports, and others may require ordering for unique packet field values, such as IP addresses, UDP/TCP ports, or other field values. For example, most IP router designs forward packets in order between two unique endpoints. In this case, the flow is determined by the combination of the IP source and destination addresses.

The flow definition required by the application may differ from the flow definition used to reorder packets. This difference is acceptable if flows used to define ordering completely contain flows as defined by the application. For example, let's say our application requires that flows be defined as sets of packets with the same source IP address, destination IP address, IP protocol number, source UDP/TCP port, and destination UDP/TCP port. Maintaining order for each of these flows may involve maintaining a lot of state. In our application, however, every packet in one of these flows is assigned the same flow ID by the IPv4 five-tuple classifier. For packet reordering, we could define a flow to be the set of packets given the same flow ID, even though multiple flows (as defined in the requirements) are given the same flow ID. Using this approach as a basis for reordering meets the requirements of the application with potentially a lot less state. This approach may mean that unrelated packets are unnecessarily kept in order, but such is the nature of an engineering tradeoff. Our sample application makes this tradeoff. So in our sample application, the flow ID given to the packet by the classifier identifies the flow for ordering purposes.

Sequence Number Assignment

The next step in our blocking reordering algorithm is to assign a sequence number to the packets. These sequence numbers are used by the packet reordering step to properly reorder the packets. For a particular packet, sequence numbers cannot be assigned until the code determines in which flow a packet belongs. In this application, we defined a flow to be the packets assigned the same flow ID. So, because the IPv4 five-tuple classification determines the flow ID for a packet, it also determines the flow for a packet. Therefore, the code cannot assign sequence numbers until after the classification completes. The sequence numbers are monotonically increasing within a particular flow. To get a sequence number, we maintain an array of sequence numbers in SRAM. The array has one entry per flow. When a thread finishes the classifier, it atomically reads and increments the number in SRAM, and sets the packet's sequence number to be the value retrieved. Here is the microengine C code that acquires a sequence number for a packet:

non_blocking_get_sequence()

```
       File: Chapter07\reorder.c
156    unsigned int non_blocking_get_sequence(
157        __declspec(sram visible)
158                non_blocking_order_flow_t* flow)
159    {
160        __declspec(sram_read_reg) unsigned int seq_number;
161        SIGNAL sram_signal;
162
163        // Retrieve the sequence number and increment it all
164        // in one shot
165        sram_test_and_incr(
166                &seq_number,
167                (void*)&(flow->next_assigned_sequence),
168                ctx_swap,
169                &sram_signal);
170
171        return seq_number;
172    }
```

Lines 165 – 169:

> This code uses an atomic SRAM operation to increment and return the next sequence number. The atomic operations are covered more extensively later in this chapter.

If you insert code after classification to assign sequence numbers, this code needs to assign sequence numbers based on the order in which the packets were received by the device, which may not be the order at which they arrive at the sequence-numbering code. So the sequence-number assignment also needs packet ordering. It sounds like a chicken-and-an-egg problem, doesn't it? Later in this chapter we'll show you a blocking packet-ordering algorithm that solves this.

Reordering Packets

Just before packets are put on scratch rings on their way to the transmit code, they are reordered so that packets within the same flow are put on the rings in the order they were received. To help reorder packets, a data structure temporarily buffers packets that come to the end of processing earlier than they should. This allows threads with out-of-order packets to start working on another packet. This data structure is a circular buffer that allows for insertion at any point in the structure and removal only from the head. We call this data structure an Asynchronous Insert, Synchronous Remove structure, or AISR for short. Figure 7.4 shows the AISR structure, and Figure 7.5 shows the complete reordering algorithm.

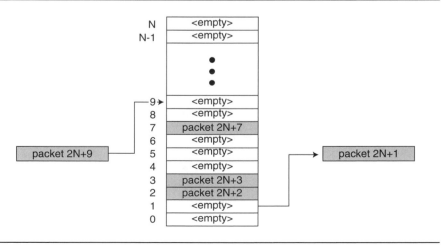

Figure 7.4 Asynchronous Insert/Synchronous Remove (AISR) Data Structure

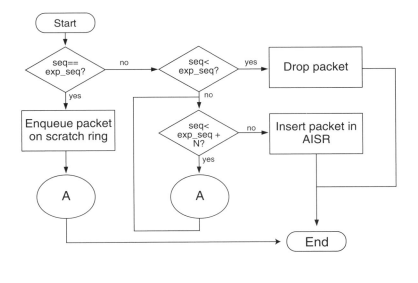

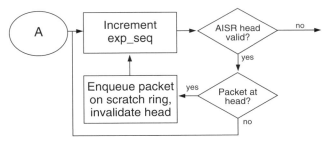

This diagram shows the algorithm that reorders packets before putting them on queues to be transmitted. The algorithm is run once for each packet, although it may result in any number of packets being enqueued. The sequence of steps in the left-hand column occurs when the packets come in order. The remaining steps use the AISR to reorder packets. In this figure, seq is the sequence number of the current packet, and exp_seq is the current expected sequence number for the flow. N is the size of the AISR array. The term "AISR head" refers to the element of the AISR indexed by exp_seq modulo N. The "Packet at head?" decision differentiates between a valid buffer handle in the AISR and an invalid packet handle indicating the packet has previously been dropped or sent to the core.

Figure 7.5 Reordering Algorithm for Non-blocking Packet Ordering

The code that reorders packets maintains an AISR for each flow. The code also maintains an expected sequence number for each flow, indicating the sequence number of the packet it expects to see next. If the reorder code receives a packet with this sequence number, it increments the expected sequence number and enqueues the packet, without accessing the AISR. If the reorder code receives a packet with a sequence number greater than the expected sequence number, it attempts to put the packet into the AISR.

Each AISR is of finite size, of course. So, if a packet arrives greater than N sequence numbers out of order, where N is the size of the AISR, the AISR has no place for the packet. To account for this, the expected sequence number is adjusted to a value ensuring the AISR has room for the new packet. Any packets in the AISR with sequence numbers less than the new expected sequence number are enqueued for transmission. This implies that later in the operation of the code, packets will arrive in this algorithm with sequence numbers *lower* than the expected sequence number that have been skipped over in this process. These packets are dropped to ensure that the reordering algorithm does not create a mis-ordering problem itself! Because dropping packets is something we want to avoid as much as possible, we must choose the size of the AISR so packet dropping happens as infrequently as possible. This decision should be based on how frequently packets get out of order and by how much. The design of the microblocks that may reorder packets and the number of threads in your design both contribute to this.

The processing code may also want to remove packets from the sequence after they have been assigned sequence numbers. For example, the application may decide to drop the packet or send it to the core. When this happens, the code sends an invalid buffer handle to the reordering code. If this happens when the expected sequence number matches the packet's sequence number, the reorder code simply increments the expected sequence number. If this happens and the packet would have normally been inserted in the AISR, the code puts the invalid buffer handle in the AISR with the packet's sequence number. When it comes time to remove the packet from the AISR, the algorithm does so without enqueuing the packet on the scratch ring. The full reordering algorithm is shown in Figure 7.5.

Although this algorithm looks complicated, it's really not that bad. If most packets come in order, the algorithm is fairly efficient, performing the steps on the left side. If a packet comes out of order by less than N places, the packet is simply inserted into the AISR. If a packet comes out of order by more than N spaces, the algorithm starts to cause performance problems and dropped packets. But N can be chosen such that these occurrences are rare.

The following microengine C code illustrates this algorithm:

non_blocking_order()

```
        File: Chapter07\reorder.c
257         expected_sequence = flow->expected_sequence;
258
259         // Check to see if this packet is coming in order
260         if (expected_sequence == data.sequence)
261         {
262             // The packet is in order. Check to see if it
263             // is an actual packet in the AISR element. If
264             // the packet had been dropped or sent to the
265             // core, this will be NULL
266             if (data.handle.value)
267             {
268                 sram_ring_put_buffer(
269                         ring_number,
270                         data);
271             }
272
273             // Now empty the AISR to the point at which the
274             // head is invalid
275             empty_aisr(flow, ring_number);
276         }
277         else
278         {
279             // The packet is out of order. Check to see if
280             // it is early or late. The late packets should
281             // almost never happen. They get dropped.
282             if (expected_sequence < data.sequence)
283             {
284                 __declspec(sram visible) aisr_element*
285                                             aisr_entry;
286                 aisr_element new_element;
287
288                 // The packet is early. Clear out the AISR
289                 // until it fits in the AISR. For most
290                 // packets this won't be necessary
```

Continues

```
291                  while (expected_sequence + AISR_SIZE <
292                        data.sequence)
293              {
294                  empty_aisr(flow, ring_number);
295                  expected_sequence =
296                               flow->expected_sequence;
297              }
298
299              // The packet now fits in the AISR. Insert
300              // it.
301              aisr_entry = flow->aisr +
302                          (data.sequence % AISR_SIZE);
303              new_element.handle = data.handle;
304              new_element.length = data.length;
305              new_element.offset = data.offset;
306              new_element.valid  = 1;
307              *aisr_entry = new_element;
308          }
309          else
310          {
311              // The packet is late. Drop it.
312              Dl_BufDrop(data.handle);
313          }
314      }
```

Line 260:

This if statement decides if the packet is in-order or out-of-order.

Line 262 – 275:

If the packet is in-order, the code checks to see whether the packet handle is valid. If it is, it puts the packet on the ring. If the packet with the current sequence number was previously dropped or sent to the core, the handle will be invalid. In either case, the empty_aisr function then performs what is marked in Figure 7.5 as subroutine "A."

Line 282:

If the packet is out-of-order, this line checks to see whether the packet is early or late.

Lines 284 – 297:

If the packet is early, this code puts the packet in the AISR. The code must first make sure there is room in the AISR. The while loop does this, emptying the AISR until there is room for the packet. This process may skip over AISR elements that represent packets that haven't arrived yet. These packets are dropped later. Hence, it is important to make the AISR large enough so that this rarely occurs. If the AISR is large enough, the body of the while loop will not be executed for most packets.

Line 312:

If the packet was previously skipped by the code just described, it is dropped here.

This algorithm requires some synchronization because multiple threads may try to run it at the same time using the same data structures. Synchronization for this code is shown later in this chapter.

Blocking Packet-ordering Algorithm

Unlike non-blocking packet-ordering algorithms, blocking packet-ordering algorithms cause threads with out-of-order packets to wait until packets that arrived earlier have been processed by the order-sensitive blocks. Although blocking packet-ordering techniques sometimes cause microengine threads to spend time waiting when they could be doing work, blocking packet-ordering algorithms tend to be less memory and processor intensive than non-blocking packet-ordering algorithms.

In the case of our sample application, the code that assigns sequence numbers for the non-blocking packet ordering algorithm above needs to process packets in the order in which they are received. This sequence number assignment happens just after IPv4 five-tuple classification.

This blocking packet-ordering algorithm is shown in Figure 7.6. To achieve this packet ordering, packets are assigned sequence numbers by the receive code. The code assigning end-to-end packet-ordering sequence numbers maintains an expected sequence number, similar to the non-blocking packet-ordering algorithm above. When a thread is ready to enter the ordered code, it blocks until the expected sequence number is the same as the packet's sequence number. Then, the thread enters the ordered code—in this case assigning a new flow-based sequence number for end-to-end packet ordering. When this code completes, the thread increments the expected sequence number.

The microengine C code that implements the part of this algorithm before the ordered code follows Figure 7.6.

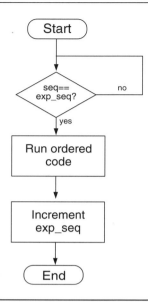

Figure 7.6 Simple Blocking Packet-ordering Algorithm

blocking_order_enter()

```
       File: Chapter07\reorder.c
72     void blocking_order_enter(
73         __declspec(scratch visible)
74                        blocking_order_flow_t* flow,
75         unsigned int sequence_num)
76     {
77         // Keep checking the current sequence number until
78         // it matches the sequence number of the packet
79         while (*flow != sequence_num)
80         {
81         }
82     }
```

Lines 79 – 81:

This code simply waits for the sequence number associated with the flow to become equal to the sequence number of the current packet.

All of these flows and sequence numbers can get pretty confusing. An easy way to think about it is: all packets belong to a flow at all points in the system. When the packet is first received, it is part of one big flow that contains every packet coming into the system. Then, as the code learns more about the packet, the flows divide into multiple flows. When a packet arrives at the system, it gets a sequence number. Every time the flow of a packet changes, it gets a new sequence number for the new flow. These sequence numbers are used to maintain packet order for the different microblocks that require packet order.

Figure 7.7 shows the relationship between flows and sequencing in our sample application design. This application has the same functionality as the ones in the previous chapters, with the processing code verifying and removing the Ethernet header, performing IPv4 five-tuple classification, adding a new Ethernet header, and performing Random Early Detection (RED) on the packets.

Alternatively, you could decide to treat all of the packets in the system as being in the same flow throughout the whole system. Having one flow is a valid design because maintaining order in a single large flow also maintains order within any component flows. If one or more flows takes substantially longer to process in the RED code than other flows, keeping the single flow throughout punishes the flows that need less processing by making them wait for the flows that need more processing. If this inefficiency outweighs the inefficiency introduced by splitting the flow, our original design choice is the correct one. This may

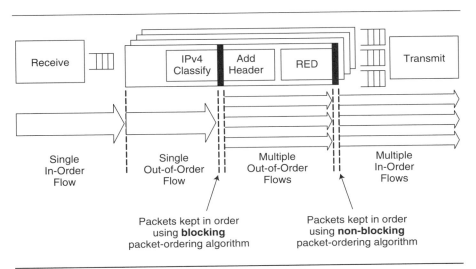

Figure 7.7 Flows and Sequencing in the Sample Application

be true in our application because congested flows take different amounts of time to process in RED than do non-congested flows. However, we have not quantified this for our application.

Other Packet-ordering Algorithms

Although we have introduced two classes of packet ordering algorithms—blocking and non-blocking—we have certainly not explained every instance of each class. The characteristics of your device design or the traffic patterns in the environment may drive you to consider variations of these algorithms or completely different algorithms altogether.

Skipping Ordered Blocks

Certain properties of our sample application make achieving packet order easier that it would be otherwise. In our application every packet goes through the blocks of code that require packet ordering. Other applications may have blocks through which only some packets go but still require packet ordering. Consider the application diagrammed in Figure 7.8.

In this application, some of the packets exiting the classifier go to a header decompression block and then to the IP routing block, while the rest go straight to the IP routing block. Let's say for the sake of argument that header decompression needs to process packets in the order they are received. Let's also say that for reordering purposes, the application has one flow throughout the whole system.

Maintaining order in the header decompression block is impossible using the blocking packet-ordering algorithm described above because the algorithm will wait for packets that never go through the header decompression block. A solution to this is to have all packets go through

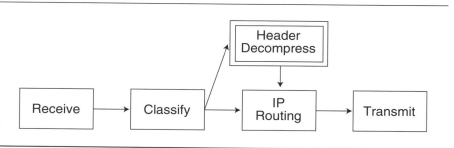

Figure 7.8 Application Example for Skipping Ordered Blocks

the packet ordering code, even if the packets do not need to be ordered. So in Figure 7.8, packets going through the IP routing microblock go through the same ordering code as packets going through the header decompression microblock, even though these packets do not need to be ordered. More complicated solutions exist, as well.

Dedicating Flows to Threads

Sometimes it is possible to use the statistical properties of network traffic to our advantage. In an environment where the packet rates of the individual flows are statistically balanced, packet ordering can be achieved by assigning flows to individual threads. Dedicating flows to threads prevents packets within flows from being reordered. In our application, we can do this by separating the processing code into different microengines. One or more microengines execute the IPv4 five-tuple classifier code. After the classifier, packets are put on queues destined for the next microengine which adds Ethernet headers and performs RED. Each thread performing the second part of the packet processing has its own queue, so after the classifier, packets are put on queues based on their flow ID. Our sample application is represented in the diagram in Figure 7.9.

This algorithm, like all of the others we have presented, has its benefits and drawbacks. If the statistical properties of the packets in your

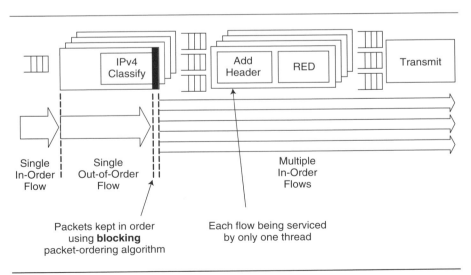

Figure 7.9 Dedicating Threads to Flows to Maintain Packet Ordering

application are such that the workload of the threads can be well balanced, this algorithm will perform very well. If, on the other hand, all of
the packets arriving in the device are part of the same flow, this algorithm will perform poorly, as only one thread is servicing the flow.

Synchronization

Like we said at the beginning of the chapter, two problems arise when
you take single-threaded packet-processing code and try to run it on
multiple threads. The first problem is packet ordering, which we have
addressed above. The second problem is synchronization, which we
address here.

When reading and writing data structures in multiple threads, software needs synchronization to ensure that these structures do not get
corrupted. For example, if the IPv4 five-tuple classification code
counted packets as they were processed, a global counter can be maintained in memory. To update this counter, the code might take the following three steps:

1. Read the counter from memory into a register.
2. Increment the counter in the register.
3. Write the counter to memory.

If one thread completes step 1 but not step 3, and another thread completes step 1, the result of both threads' actions is a single incrementing
of the counter, which is incorrect. If the code synchronizes its activities—only allowing one thread to perform these steps at a time—then
the proper behavior results.

The IXP2XXX microengines have some hardware features that help
support many synchronization methods. This chapter outlines six of
them: atomic test operations, atomic logical and arithmetic operations,
Deli Ticket Server (DTS), the CAM unit, register/local memory bit spin
loop, and synchronization servers. No single synchronization method is
appropriate for every scenario. The following properties vary from one
synchronization method to another:

■ Scope—Some methods only work within a single microengine and
others work across microengines. For the locks described in this
book, the scope is either intra-microengine or inter-microengine.

- Potential Locks—Some methods only provide for a very small number of potential locks, and others allow for many.

- Outstanding Locks—Independent of the number of potential locks allowed by the synchronization method, some methods limit the number of outstanding locks. For example, using the CAM unit to provide locks allows for 2^{32} potential locks, but only 16 can be locked at any one time.

- Ordering—Some synchronization methods guarantee that threads gain access to a critical section in the same order they request access.

- Starvation—Some methods guarantee that a thread requesting access to a critical section eventually gets access. Others do not.

- Performance—The performance of these synchronization methods varies. Some require polling of external memory, which is slow. Some allow threads to wait for a signal, which is fast.

This section covers the synchronization methods that are appropriate for unordered thread execution, applying some to the synchronization issues in the sample code. The IXP2XXX processor also has a very efficient, coarse granularity, cross-microengine synchronization method that works for ordered thread execution that is covered in Chapter 9.

Atomic Test Operations

The SRAM controller and scratchpad memory unit provide atomic test operations that atomically perform a read, a modification, and a write on a single 32-bit location in memory. These operations can be used in a loop to provide synchronization for multiple threads. The flow chart in Figure 7.10 shows an example implementation of this using atomic test-and-set. This particular instruction sets one or more bits in the memory location and returns the original value in a transfer register. Table 7.1 shows the properties of using atomic test operations for synchronization.

The SRAM controller also supports test-and-clear, test-and-increment, test-and-decrement, and test-and-add. The scratchpad memory unit supports all of these operations as well as a test-and-subtract operation.

In our sample application, the code that implements the reordering algorithm in Figure 7.5 requires a synchronization method that works across multiple microengines that can provide synchronization for the entire length of the algorithm. For this case, atomic test-and-set works well. One memory bit per queue is used as the lock bit. The following microengine assembly code is placed in front of the reorder algorithm to provide synchronization:

```
// First, we need to grab the lock for this flow.
.reg $lock
.sig lock_signal
.repeat
    sram_bits_test_and_set($lock, 0x1, in_flow,
                           END_TO_END_ORDER_LOCK,
                           lock_signal, lock_signal,
                           ___)
.until (!$lock)
```

When the reorder algorithm has completed, the atomic bit clear operation is used to allow other threads to reorder packets for the same queue. The following microengine C code performs this operation:

```
// Now, unlock the flow
sram_bits_clr(0x1, in_flow, NON_BLOCKING_ORDER_LOCK,
              lock_signal, lock_signal, ___)
```

This code uses an atomic SRAM operation to clear the lock bit.

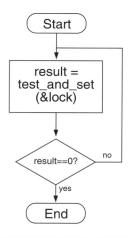

Figure 7.10 Algorithm for Entering a Critical Section Using Atomic Test-and-set

Table 7.1 Properties of Synchronization Using Atomic Test Operations

Property	Atomic Test Operations Support
Scope	Inter-microengine
Potential Locks	Limited by number of bits in memory
Outstanding Locks	Limited by number of bits in memory
Ordering	Not ordered
Starvation	Possible
Performance	Slow (polling memory)

Atomic Logical and Arithmetic Operations

If the operation that needs to be synchronized is a simple logical or arithmetic operation, the atomic read-modify-write operations described above may be enough to do all of the necessary synchronization. For example, if an algorithm reads a value from memory, adds another value to the original value, and replaces the original with the sum, a single atomic SRAM or scratch add instruction suffices. In this case, the "test" part of the instruction is not necessary. The operation itself is sufficient.

On the IXP2XXX processor, if the scratchpad memory and SRAM controller support a particular atomic test operation, they also support an atomic logical or arithmetic operation of the same type. For example, the SRAM controller supports both `incr` and `test_and_incr`. Table 7.2 shows the properties of this synchronization method.

Table 7.2 Properties of Synchronization Using Atomic Logical and Arithmetic Operations

Property	Atomic Logical and Arithmetic Operations Support
Scope	Inter-microengine
Potential Locks	Limited by number of long-words in memory
Outstanding Locks	Limited by number of long-words in memory
Ordering	Ordered
Starvation	Not possible
Performance	Medium (accessing memory)

Sometimes, you might want to use these atomic operations even when you don't need synchronization because they combine what would be two memory operations into one. Combining memory operations gives your code a performance benefit because the latency incurred getting a command from the microengine to the scratchpad memory or the SRAM controller is only incurred once, instead of twice. This does not change the amount of latency observed due to the actual memory itself, however, because the hardware still internally performs a read and a write.

Our sample application uses an atomic operation when incrementing the expected sequence number to leave a section of code using our simple partial packet order algorithm.

Deli Ticket Server

Another method for synchronization that works across microengines is called the "Deli Ticket Server" or DTS for short. The DTS method is modeled after grocery store delis or other commercial settings where customers take a numbered piece of paper to determine when they get service.

The DTS algorithm is very similar to the algorithm described in the Non-blocking Packet-ordering Algorithm section above, where the sequence number is instead a ticket number. Rather than the ticket number being assigned in advance, the code gets the ticket number at the point in time at which it tries to enter the critical section. Figure 7.11 shows the algorithm for entering a critical section using the DTS algorithm.

To exit the critical section, the expected ticket number (exp_ticket in Figure 7.11) is incremented using the atomic increment operation.

The properties of the DTS method of synchronization are shown in Table 7.3.

CAM Unit

The CAM unit in each microengine can also be used to provide synchronization. Remember that the CAM allows for the lookup of arbitrary 32-bit values, and each CAM entry can have 4 bits of state associated with it. Also remember that the CAM only contains 16 entries. The

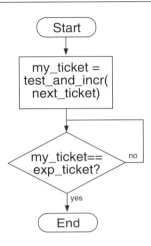

Figure 7.11 Algorithm for Entering a Critical Section Using DTS

Table 7.3 Properties of Synchronization Using Deli Ticket Server

Property	Deli Ticket Server Support
Scope	Inter-microengine
Potential Locks	Limited by number of long-words in memory divided by two
Outstanding Locks	Limited by number of long-words in memory divided by two
Ordering	Ordered
Starvation	Not possible
Performance	Slow (polling memory)

algorithms described in Figure 7.12 and Figure 7.13 show how to use the CAM to synchronize code based on a 32-bit "lock ID." This lock ID can be a pointer into memory or any other application-defined identifier.

The properties of using the CAM unit for synchronization are shown in Table 7.4.

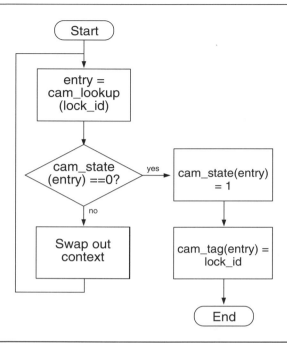

Figure 7.12 Algorithm for Entering a Critical Section Using the CAM

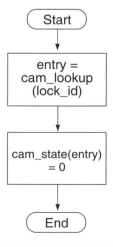

Figure 7.13 Algorithm for Leaving a Critical Section Using the CAM

Table 7.4 Properties of Synchronization Using the CAM Unit

Property	CAM Unit Support
Scope	Intra-microengine
Potential Locks	2^{32}
Outstanding Locks	16
Ordering	Not ordered
Starvation	Not possible
Performance	Fast (polling the microengine CAM)

Of course, this algorithm only works because microengine threading is not preemptive. If the microengines were able to change contexts in the middle of entering or leaving a critical section, this algorithm would fail.

Register/Local Memory Bit Spin Loop

The same algorithm shown in Figure 7.10 using atomic test operations can also be used with registers or local memory on a microengine to provide synchronization on just a single microengine. Even though the microengines have no atomic test operation on registers or local memory, the thread arbiter makes this method function properly. Remember from Chapter 2 that the microengine threading hardware does not preempt microengine threads. So, the atomic read and write can be guaranteed by simply not releasing the microengine context in between the read and write.

The properties of using the registers or local memory for synchronization are shown in Table 7.5.

Synchronization Server

A synchronization server can be used to turn one of the single microengine synchronization methods into a multiple microengine synchronization method by sacrificing a microengine to the cause. The microengine used has an input queue in scratchpad memory or SRAM for lock and unlock requests. It then honors those requests using any of a number of methods. For microengine threads blocking on a lock request, their thread number and a signal number are queued up with

Table 7.5 Properties of Synchronization Using a Register/Local Memory Spin Loop

Property	Register/Local Memory Spin Loop Support
Scope	Intra-microengine
Potential Locks	Limited by number of bits in registers/local memory
Outstanding Locks	Limited by number of bits in registers/local memory
Ordering	Not ordered
Starvation	Not possible
Performance	Fast (polling the registers/local memory)

the request. After the request is sent, the requesting microengine thread blocks on the signal. The synchronization server then signals the thread using the specified signal when the lock is acquired. The operation of the synchronization server is diagrammed in Figure 7.14.

The properties of using a Synchronization Server for synchronization are shown in Table 7.6.

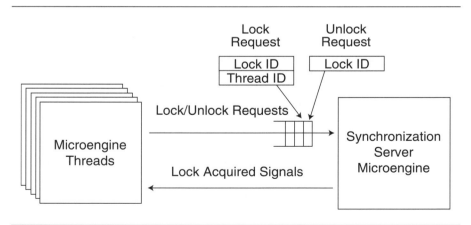

Figure 7.14 Synchronization Server

Table 7.6 Properties of Synchronization Using a Synchronization Server

Property	Register/Local Memory Spin Loop Support
Scope	Inter-microengine
Potential Locks	Depends on Intra-microengine method used internally
Outstanding Locks	Depends on Intra-microengine method used internally
Ordering	Ordered
Starvation	Not possible
Performance	Fast (enqueue then wait for a signal)

A Performance Improvement: A Dispatcher

If you were to write and run the code as we have described it thus far and used all 14 remaining IXP2800 microengines for the processing task, you would find that it runs very poorly. Examining the thread states of the machine would show many threads stalled waiting for scratch ring "get" instructions. Because our receive code is so much slower than our processing code at this point, the processing code is spending an enormous amount of time trying to get packets from the receive code. The problem is that all of these scratch ring accesses are having a large negative impact on the system as a whole because hardware queues on the way out of the microengines and on the way into the Scratchpad, Hash and CAP (SHaC) are full.

To alleviate this, you can use an alternative to packet rings for getting packets from the receive code to the processing code. This alternative is called a "dispatcher". With a dispatcher, a scratch ring is still needed, but information on this scratch ring flows in the opposite direction of normal: from the processing code to the receive code.

The data on this ring is not packets, however. Instead, a processing thread enqueues information about itself when it is available to process packets. The receive code then uses this information to "dispatch" packets to the processing code. The information on the ring is a thread ID and the index into a reserved region of transfer registers. When the receive code has a packet and thread information from the ring, it puts the packet information into the thread's transfer registers using the reflector bus and signals the thread. This is shown in Figure 7.15.

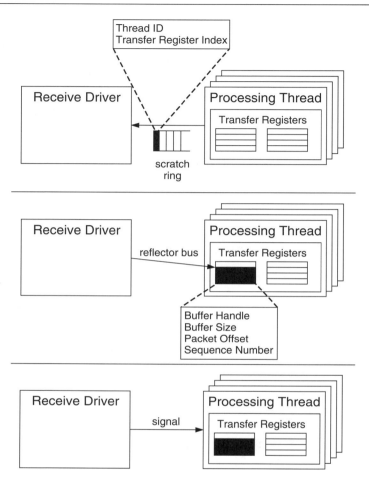

The dispatch process is illustrated in three steps. The first step shows one of the processing threads putting information on a scratch ring being read by the receive driver. This information includes the processing thread's thread ID and an index into a reserved area of its transfer registers. After this, the processing thread waits for a previously agreed upon signal. In the second step, the receive thread takes packet data for a newly received packet and puts it into the processing thread's transfer registers. Finally, in the third step, the receive thread signals the processing thread to process the new packet.

Figure 7.15 Packet Dispatch Algorithm

This algorithm can be more efficient than using scratch rings directly, especially when the processing threads are faster than the receive threads. In this scenario, using scratch rings to pass packets would result in many scratch memory accesses. Using the dispatcher algorithm, however, idle processing threads are instead blocking on a signal, using no compute or memory resources. This algorithm also lets us show you the usage of the reflector bus.

The sample application code has an implementation of packet dispatch. On the CD in the back of the book we have included a microengine assembly version and a microengine C version. Here is the microengine C code used in the processing thread to get packets from the receive code:

dispatch_get_packet()

```
       File: Chapter07\dispatch.h
173       // Set up the data to put on the scratch ring for
174       // the dispatcher
175       free_thread.me_num = __ME();
176       free_thread.thread_num = ctx();
177       free_thread.xfer_reg_num =
178                    __xfer_reg_number(&packet_info);
179
180       // Put the data on the ring
181       free_thread_xfer = free_thread;
182
183       scratch_put_ring(&free_thread_xfer,
184                    ring_addr,
185                    sizeof(free_thread_xfer)
186                        / sizeof(unsigned int),
187                    ctx_swap,
188                    &ring_signal);
189
190       // Now, wait for the assignment to arrive
191       __assign_relative_register(&packet_ready_sig,
192                            DISPATCH_SIGNAL_NUMBER);
193       wait_for_all(&packet_ready_sig);
194
195       *buffer = packet_info.buffer;
196       *length = packet_info.length;
197       *offset = packet_info.offset;
198       *sequence = packet_info.sequence;
```

Lines 175 – 178:

> These lines pack the information that must go on the ring being read by the receive code. This information consists of the microengine number, the thread number within the microengines, and the transfer register number of the first transfer register that will eventually contain the packet information.

Lines 181 – 188:

> These lines take this data and put it on the scratch ring for the receive code to get later.

Lines 191 – 193:

> Here the code waits for the receive code to signal a previously agreed upon signal number.

Lines 195 – 198:

> After the signal is received, the code uses the information placed in the transfer registers by the receive code.

In the microengine assembly version of the sample code, the code used by the receive code to send packets to the processing code is shown here:

---

dispatch_assign_packet()

```
        File: Chapter07\dispatch.uc
174     #macro dispatch_assign_packet(IN_RING_NUM, in_buffer, \
175                                   in_length, in_offset, \
176                                   in_sequence)
177         .begin
178         .reg $free_thread ring_addr
179         .reg cap_addr me_num thread_num xfer_num
180         xbuf_alloc($packet_info,
181                 DISPATCH_PACKET_INFO_SIZE_LW, WRITE)
182         xbuf_alloc(packet_info_gp,
183                 DISPATCH_PACKET_INFO_SIZE_LW, READ_WRITE)
184         xbuf_alloc($free_thread,
185                 DISPATCH_FREE_THREAD_SIZE_LW, READ)
186         .sig ring_signal
187         .sig reflector_signal
188         .addr reflector_signal DISPATCH_SIGNAL_NUMBER
189         .sig remote packet_ready_sig
190
```

Continues

```
191        // Get a free thread from the pool
192        immed32(ring_addr, (IN_RING_NUM<<2))
193        scratch[get, $free_thread[0], ring_addr, 0,
194               DISPATCH_FREE_THREAD_SIZE_LW],
195                  ctx_swap[ring_signal]
196        xbuf_extract(me_num, $free_thread,
197                  DISPATCH_FREE_THREAD_ME_NUM)
198        xbuf_extract(thread_num, $free_thread,
199                  DISPATCH_FREE_THREAD_THREAD_NUM)
200        xbuf_extract(xfer_num, $free_thread,
201                  DISPATCH_FREE_THREAD_XFER_NUM)
202
203        // Now use the reflector to write the packet to
204        // the transfer registers of the thread
205        .reg offset
206        move(offset, in_offset)
207
208        // Convince the assembler we know what we're doing
209        // This preprocessor loop emits a .set for each
210        // register in the five_tuple xbuf
211        #define_eval LOOP (DISPATCH_PACKET_INFO_SIZE_LW-1)
212        #while (LOOP >= 0)
213        .set packet_info_gp[LOOP]
214        #define_eval LOOP (LOOP-1)
215        #endloop
216        #undef LOOP
217
218        // Put the packet info into a series of general
219        // purpose registers and then copy them into write
220        // transfer registers.
221        xbuf_insert(packet_info_gp, in_buffer,
222                  DISPATCH_PACKET_INFO_BUFFER)
223        xbuf_insert(packet_info_gp, in_length,
224                  DISPATCH_PACKET_INFO_LENGTH)
225        xbuf_insert(packet_info_gp, offset,
226                  DISPATCH_PACKET_INFO_OFFSET)
227        xbuf_insert(packet_info_gp, in_sequence,
228                  DISPATCH_PACKET_INFO_SEQUENCE)
229        xbuf_copy($packet_info, 0, 0, packet_info_gp, 0, 0,
230                  (DISPATCH_PACKET_INFO_SIZE_LW * 4), 0)
231
232        // Compute the CAP address for the transfer
233        // registers on the other microengine.
234        immed32(cap_addr,
235               (1<<CAP_ADDR_REFLECT_BIT_SHIFT_LEFT))
236        or_shf_left(cap_addr, cap_addr, me_num,
237                  CAP_ADDR_ME_NUMBER_SHIFT_LEFT)
```

Continues

```
238          or_shf_left(cap_addr, cap_addr, thread_num,
239                      CAP_ADDR_CONTEXT_SHIFT_LEFT)
240          or_shf_left(cap_addr, cap_addr, xfer_num,
241                      CAP_ADDR_XFER_SHIFT_LEFT)
242
243
244          // Use the cap instruction to write the other
245          // microengine's transfer registers via the
246          // reflector bus.
247          #define          CONSUMER_ME          1
248          cap[write, $packet_info[0], cap_addr, 0,
249              DISPATCH_PACKET_INFO_SIZE_LW],
250              sig_done[reflector_signal],
251              sig_remote[packet_ready_sig, CONSUMER_ME]
252          ctx_arb[reflector_signal]
253
254          xbuf_free($packet_info)
255          .end
256      #endm
```

This code is not nearly as scary as it looks. Here's some explanation:

Lines 193 – 195:

> The first thing this code does is to get the consuming thread's information from the scratch ring. This information consists of the consuming thread's microengine and thread numbers, as well as the transfer register index into which the producer should put the packet information.

Lines 208 – 230:

> The xbuf_insert macros in this part of the code insert the packet information into a series of general-purpose registers. These general-purpose registers are then copied into transfer registers. This code is written without knowledge of the structure of the packet information. A set of defined constants with names starting with DISPATCH_PACKET_INFO_ define how the various fields are packed into the final structure. Because some of these fields may not be 32-bit aligned, the code must build the complete structure in general purpose registers instead of directly in write transfer registers (write transfer registers are write only).

> The preprocessor loop starting at line 211 suppresses assembler warnings that result from the xbuf_insert macros reading from registers that have not been explicitly set. Because that is the desired behavior in this situation, we generate some .set directives to convince the assembler that we know what we are doing. The preprocessor loop lets us do this without knowing how large the data structure is, instead relying on defined constants to make the correct number of .set directives.

Lines 232 – 241:

> To use the reflector to write to a transfer register on a thread when neither is known at compile time, the `cap` instruction must be used in calculated addressing mode. In this mode, the address used to perform the `cap write` command tells the unit the thread and transfer register to which to write the packet data. These lines build up this address based on the thread and transfer register information received on the scratch ring.

Lines 244 – 252:

> This code performs the actual write on the reflector bus using the `cap` command. The consuming thread should be waiting for a signal at this point. The reflector write can signal both the consuming and producing thread when the write is complete, but only with the same signal number. To accomplish this, the `.addr` command ensures that a named signal is mapped to a specific signal number, set by a defined constant. The `dispatch_get_packet` macro does the same to map a named signal to the same signal number as is used here.

Performance

If you run the sample packet-processing code on all eight threads of one microengine, it performs somewhat better than the code from Chapter 6. If you look at the scratch ring used for packet dispatch between the receive code and the processing code, you will notice it spends most of its time being empty. The dispatch ring being empty is a good indication that the processing code is now slower than the receive code. Furthermore, if you add more microengines, you'll notice that the throughput actually decreases. What's going on here?

A couple of forces are at work here to make our sample code slower than it could be. For one, all of the packets going through the system are part of the same flow. So lock contention for the RED data structures and the end-to-end reordering code is very high. In the next chapter, you'll see a scheduler in between processing and transmit, which will allow us to send in multiple flows, reducing this lock contention. Another factor is the type of locks the sample application is using for the RED data structures and the end-to-end reordering data structures. The atomic test operation method of synchronization does not guarantee that threads are granted the lock in the order they request them. This causes a higher number of packets reaching the end-to-end ordering code out-of-order than would be seen otherwise. Because the reordering algorithm is somewhat more expensive when the packets are out of order, this property of the atomic test operations works against us. Perhaps the usage of the DTS method would help. We'll leave that as an exercise for you to do.

As you can see, the performance and characteristics of the synchronization methods chosen in a design greatly impact the system's performance. In some instances, the cost of synchronization drives designers to put packet-processing blocks on a single microengine, making some of the single microengine synchronization methods available. This, of course, must be balanced with the limited numbers of threads and CPU cycles available on a single microengine. Another way to address synchronization performance for some applications is to use ordered thread execution, which uses an extremely efficient cross-microengine synchronization method. This is described in more detail in Chapter 9.

Summary

Unordered thread execution is an ideal way to write multithreaded microengine software in many applications. The issues of packet ordering and synchronization must be carefully considered, however. Thankfully, the IXP2XXX hardware provides some services to help make packet ordering and synchronization efficient and not too difficult to program. The hardware facilities used to achieve packet ordering and synchronization depend very much on the application requirements and the design of the software.

Chapter 9 describes another way to write multithreaded microengine software, predictably called "ordered thread execution." This programming model makes packet ordering and synchronization much simpler, but some applications do not perform well when it is used. Chapter 9 also discusses some reasons why you would choose one method over the other.

Chapter 8

Context Pipeline Stages

In Chapter 7, we wrote code under the assumption that the code must be able to run on any number of microengines. This assumption is appropriate for most processing code, like that of Chapter 7, which exhibits high degrees of packet-level parallelism. However, what if one of the functions in your application does not exhibit this characteristic? For such functions, you might wonder whether it is better to remove the assumption that the code is executing on multiple microengines, and the answer is: quite possibly!

Consider what would happen if you could assume that your microblock was only going to run on one thread, or more realistically, one microengine. Synchronization across the threads would become trivial and fast through the use of absolute GPRs and local memory. In addition, other assumptions regarding microengine resource availability, for example use of the CAM, could be made. Writing code under this single-microengine assumption is called a context pipeline stage.

Of course, context pipeline stages have their own set of restrictions, such as limited numbers of threads and strict performance guarantees because no other microengine can share the workload. We explore both the benefits and consequences of context pipeline stages in this chapter through an example of packet scheduling. And, as a bonus, implementing a packet scheduler nicely completes our example code!

Deficit Round-Robin Scheduling

The packet-processing code in the previous two chapters classifies packets into flows and then performs congestion avoidance on those flows. While all of this processing exposes many features of the IXP2XXX hardware, from an application perspective, something is missing. In particular, how should the transmit code deal with the notion of multiple incoming flows? It seems a bit silly to expend the effort of identifying packet flows only to ignore this classification during the transmit operation. The solution to this deficiency is a new microengine task that schedules flows of packets for transmission using different priorities for each flow. When we put the previous code with this new scheduler, the resulting application resembles a quality-of-service (QoS) system which can identify and prioritize different flows of IP traffic.

This section is a brief overview of the deficit round-robin (DRR) algorithm implemented in this chapter. In no way do we attempt to cover packet scheduling in a comprehensive manner. Instead, just enough detail is presented to motivate the need for packet scheduling and explain the DRR algorithm implemented in this chapter. If you're a queuing theorist and are not looking for a good laugh, skip this section and go straight to the implementation details. Remember, we are trying to explain context pipeline stages!

Scheduling occurs nearly everywhere, not just in network devices. Scheduling is needed anytime a single resource is used by more than one user. The need for packet scheduling within network devices arises when multiple packets are ready to be sent on the same transmission link. In this domain, the scheduler is responsible for determining which packet, out of the currently available packets, should be transmitted next. Figure 8.1 shows where a packet scheduler is needed in our example software application. After the packet processing tasks have placed packets onto multiple queues for transmission, a scheduler decides which packet is transmitted next. This scheduling typically occurs for each outgoing port independently.

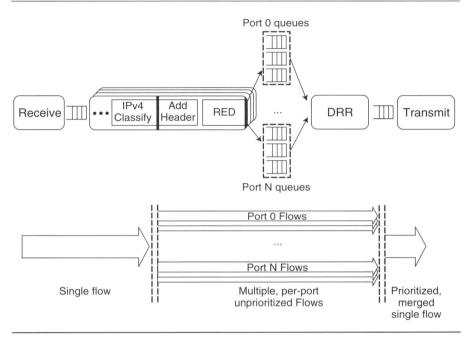

Figure 8.1 An Illustration of Where Packet Scheduling is Needed in a Packet-Processing Pipeline

Separating Scheduling and Queue Management

Strictly speaking, Figure 8.1 exposes the need for two functions in our application: a scheduler and a queue manager. The queue manager deals with enqueueing and dequeueing packets under the control of the scheduler. In this chapter, both of these functions are merged into the micro-engine executing DRR. However in the Intel IXA SDK 3.0 reference designs, these two functions are explicitly separated.

Explicit separation has several advantages like the ability to easily replace the scheduling algorithm without changing the queue manager. In addition, such separation can result in much faster code, especially for applications that require large numbers of queues because both the queue manager and scheduler can utilize their individual local memories as a cache for queue and scheduling state information respectively. Of course, the downside is more complexity, which is why we defer the discussions about a queue manager until Chapter 12.

Each queue of packets has a value associated with it called a "deficit". The DRR algorithm schedules the next packet from the next available non-empty queue that has built up enough deficit. The packet(s) at the head of each queue can be transmitted only when the deficit for that queue is greater than or equal to the length of the packet(s) (usually defined in bytes). A flowchart for DRR is shown in Figure 8.2, along with an example operation of DRR in Figure 8.3.

As shown in Figure 8.2, the DRR algorithm cycles through each queue in order. A *round* is one cycle through all of the queues. During

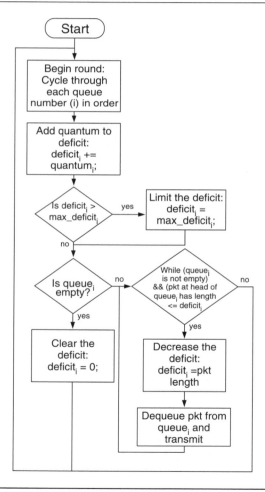

Figure 8.2 The Flowchart for the DRR Algorithm

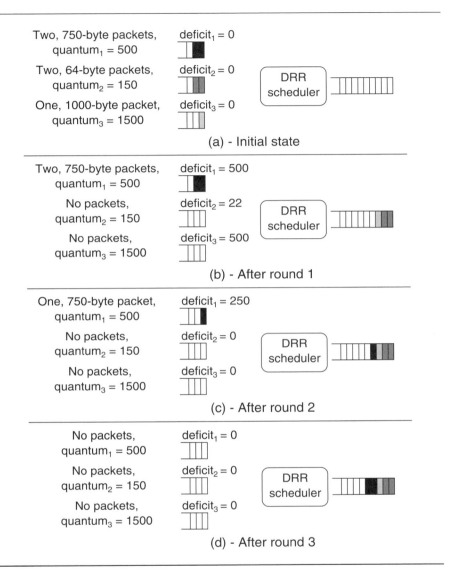

Figure 8.3 An Example of DRR Scheduling

each round, the first operation performed by the DRR scheduler is to add, up to a per-queue limit, a certain amount to the current queue's deficit. The amount of additional deficit a queue obtains in a given round is called the quantum for the queue. DRR can therefore create different priorities by providing different quanta for each queue.

Next, the current queue is checked to see whether it contains any packets. If the queue is empty, the deficit for the queue is cleared (i.e., set to zero). This action ensures that a queue does not build up any deficit while idle. You could imagine allowing the queue to build a deficit (up to the maximum deficit) even when the queue contained no packets. Indeed, you can imagine many variations on the DRR algorithm, some of which we discuss in the sidebar titled "DRR on the Intel IXA SDK 3.0." We have decided to clear all deficits to ensure that an idle queue cannot artificially build a large deficit.

If the queue is not empty, packets are dequeued from the head of the queue so long as the length of the packets are less than or equal to the deficit. For each dequeued packet, the deficit is decreased by the length of the packet. So, intuitively, the deficit indicates how many bytes a given queue can transmit in a given round.

For example, Figure 8.3(a) shows the initial state of the DRR scheduler dealing with three queues. The first queue has two packets, each 750 bytes long and a quantum of 500.[1] The second queue has two packets, each 64 bytes long and a quantum of 150. The third queue has one packet 1000 bytes long and a quantum of 1500. All of the queues have a large enough maximum deficit so that we simplify this explanation by ignoring that detail.

During the first round, the DRR scheduler begins by adding 500 to the first queue's deficit. Because the packet at the head of this queue is larger (in bytes) than the deficit, the packet is not transmitted.

The scheduler then adds 150 to the second queue's deficit. The first 64-byte packet is scheduled and the deficit is decreased by 64. Because the next packet on the second queue also fits within the deficit, this packet is transmitted as well, and the deficit is decreased. No packets remain on the queue so the algorithm progresses to the third queue.

Again, the quantum is added to the deficit of the third queue, the packet is transmitted, and the deficit is decreased. This cycle completes the first round of the DRR algorithm as shown in Figure 8.3(b).

In the second round, the first queue gets an additional 500 in deficit, and its first packet is transmitted. The second and third queues, because they have no packets, lose their deficits entirely. The resulting state of the system is shown in Figure 8.3(c).

Finally, after four rounds all packets have been transmitted and all deficits are reset to zero. The resulting packet output order is shown in

[1] The units of the quantum are omitted because it is unit-less. However, if you want to think of the quantum as being in units of bytes, go ahead, we won't tell.

Figure 8.3(d). Notice that while the second queue has the smallest quantum, its packets are transmitted first because its packets were much shorter in length. In general, larger quanta equate to higher priorities. Indeed, had both the second and third queue, for example, each had ten, 64-byte packets, the second queue would have been able to transmit two packets during each round whereas the third queue would have been able to transmit all of its packets during the first round.

DRR on the IXA SDK 3.0

Our implementation of the DRR algorithm differs from the algorithm implemented on the Intel IXA SDK 3.0. While both implementations are roughly equivalent, you should understand the differences to avoid any confusion. The main difference between our algorithm and that of the Intel IXA SDK 3.0 is that the latter allows negative deficits.

The IXA SDK 3.0 implementation of the DRR algorithm uses "negative" deficits. In this implementation, the code continues to transmit packets on a queue until the deficit goes negative. Negative deficits ensures that the code does not perform an "unnecessary" rounds (i.e., a round where packets are available but no queue has a large enough deficit).

For example, consider what can happen with our implementation. By clearing the deficit, we ensure that bursty traffic cannot dominate the bandwidth of the outgoing link. We also ensure that queues, which have no data, do not need any updates per-round (except for the first round, of course). However, this also means that our algorithm may instead go through multiple rounds before transmitting a packet, which would represent an unnecessary delay in the forwarding of a packet.

So why don't we use negative deficits? Mostly for simplicity, but also because we can avoid the problem of unnecessary rounds by ensuring that the smallest quantum in the system is at least as large as the maximum packet size.

Context Pipeline Stages

In Chapter 3, we posed three main questions to answer when implementing a function (microblock, driver, or other) on the IXP2XXX processor. These questions were: where is the function's state stored (i.e., the memory allocation)? On which microengine(s) should the function run (i.e., the processor allocation)? And, what hardware accelerators should the function utilize? All of these questions must be answered for our DRR algorithm before the code can be written.

In the previous chapter we explored the unordered thread execution model in which microblocks mapped their state into shared memory (e.g., scratchpad, SRAM, and DRAM) and ran on multiple microengines. This approach is good for microblocks that have variable amounts of packet processing time and a lot of packet-level parallelism. The performance penalty associated with accessing state in memory is offset by the large number of threads executing in the pool.

DRR, however, does not have these same characteristics. Each round of DRR needs to run sequentially. The algorithm does not allow for one queue to start the second round until all other queues have finished the first round, and, within each round, each queue is treated sequentially. As shown in Figure 8.1, the DRR algorithm can run independently for each port's set of queues, but since the number of ports is typically small, DRR does not benefit from running on a large number of microengines like in the unordered and ordered thread execution approaches.

Moreover, the amount of processing in DRR of any given queue is fairly uniform. The only reason one queue would take longer to process would be because it had more packets to transmit within its deficit. Even in this case, it is appropriate for DRR to spend more time processing such a queue as it likely indicates that this queue requires more 'attention' (i.e., has a higher deficit).

Finally, the amount of state associated with any queue is fairly small— the quantum, current, and maximum deficits—but is key to almost all of work done in any round of DRR. Thus, DRR would benefit from the fastest possible access to this state information.

So DRR is not a good match for an unordered thread execution model. Instead, DRR can reasonably be mapped onto a single microengine. With this assumption, the state information can be mapped into registers and local memory, wherever possible, to provide the smallest possible access latencies. Such an approach to microblock design, namely mapping a single microblock to a single microengine, is called a context pipeline stage in the Intel IXA SDK 3.0 framework.

Chapter 3 introduced the concept of context pipeline stages. Context pipeline stages have been described in many ways. One description has been microblocks that move the 'context' of the processing, as opposed to the function. A second description has been those pipeline stages that do not modify the packet itself, but instead work only with the 'context' of the packet. None of these definitions is categorically correct because exceptions to these descriptions exist. For example, a meter is usually considered a good fit for a context pipeline stage because it primarily works with the context (i.e., arrival rate) of the packet, but even meters modify the packet to mark, for example, the Diffserv codepoint for non-conforming packets.

Instead of such generalizations—which help to frame the problem but also spark a lot of debates!—the best way to define a context pipeline is through the fundamental property of such a stage. Namely, every context pipeline stage contains a single function written with the knowledge that it is running alone on a single microengine.

Notice the key difference between such a function and the microblocks written for the unordered thread execution model. The microblocks using the unordered thread execution model had to assume that other microblocks were running on the same microengine and were, possibly, modifying local memory, using the CAM, changing the T_INDEX register, etc. Even a microblock that is the only microblock in the unordered thread execution model still must make these same assumptions. A function written as a context pipeline stage on the other hand, is free to assume that it has exclusive access to all of the microengine's resources.

Context pipeline stages are therefore advantageous for functions that don't require the processing resources of multiple microengines and have some state that would benefit from being located in fast local memory or even registers.

Context pipeline stages also have drawbacks. First, rarely does the code associated with a context pipeline stage use more than just a fraction of the microengine's instruction store. Because no other functions run on the same microengine as a context pipeline stage, this entire unused code store represents a lost resource. Second, context pipeline stages don't enjoy the benefit of extra processing time that comes with additional microengines. As discussed in Chapter 3, a context pipeline stage must retire (i.e., process) packets as fast as they arrive.

Implementing a Context Pipeline Stage: DRR Scheduling

Let's implement DRR now that both the algorithm and our approach (i.e., a context pipeline stage) are known. We do this in an inside-out manner. First, the inner loop, which processes a single queue, is developed, and second, the outer loop, which cycles through all queues to complete a round, is developed.

The Inner Loop: Servicing a Single Queue

The first place to start is with a routine that can perform the inner-loop of the DRR algorithm. The following code takes in a queue and the DRR state information about that queue and dequeues the appropriate number of packets. The code mirrors the flowchart shown in Figure 8.2 closely.

_drr_run_queue()

File: Chapter08\drr_no_ffs.c

```
253  void _drr_run_queue(
254      drr_state_t *state,
255      unsigned int ring_num)
256  {
257      ring_data_t ring_data;
258
259      while(1)
260      {
261          // Peek a packet from the ring
262          _drr_ring_peek_buffer(ring_num);
263
264          // Is there enough deficit to transmit?
265          if (dlBufHandle.value != 0 &&
266              state->cur_deficit &&
267              state->cur_deficit >= dlMeta.bufferSize)
268          {
269              // Decrease the deficit
270              state->cur_deficit -= dlMeta.bufferSize;
271
272              // Dequeue the packet and transmit it
273              drr_ring_get_buffer(ring_num);
274
275              // Pass the packet to be transmitted
276              dlNextBlock = DRR_NEXT_BLOCK;
277              dl_sink();
278          }
279          else
280          {
281              break;
282          }
283      }
284  }
```

Line 254:

For each queue, the current deficit, maximum deficit, and quantum are maintained in a structure defined as `drr_state_t`, as shown in the following code:

```
typedef struct s_drr_state
{
    unsigned int cur_deficit; // The current deficit
    unsigned int quantum;     // The per-round quantum
    unsigned int max_deficit; // The maximum deficit
} drr_state_t;
```

Line 262:

First, the first packet on the ring is "peeked" (i.e., retrieved but not removed from the ring). The implementation of this peek routine is shown in the next section.

Lines 265 – 282:

If the current deficit is greater than or equal to the length of the packet (line 267), the deficit is decreased (line 270) and the packet is removed from the ring and placed on the ring for transmit (lines 273 and 277, respectively).

Implementing ring "peek"

In the inner loop code above, a new routine `_drr_ring_peek_buffer` was used to retrieve, but not remove, the first packet handle and meta-data from a given SRAM ring. No such peek operation natively exists on the SRAM rings in the IXP2XXX hardware. Instead, we built this routine by dequeuing the packet information from the SRAM ring and then caching it in local memory, as shown in the following code.

_drr_ring_peek_buffer()

```
     File: Chapter08\drr_no_ffs.c
133  void _drr_ring_peek_buffer(
134      unsigned int ring_num)
135  {
136      ring_data_t state;
137
138      // If the information in local memory
139      // is invalid, then dequeue from the
140      // SRAM ring and store the value in
141      // local memory
```

Continues

```
142        if (peek_state[ring_num].handle.value == 0)
143        {
144            dl_source();
145            state.handle = dlBufHandle;
146            state.length = dlMeta.bufferSize;
147            state.offset = dlMeta.offset;
148            state.sequence = dlSequenceNum;
149            peek_state[ring_num] = state;
150        }
151        // Otherwise, just retreive the
152        // information from local memory
153        else
154        {
155            state = peek_state[ring_num];
156            dlBufHandle        = state.handle;
157            dlMeta.bufferSize  = state.length;
158            dlMeta.offset      = state.offset;
159            dlSequenceNum      = state.sequence;
160        }
161    }
```

Lines 142 – 150:

The routine first checks the local memory cache for the given ring number. The local memory cache, defined as an array of ring elements, is stored in local memory. This array has 16 elements, which represents the total number of rings supported in the code. A larger version of the array could be moved into scratchpad or SRAM memory for applications requiring more rings. The definition for this cache is as follows:

```
static
__declspec(local_mem) ring_data_t peek_state[16] = {0};
```

If the cache has no data in it for the ring, the packet information is retrieved from the ring using the dl_source routine, placed in the local memory cache, and then returned to the caller.

Lines 153 – 160:

Otherwise, the data from the cache is returned to the caller of the routine and the SRAM ring is not accessed.

Although not shown, the _drr_ring_get_buffer routine must also understand the notion of this local-memory cache. When _drr_ring_ get_buffer is called, the local-memory cache must be checked, and if packet information exists in this cache, it must be removed from the cache and returned to the caller.

Finally, realize that this algorithm only works when the callers of the peek and get routines are on a single microengine. Yet another optimization made possible because the code is written as a context pipeline stage.

Refining the Inner Loop Using Next-Neighbor Registers

After the inner loop schedules a packet, it must provide this packet to the transmit driver. Following the code developed in previous chapters, this would involve putting the packet data on a scratchpad or SRAM ring. These in-memory rings were previously chosen because multiple microengines needed to give packets to the transmit driver.

Now, however, DRR is the only microengine giving data to the transmit driver, which is also on only one microengine, and so an optimization can be made because both the DRR scheduler and transmit driver are context pipeline stages. Specifically, the in-memory ring can be replaced with a faster next-neighbor ring.

Chapter 2 showed that every microengine contains a set of next-neighbor registers that can be accessed like a ring with put and get operations. A microengine can read from its own set of next-neighbor registers and can write to those of the numerically-next microengine.[2]

Of course, next-neighbor registers only work between two sequential (i.e., directly-connected) microengines. This situation is exactly what we have with DRR and the transmit driver: two context pipeline stages which can be placed on sequential microengines.

So let's replace the scratchpad ring between DRR and the transmit driver with a faster ring built using next-neighbor registers. First, to initialize a next-neighbor ring the consuming microengine must write the NN_Put and NN_Get microengine CSRs, as shown in the following code.

nn_ring_init()

```
        File: Chapter08\nn_rings.c
39      void nn_ring_init()
40      {
41          local_csr_write(local_csr_nn_put, 0);
42          local_csr_write(local_csr_nn_get, 0);
43      }
```

---

[2] Actually, a microengine can also be configured in a 'loopback' mode in which it writes to its own next-neighbor registers. This usage model is not covered in this book. For more details, refer to the *Programmer's Reference Manual* (Intel 2002).

When the consuming microengine gets an element from the next-neighbor ring, the NN_Get CSR is used as an index into the next-neighbor registers, as shown in the following code.

nn_ring_get_buffer()

```
      File: Chapter08\nn_rings.h
70    void nn_ring_get_buffer(ring_data_t      *data)
71    {
72        if (nn_ring_empty())
73        {
74            data->handle.value = 0;
75            return;
76        }
77
78        data->handle.value = nn_ring_dequeue_incr();
79        data->length       = nn_ring_dequeue_incr();
80        data->offset       = nn_ring_dequeue_incr();
81        data->sequence     = nn_ring_dequeue_incr();
82    }
```

Lines 72 – 76:

Before removing elements from the ring, the ring is checked to make sure it is not empty. The hardware provides a state signal to the microengine when the next-neighbor ring is empty. In this example, the routine nn_ring_empty simply tests this state signal and returns an indication of whether the ring is empty.

Lines 78 – 81:

In these lines of code, the consuming microengine gets elements from the next-neighbor ring using the nn_ring_dequeue_incr() instrinsic. This intrinsic returns the value of the next-neighbor register indexed by the NN_Get CSR and atomically increments the NN_Get CSR afterwards.

Similar to getting elements from a next-neighbor ring, when the producing microengine puts an element on the next-neighbor ring, the NN_Put register (of the consuming, or neighboring, microengine!) is used as an index into the next-neighbor registers, as illustrated in the following code segment.

nn_ring_put_buffer()

File: Chapter08\nn_rings.c

```
119    void nn_ring_put_buffer(ring_data_t       data)
120    {
121        while (nn_ring_full())
122        {
123            ctx_swap();
124        }
125
126        nn_ring_enqueue_incr(data.handle.value);
127        nn_ring_enqueue_incr(data.length);
128        nn_ring_enqueue_incr(data.offset);
129        nn_ring_enqueue_incr(data.sequence);
130    }
```

Lines 121 – 130:

Analogous to the next-neighbor get routine, the code first ensures the ring is not full (based on another state signal).

Lines 126 – 129:

Once the code has determined the ring is not full, the data is placed on the ring using the `nn_ring_enqueue_incr()` instrinsic. This intrinsic returns the value of the next-neighbor register indexed by the NN_Put CSR and atomically increments the NN_Put CSR afterwards.

Simple, right? And fast as well.

> **Note**   The next-neighbor ring code contains no locks and yet is still thread-safe! The 'put' and 'get' routines can only be accessed by one microengine each; these are next-neighbor registers after all. And because the code that accesses the rings (i.e., the instrinsics) does not release control of the microengine, the non-preemptive nature of the microengine thread arbiter ensures one thread places data on the ring atomically.

The Outer Loop: DRR Rounds

Implementing a round in DRR involves two key tasks: first, retrieving the next queue to service, and second, retrieving the DRR state for this next queue.

Selecting the next queue in a naïve manner is easy. Simply maintain a queue number and increment it. This approach is not great when many of the queues are empty, but we start with this approach anyway and discuss ways to refine it in a subsequent section.

Retrieving the DRR state for the next queue depends on how many queues and ports need to be supported. If many queues or many ports need to be supported, this state information may need to be stored in scratchpad or SRAM memory. In this chapter only 16 queues for a single port are supported, so these data structures can be placed in local memory. This design choice highlights one advantage of context pipelines, namely the ability to make assumptions about access to microengine resources.

The following code illustrates how to implement the outer loop of DRR.

drr()

```
            File: Chapter08\drr_no_ffs.c
308    void drr()
309    {
310        unsigned int next_ring;
311        ring_data_t      ring_data;
312        drr_state_t cur_state;
313
314        // This code should be single-threaded per port.
315        // Since we only deal with one port, this is simply
316        // single threaded code
317        next_ring = 0;
318        while(1)
319        {
320            // Is the ring empty?
321            dlMeta.flowId = next_ring;
322            if (dl_get_source_size() == 0)
323            {
324                // Yes, the clear the deficit
325                drr_state[next_ring].cur_deficit = 0;
326            }
327            else
328            {
329                // Otherwise, add the quantum to the
330                // current deficit
331                cur_state = drr_state[next_ring];
332                cur_state.cur_deficit +=
```

Continues

```
333                    cur_state.quantum;
334                if (cur_state.cur_deficit >
335                    cur_state.max_deficit)
336                {
337                    cur_state.cur_deficit =
338                        cur_state.max_deficit;
339                }
340
341                // Run the DRR inner loop
342                _drr_run_queue(&cur_state,
343                                next_ring);
344
345                // Update the state
346                drr_state[next_ring] = cur_state;
347            }
348
349            // Select the next ring
350            if (++next_ring == 16)
351            {
352                next_ring = 0;
353            }
354        }
355    }
```

Lines 321 – 326:

First, the next ring in the round is checked for empty. In this code, the `dl_source` and `dl_get_source_size` routines use the `flowId` field in the dispatch loop metadata to identify the queue number. If the ring is empty, the deficit for the ring is zeroed and the next ring is selected.

Lines 331 – 339:

If the ring does have data, the quantum is added to the current deficit for the current ring, while adhering to a limit on the deficit.

Lines 342 – 346:

Finally, after the DRR state has been updated, the DRR inner loop is executed on the ring, and the state is written back into local memory.

Refining the Outer Loop

As you can imagine, a design which mercilessly checks queues or rings for data is detrimental to the entire system's performance. Since DRR is checking for data from many rings (sixteen in our code, but possibly thousands in a commercial application), we want to avoid polling each queue to find out whether it has data. If the code could detect which rings have data, many accesses of DRR state and ring peeks could be avoided.

To solve this problem, one or more bit-vectors indicating which rings currently have packets can be maintained. These extra bit-vectors have a bit for each ring, possibly arranged in a hierarchy as shown in Figure 8.4. In this figure, the top-most bit vector indicates which ports have data available. A port has data available whenever any queue associated with that port has data (i.e., the logical OR of the per-port bit vector). You can certainly create more levels in the hierarchy if necessary to support the number of queues in your application.

But how do such bit vectors eliminate the polling-of-queues problem? Well, instead of polling queues, you can simply read the appropriate bit vector(s) and search for bits that are set in these bit vectors. But isn't such a search operation expensive, you ask? Actually no, not on the IXP2XXX processor at least, because of the existence of the find-first set instruction on the microengines. The find-first set instruction searches one or more registers for the location of the first bit that is set (i.e., of value 1). The result is the location (bit position) of that first set bit. Using such a solution, the outer loop code could very efficiently search a bit vector of queues with data to determine the current state of all queues being serviced by DRR.

The only tricky issue when using bit vectors in this manner is where to store the bit vector itself. You might be tempted to use the atomic bit operations in either scratchpad or SRAM memory, but then you are really not avoiding the original problem which was multiple memory accesses! It is much better to store these bit vectors in either registers or local memory on the scheduler's microengine.

The leaf (bottom-most) bit vectors represent data availability of an individual queue. A bit set means the corresponding queue has data available. All non-leaf bit vectors represent the logical OR of another, lower-level, bit vector. For example, the port-ready bit vector's first bit would be set whenever any bit in the "Queues in Port 0 bit vector" is set.

Figure 8.4 An Example of Hierarchical Bit Vectors Used to Indicate Queue Readiness

However, storing these bit vectors on the scheduler's microengine also presents a problem: how can the processing code access these bit vectors to update them when new data is placed on a queue? Using bit vectors to eliminate the polling of queues means that the code, which puts packets into a ring, needs to set the appropriate bit(s) in these bit vectors. Similarly, the code that gets packets needs to be modified to clear the bit vector when the queue is empty.

One solution might be to use the reflector bus to have the code which performs the enqueue update transfer registers in the scheduler's microengine with some message indicating which queue was modified. Then, the scheduler could read this message and update its local copy of the bit vectors. While this solution works and is an improvement over using the atomic bit operations in scratchpad or SRAM, it still suffers one major drawback: you still must coordinate access to the transfer registers on the scheduler's microengine.

A better solution can be found in the Intel IXA SDK 3.0 reference designs. In the Intel IXA SDK 3.0 reference designs, the queue manager (see Chapter 12) receives enqueue requests from the processing tasks via a single scratch ring. The queue manager then can process these requests and send the scheduler messages on how to update its bit vectors via a next-neighbor ring (or via the reflect bus because only one function would be writing into the schedulers transfer registers). We cover the design of a queue manager in Chapter 12, and, of course, you can find all of the details in the Intel IXA SDK 3.0 code itself.

Enhancing RED Using Timestamps

Now that our application for classifying, managing, and scheduling packets is complete, we need to tie up one loose end: namely, the empty ring condition in RED. Recall from Chapter 6 that when the RED algorithm puts a packet on an empty ring, the average depth of the ring is computed based on previous average depth and how long the ring has been empty. Intuitively, the longer the ring has been empty, the smaller the new average depth.

Thus, some notion of time must get embedded into the ring whenever the scheduler empties (i.e., removes all of the packets from) a ring. On the IXP2XXX processor, obtaining such a timestamp is done by reading one or two microengine CSRs. Together the TIMESTAMP_LOW and TIMESTAMP_HIGH microengine CSRs represent a 64-bit timestamp that increment every 16 clock cycles. The following code segment reads the

TIMESTAMP_LOW CSR and saves it in a per-ring data structure maintained in scratchpad memory. This timestamp can subsequently be retrieved by the RED algorithm.

```
// If the ring is now empty, update the timestamp
if (!g_rings[ring_number].num_packets)
{
    g_rings[ring_number].last_empty_timestamp =
        local_csr_read(local_csr_timestamp_low);
}
```

Note You are probably wondering how you can read both the TIMESTAMP_LOW and TIMESTAMP_HIGH CSRs atomically. Well, you don't have to actually. Once you read the TIMESTAMP_LOW CSR, the IXP2XXX hardware latches the value of the TIMESTAMP_HIGH CSR. When (or if) you subsequently read the TIMESTAMP_HIGH CSR, the latched value is returned. Thus, you can easily get a valid 64-bit timestamp from the IXP2XXX hardware. Just be sure the read the TIMESTAMP_LOW CSR before the TIMESTAMP_HIGH CSR.

Having the timestamp available in microengine CSRs provides fast access to the timestamp, but it does present a problem. Namely, how can the timestamp from one microengine be correlated to the timestamp from another microengine? Luckily, all timestamps can be reset to a specific value and simultaneously started by writing the MISC_CONTROL CSR and the CAP. Moreover, all timestamp CSRs are set to a value of zero during a chip reset and so they are naturally "synchronized."

Thus, the microengine timestamp CSRs represent a fast mechanism to compute relative time differences in microengine applications. In Chapter 12, we show how timers can be built which signal microengine threads after a given amount of time has expired. Together, timers, which are also microengine-local and thus fast to access and use, and timestamps, represent an extremely efficient way to build temporal-dependent applications.

Summary

A context pipeline stage is a function written with the knowledge that it executes alone on a single microengine. Many optimizations are possible when using context pipeline stages because the full resources of the microengine (e.g., registers and local memory) can be assumed to belong to the context pipeline stage.

One such resource is the next-neighbor registers. These registers, which connect pairs of microengines together, are accessed like a small, high-speed ring between the two neighboring microengines. When one context pipeline stage needs to pass packets or other data to a second context pipeline stage, next-neighbor registers can be used. In this chapter, DRR uses next-neighbor registers to pass packet information to the transmit driver.

The find-first-set instruction searches one or more registers for the location the first 'set' bit (i.e., the first 1). The result of the instruction is the index of this first set bit. The find-first-set instruction is useful for maintaining bit vectors of status information.

Each microengine contains a 64-bit counter which increments at $1/16^{th}$ the frequency of the processor. In effect, this counter represents a relative-timestamp for the microengine programmer. The timestamps on all microengines can be synchronized.

When scaling a scheduler to deal with more queues than are supported by the SRAM controllers, a fundamentally different design is necessary. In Chapter 12, we cover the basic design of a queue manager which interfaces to a scheduler and provides a scalable solution to dealing with any number of queues. The Intel IXA SDK 3.0 contains a working implementation of such a queue manager.

Chapter 9

Ordered Thread Execution

In Chapter 7, you learned about one model for processing packets on multiple threads and multiple microengines called "unordered thread execution." This chapter describes another programming model for processing packets on multiple threads. This model is creatively called "ordered thread execution." In this chapter, you will take the packet-processing sample code from Chapter 7 and modify it to use the ordered thread execution method.

Ordered thread execution has some advantages over unordered thread execution for some applications. However, for other applications, ordered thread execution is a poor choice or even completely unworkable. This chapter concludes with a discussion of when each method is most appropriate.

Simple Ordered Thread Execution

Ordered thread execution can take many forms. In this section, we'll start with a description of the simplest form. Later, you'll see more advanced forms.

For the purpose of this simple form of ordered thread execution, "ordered" means that certain critical drivers and microblocks run on multiple threads one at a time in thread numerical order. Is that confusing enough? It's actually not as difficult as it sounds. Figure 9.1 shows an

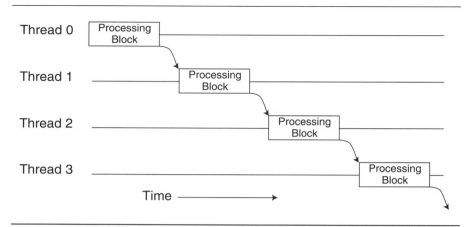

Figure 9.1 Simple Ordered Thread Execution Example

illustration of a single packet processing microblock running in order on four threads using the simplest form of ordered thread execution.

Figure 9.1 shows four threads running code that includes an ordered packet-processing microblock. Thread 1 does not run this microblock until thread 0 has left the microblock, and so on. Thread 0 does not run this microblock until the last thread has left the microblock, completing a loop through all of threads running the microblock, even if those threads span multiple microengines.

In this form of ordered thread execution and in more advanced forms, the ordering is implemented in a very efficient manner using a hardware feature of the IXP2XXX processor called inter-thread signaling. Inter-thread signaling allows a thread to assert any signal on any other thread on the chip. The signals used for inter-thread signaling are the same as those used for accessing memory, hash, and other hardware units. Using inter-thread signals, the threads running a particular ordered microblock agree on a signal number to use for that microblock, wait for the signal to assert before entering the microblock, and signal the next thread after leaving the microblock. This enforces the ordered execution as shown in Figure 9.1.

Because the IXP2XXX processor has 15 usable signal numbers, a group of threads can have more than just one ordered microblock. When threads have multiple ordered blocks, different signal numbers are used for each microblock. Figure 9.2 shows four threads running three different ordered blocks.

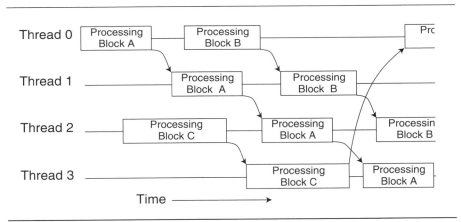

Figure 9.2 Example Showing Three Ordered Blocks on Four Threads

Ordered thread execution helps microblocks achieve characteristics that are more difficult in unordered thread execution. The obvious characteristic is that ordered microblocks need no synchronization other than the inter-thread signals because only one thread will ever be running the same microblock at a given time. Packet ordering is also achieved using ordered thread execution.

In the sample code for this chapter, we use this simple form of ordered thread execution to provide packet ordering for enqueuing and dequeuing packets in the processing block. Remember from Chapter 7 that imposing packet ordering for these blocks allows us to meet the end-to-end ordering requirement. And of course, imposing packet ordering for other blocks allows us to meet any partial order requirements of those blocks.

To use ordered thread execution, the code has to be able to signal the next thread in a rotation of threads. The IXP2XXX hardware provides four different control status registers (CSRs) for performing inter-thread signaling, three of which are useful for ordered thread execution. The CSRs are SAME_ME_SIGNAL, NEXT_NEIGHBOR_SIGNAL, and INTERTHREAD_SIG. A thread can write to the SAME_ME_SIGNAL to assert a signal on another thread in the same microengine, NEXT_NEIGHBOR_SIGNAL to assert a signal on a thread in the next higher numbered microengine, and INTERTHREAD_SIG to assert a signal on any thread on the chip. A fourth register, PREV_NEIGHBOR_SIGNAL, can be used to assert a signal in the next lower numbered microengine, which is not useful to ordered thread execution. The SAME_ME_SIGNAL, NEXT_NEIGHBOR_SIGNAL, and

PREV_NEIGHBOR_SIGNAL CSRs are microengine local CSRs, so accessing them is much more efficient than accessing the INTERTHREAD_SIG CSR, which is a CSR in the SHaC unit.

The following microengine C code implements a function that signals the next thread in an ordered thread execution group. This function is used by the dl_source and dl_sink macros on the processing microengines to help provide packet ordering.

exit_block()

File: Chapter09\ordered_signal.h

```
78   static __forceinline void exit_block(SIGNAL* sig)
79   {
80       // There are three different ways to perform an
81       // inter-thread signal.  If the current context is
82       // the last context on the last microengine, the CAP
83       // must be written to signal the first thread.  If
84       // the current context is the last context on any
85       // other microengine, the signal_next_ME() intrinsic
86       // can be used.  If the current context is one that
87       // does not fall into either of these categories,
88       // the signal_same_ME_next_ctx() intrinsic can be
89       // used.
90       if (ctx() != 0x7)
91       {
92           // Signal the next thread on the same
93           // microengine
94           signal_same_ME_next_ctx(
95                           __signal_number(sig));
96       }
97       else
98       {
99           if (__ME() != LAST_ORDERED_ME)
100          {
101              // Signal the next microengine's first thread
102              signal_next_ME(__signal_number(sig), 0);
103          }
104          else
105          {
106              // Use the CAP
107              __declspec(sram_write_reg) INTERTHREAD_SIG_t
108                                         signal_info;
109              INTERTHREAD_SIG_t signal_info_gp;
```

Continues

```
110                    SIGNAL cap_signal;
111                    signal_info_gp.RES = 0;
112                    signal_info_gp.ME_NO = FIRST_ORDERED_ME;
113                    signal_info_gp.THD_NO = 0;
114                    signal_info_gp.SIG = __signal_number(sig);
115                    signal_info = signal_info_gp;
116                    cap_csr_write(&signal_info,
117                                  csr_interthread_sig, ctx_swap,
118                                  &cap_signal);
119                }
120            }
121        }
```

Lines 90 – 96:

> If the current thread is not the last on any microengine, it uses the
> `signal_same_ME_next_ctx` intrinsic to signal the next thread on the same
> microengine. This intrinsic writes to the SAME_ME_SIGNAL CSR.

Lines 99 – 103:

> This code checks to see whether the current thread is the last thread
> in the group of threads participating in the signaling loop. The LAST_
> ORDERED_ME and FIRST_ORDERED_ME symbols are defined at compile time
> to be the numbers of the last microengine and the first microengine in the
> signaling loop, respectively. If the current thread is not the last in the
> group, the `signal_next_ME` microengine C intrinsic is used to signal the
> first thread on the next microengine. This intrinsic writes to the NEXT_
> NEIGHBOR_SIGNAL CSR.

Lines 104 – 120:

> If the current thread is the last of all threads on all microengines, this code
> uses the INTERTHREAD_SIG CSR to signal the first thread on the first
> microengine.

Waiting for a signal from the previous thread in ordered thread execution is no different than waiting for any other signal. In microengine
assembly, use the `ctx_arb[]` instruction; while in microengine C, use
the `wait_for_all()` instrinsic. In the microengine C sample code we
provided a function, called `enter_block()`, which waits for the signal.
In microengine assembly, the sample code has a macro with the same
name.

With the ability to signal and wait for signals, changing our code from
unordered thread execution to the simpler form of ordered thread

execution is simple. For example, to enter the critical section in the dl_ source driver the following function call does the trick:

```
// This needs to use signals to keep this in order
enter_block(&dl_source_sig);
```

To exit the critical section, this code is used:

```
// Signal the next thread to run this
exit_block(&dl_source_sig);
```

These same macros with different signals can also be used by the RED microblock to provide synchronized access to the RED data structures. When doing so, the granularity of the synchronization is very coarse. Because only one signal can be used by RED, the code can only process one packet at a time, even if the packets are from completely unrelated flows. Later in this chapter, we resolve this issue using a more advanced form of ordered thread execution.

Dispatch Loops in Ordered Thread Execution

Using ordered thread execution changes how we organize microblocks into dispatch loops. Some of the packets that go through the processing microengines in the sample application are dropped before they reach the RED code or the enqueue code in the dl_sink driver. The sample code we have built to this point doesn't handle this well at all. Figure 9.3 illustrates why.

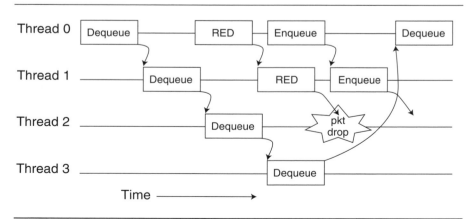

Figure 9.3 Example of a Packet Being Dropped in Ordered Thread Execution

In Figure 9.3, the packet processing code drops the packet being processed by thread 2. Packets can be dropped for any number of reasons, such as the packet's five-tuple not being present in the classifier's lookup table. When the packet is dropped, the code skips the RED and enqueue code and instead waits to dequeue another packet to process. However, when thread 1 finishes the RED and enqueue blocks, it signals thread 2. Because thread 2 does not enter those blocks, it does not wait for those signals, nor does it produce these signals for thread 3. After dequeuing a packet to process, thread 3 waits forever for the signal from the RED microblock, locking up the system.

To fix this issue, the code needs to be written so that when an ordered microblock is skipped, the thread still participates in the signaling loop. Figure 9.4 shows a corrected version of the example shown in Figure 9.3.

In Figure 9.4, the two small boxes after the dequeue block on thread 2 indicate code that waits for a signal and passes the signal on to the next thread when a microblock is skipped. Participating in the signaling even when a packet is dropped keeps the signal moving through the thread rotation. As the diagram shows, when a thread drops a packet, it still must wait for signals from the other ordered blocks that would have otherwise been run. Although waiting for the signal does not use any compute resources, it does put this thread in a state where it is not doing useful work.

The Intel IXA SDK 3.0 provides a different dispatch loop structure for ordered thread execution than the dispatch loop structure you've seen

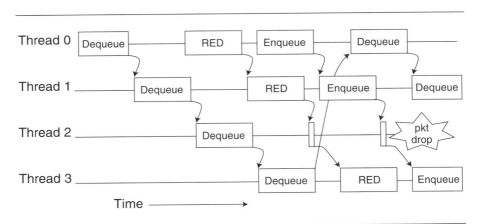

Figure 9.4 Corrected Example of Dropping a Packet in Ordered Thread Execution

in previous chapters. Instead of testing the next-block value in the dispatch loop after every microblock, the microblocks themselves test the next-block value. Testing the next-block value in the microblocks allows them to do whatever actions are necessary to keep the signal rotation going. The dispatch loop then calls all of the microblocks in order, without attempting to decide whether a particular microblock actually needs to be run. For example, the following microengine assembly code implements the ordered thread execution dispatch loop for our example code:

main()

```
         File: Chapter09\dispatch_loop\process_dl.uc
57          .while(1)
58              // Work around a weirdness in SDK code
59              immed[dl_exception_reg, 0]
60
61              // Dequeue a packet from the source
62              dl_source()
63
64              // Verify that this packet is an acceptable
65              // Ethernet packet and that it is locally
66              // addressed.
67              ethernet_validate()
68
69              // At this point we know we have an Ethernet II
70              // packet. Before we send it to the IPv4
71              // classifier, we have to make sure that it is an
72              // IP packet.  Then, since the classifier is L2
73              // agnostic, we  have to move the packet data
74              // pointer past the Ethernet header.
75              ethernet_strip_header()
76
77              // Now that we have a packet, send it the
78              // IPv4 5-tuple classifier.  The classifier
79              // will assign a flow ID that will be used
80              // by RED, and a next hop ID that will be
81              // used by ethernet_add_header.
82              ipv4_five_tuple_class()
83
84              // Before we transmit the packet, we have to
85              // add the Ethernet header back on.  We do this
86              // based on the next hop ID retrieved
87              // from the classifier.
```

Continues

```
88              ethernet_add_header(0x0800)
89
90              // Now that the flow ID is assigned, send
91              // it to the RED buffer manager to either
92              // enqueue or drop
93              red();
94
95              // Enqueue the packet
96              dl_sink()
97          .endw
```

Notice that this code does not test the dl_next_block register at any point. Instead, the microblocks themselves test this value. For example, the dl_sink macro for the processing microengines has code like this:

dl_sink()

File: Chapter09\dispatch_loop\dl_source.uc

```
245     // This needs to use signals to keep this in order
246     enter_block(dl_sink_sig)
247
248     //  In the case of an exception packet, it needs to
249     //  be sent to the core (Xscale)
250     //  through a different ring.
251     //  For now just drop the packet.
252     br=byte[dl_next_block, 0, IX_EXCEPTION, drop_packet#]
253     br=byte[dl_next_block, 0, IX_DROP, drop_packet#]
254
255     .reg ring_to_tx_num
256     dl_meta_get_flow_id(ring_to_tx_num)
257     dl_meta_get_buffer_size(buf_length)
258     dl_meta_get_offset(offset)
259     sram_ring_put_buffer(
260                 ring_to_tx_num,
261                 dl_buf_handle,
262                 buf_length,
263                 offset,
264                 0)
265
266     exit_block(dl_sink_sig)
267
268     br[done#]
269
```

Continues

```
270    drop_packet#:
271        exit_block(dl_sink_sig)
272
273        dl_buf_drop(dl_buf_handle)
274
275        br[done#]
```

Line 246:

> Regardless of the contents of the dl_next_block register, the code needs
> to participate in the signaling rotation. So this line calls the enter_block
> macro, which waits for the specified signal.

Line 253:

> Here the code checks the value of the dl_next_block register. If it indi-
> cates the packet should be dropped, the code jumps to the drop_packet#
> target. Otherwise it continues. Because the example code does not send
> packets to the core, packets with a next block ID of IX_EXCEPTION are
> dropped as well.

Lines 255 – 264:

> If the packet does not need to be dropped, these lines of code put the
> packet on the proper SRAM ring.

Line 266:

> After the packet has been placed on the ring, the exit_block macro sig-
> nals the next thread to let it know it can enter the critical section.

Lines 270 – 275:

> If the packet needs to be dropped, this code runs the same exit_block
> macro that would have been run if the packet did not need to be dropped.
> Then, the code drops the packet. The dl_buf_drop macro does not need
> to be between the enter_block and enter_block calls because it has no
> synchronization or packet ordering requirements. So instead of making
> the next thread wait for the packet to be dropped, the thread sends the
> signal before dropping the packet.

Regardless of whether or not an ordered microblock is logically
skipped, the code waits for the signal and signals the next thread. It is
tempting to write the code such that it doesn't wait for the signal or
delays waiting for the signal because it doesn't need to wait for the signal to fulfill any synchronization or ordering requirements. Doing so
would be a mistake, as failing to wait for the signal before signaling the
next thread can cause a thread to be signaled with the same signal

twice. Because microengines do not queue signals, the results are lost signals and locked up processing code.

Complicated Applications using Ordered Thread Execution

The dispatch loop of our sample application is very easy to implement using ordered thread execution. Some dispatch loops are not so easy, however. Consider the series of blocks shown in Figure 9.5.

If the application graph has two parallel branches like the on in Figure 9.5, and the parallel microblocks (C and D in the figure) are not ordered microblocks, the implementation is no more complicated than what has already been described. If one or more of the parallel microblocks is ordered, however, the implementation is more complicated.

An application with ordered parallel microblocks can be implemented in one of two ways. The first way to implement ordered thread execution with ordered parallel microblocks is to wait for, and signal, the signal for all microblocks that are not executed while processing a particular packet. In essence, the ordered parallel microblocks are 'flattened' so one microblock (e.g., microblock C) executes before the other microblock (e.g., microblock D). So, if the code determines that an ordered microblock is to be skipped, it runs the same signal passing code for that microblock that would have been run if the packet had been dropped. See Figure 9.6 for an example.

Figure 9.6 is an example based on the graph shown in Figure 9.5. In this example, blocks C, D, and E are the only ordered blocks in the graph. Threads 0, 1, and 3 are processing packets that go through blocks C and E, while thread 2 is processing a packet that goes through blocks D and E. Notice that although threads 0, 1, and 3 do not execute microblock D, they still participate in the signaling rotation using the

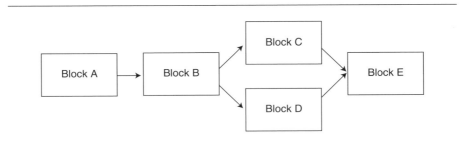

Figure 9.5 Ordered Thread Execution Example with a Branch

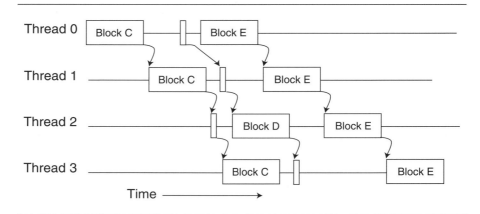

Figure 9.6 Ordered Thread Execution with a Branch Example Showing Signaling

same code that is used when packets are dropped. Similarly, thread 2 does not execute microblock C, but it still must participate in the signaling rotation for this microblock.

Another way to implement ordered thread execution for ordered parallel blocks is to get both blocks to agree on the same signal number. Using this approach, the processing flow of our example from Figure 9.6 looks like Figure 9.7, with blocks C and D agreeing on, and using, the same signal.

This second method will likely increase performance because no time is spent in 'unused' blocks, but may reduce the reusability of the

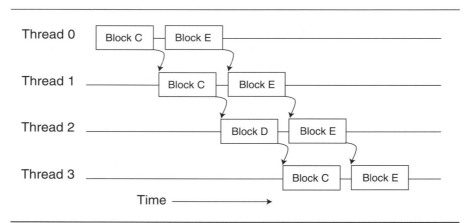

Figure 9.7 Ordered Thread Execution with a Branch Example Showing Shared Signaling

microblocks if the microblocks are written assuming they are being used with other microblocks on a parallel branch.

Some types of microblock graphs defy all attempts to implement them in ordered thread execution. For example, a graph with a loop that includes an ordered microblock, like the one in Figure 9.8, cannot be implemented in ordered thread execution. These graphs must either be split up into multiple separate graphs without loops running on separate microengines, or implemented using unordered thread execution.

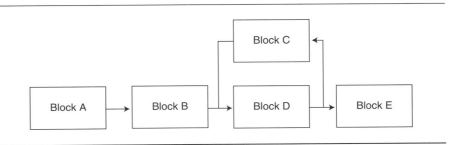

Figure 9.8 Microblock Graph with a Loop

Using Local Memory as a Cache

In Chapter 7, the sample code used local memory to store some commonly-used small read-only data structures. Local memory is also used in some designs as a cache for larger read-write data structures that don't completely fit into a microengine's local memory. This technique is called "folding" and can only be done inside a block using ordered thread execution. The CAM unit that comes with each microengine is helpful for implementing this cache. In this section you'll learn how to build a cache for large data structures using local memory and the CAM unit. You'll also see how this caching ability can be used to speed up the RED code in the sample application.

In case you forgot from Chapter 2, microengines perform CAM lookups by giving the CAM unit a 32-bit quantity. The CAM compares this 32-bit quantity to all of its 16 entries in a very short amount of time. If the lookup value matches a CAM entry, the CAM returns information about that entry to the microengine. If the lookup value does not match a CAM entry, the CAM returns the information about the least recently used (LRU) entry to the microengine. The LRU entry is the entry that has been added or found as a result of a lookup least recently. Conveniently, LRU is often used as a cache replacement algorithm in other caching systems.

To show how you can use this functionality to implement a cache, the sample RED code has been modified to use local memory and the CAM to cache queue entries. First, the RED code reserves a 16-element array of queue_info data structures in local memory. The queue_info data type is the same used for the larger SRAM queue information table, indexed by ring number. Here is the microengine C version of the code that reserves the local memory space:

```
static __declspec(shared local_mem)
                    queue_info g_queue_data_cache[16];
```

This code reserves space for all of the cached entries. The size of this array is 16—the number of entries the CAM can hold. Now, when the code needs to look up the queue information as part of the RED algorithm, it first looks up the queue entry's SRAM address in the CAM with this code:

```
lookup_info = cam_lookup((unsigned int)mem);
```

The CAM lookup returns two pieces of information useful for caching: a bit indicating whether or not the lookup value is in the CAM and a CAM entry number. If the bit indicates the lookup value is not in the CAM (a miss), the CAM entry number is the LRU CAM entry. If the bit indicates the lookup value is in the CAM (a hit), the CAM entry number is the number of the entry that matched the lookup value. The entry number can then be used as the local memory array index. Therefore, the RED code reads the queue information from local memory using this code:

```
queue = g_queue_data_cache[cam_entry];
```

If the CAM lookup resulted in a miss, the queue information is read from SRAM. To put the information in the cache, the LRU CAM entry number is used to write the data into the local memory array. Then, the CAM is written so that it generates a hit the next time this code looks up this address.

Of course, overwriting the LRU entry may replace an entry put there earlier by the RED microblock. So if a microblock needs to modify a table entry, it must do so in the cache as well as in the memory holding the complete table. If the microblock just modifies the cache, the changes can be lost when the microblock kicked its CAM entry out of the CAM. Therefore, when modifying the queue information, the RED code writes the data to SRAM as well as the cache.

The original RED algorithm is shown in Figure 9.9. With all of these changes in place, the RED algorithm now looks like Figure 9.10.

If this algorithm is run on multiple microengines, the local memory caches may have incorrect data. As one microengine modifies its local memory cache and SRAM, another microengine believes its local memory cache is up-to-date. To prevent this from happening, the algorithm needs to clear the CAM of all entries before the first thread on a particular microengine starts to use it. How do you know if a thread is the first thread on a microengine to run a microblock? Only if you are using ordered thread execution is this task simple. Using ordered thread execution, thread zero is always the first thread on a microengine to run an ordered microblock. When thread zero receives a signal allowing it to enter the microblock, it clears the CAM. Although this solves our problem, it also limits the number of microblocks using local memory as a cache to one, as clearing the CAM can have negative effects on any other microblock using the CAM.

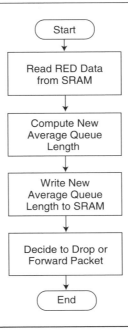

Figure 9.9 RED Algorithm before Ordered Thread Execution and Folding

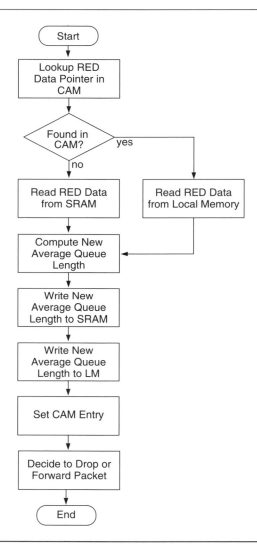

Figure 9.10 RED Algorithm with Folding

As with the unordered thread execution version of RED, the algorithm needs some synchronization to prevent the data structures from being corrupted. Conveniently, ordered thread execution provides this synchronization as well. With ordered thread execution added to RED, the algorithm now looks like Figure 9.11.

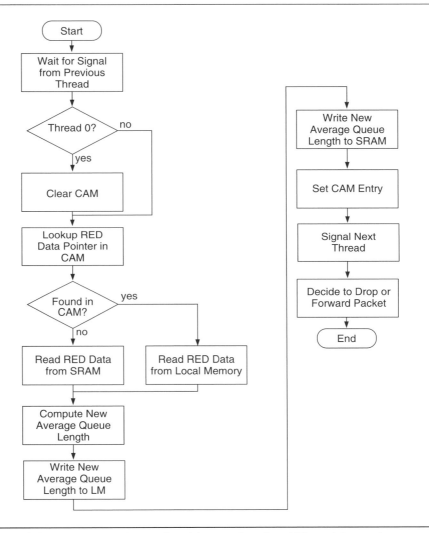

Figure 9.11 RED Algorithm with Folding and Ordered Thread Execution

Advanced Ordered Thread Execution

By modifying the algorithm as we describe in this section, we can achieve some performance gains. This performance increase comes from leveraging an aspect of the synchronization requirements of the RED microblock. The RED microblock really only needs synchronization between threads processing the same flow, as identified by the flow ID.

But, ordered thread execution provides synchronization for all threads running the RED code. It would be great to get some of that parallelism back!

Luckily, there is a way to allow code working on different flows to achieve some parallelism. The microblock is logically split into a read phase and a write phase. The read phase is the phase where data is read from either SRAM or local memory and continues until the data needs to be updated. The write phase is the phase where the data is updated in SRAM and/or local memory. This modified algorithm is shown in Figure 9.12 with the phases highlighted.

In the beginning of the read phase, the modified algorithm waits for a signal from the previous thread and looks up the queue data in the CAM, just as the original version of the algorithm does. However, in the new algorithm, the signal to the next thread is given right away. Then, the CAM state bits are used to provide synchronized access to the queue data structure, as described in Chapter 7. Using the state bits for synchronization allows threads processing packets from unrelated flows to perform computations at the same time because each CAM entry is associated with a different flow. The microengine assembly code implementing this is shown here:

start_read_phase()

```
        File:  Chapter09\ordered_signal.uc
150     #macro start_read_phase(out_lm_index, \
151                             out_data_in_lm, \
152                             in_block_sig, \
153                             in_mem)
154        .begin
155        .reg csr_val lookup_info
156
157        // Wait for a signal from the previous thread
158        ctx_arb[in_block_sig]
159
160        // We can't let another thread into this code until
161        // the CAM state is correct. This can be ensured by
162        // the fact that microengine threading does not swap
163        // contexts until the code releases the context.  So
164        // it's OK to signal the next thread now, since our
165        // next context swap is after the CAM is set up.
166        shf_left(csr_val, &in_block_sig, 3)
167        or_shf_left(csr_val, 0x80, csr_val, 0)
```

Continues

```
168         local_csr_wr[SAME_ME_SIGNAL, csr_val]
169
170         // The first thread has to clear the CAM
171         .if (ctx() == 0x0)
172             cam_clear
173         .endif
174
175         // Try to find the queue information in the local
176         // memory cache
177         cam_lookup[lookup_info, in_mem]
178
179         // If the lookup generated a hit, the data is or
180         // soon will be in the local memory cache thanks to
181         // a previous thread on this microengine.
182         immed[out_data_in_lm, 0]
183         .if (bit(lookup_info, 7))
184             // If the CAM entry has a state bit on, that
185             // means a previous thread is still working
186             // on putting the data into the CAM
187             .while (bit(lookup_info, 8))
188                 ctx_arb[voluntary]
189                 cam_lookup[lookup_info, in_mem]
190             .endw
191
192             immed[out_data_in_lm, 1]
193         .endif
194
195         // Mark the CAM entry as being locked by setting the
196         // state bit.  This tells the other threads that
197         // it is being used.
198         and_shf_right(out_lm_index, 0xf, lookup_info, 3)
199         cam_write[out_lm_index, in_mem, 1]
200
201         .end
202   #endm
```

Line 158:

The code waits for a signal from the previous thread.

Lines 160 – 168:

Here the code signals the next thread, even though it hasn't yet properly set up the CAM. Because the code doesn't swap out this context until after the CAM has been set up, signaling early doesn't hurt thanks to the non-preemptive nature of microengine threading. Notice the thread signals the next thread on this microengine. If this thread were the last thread on the microengine, the signal would go to thread zero of this microengine. The code can't let other microengines into this microblock until this microengine has written any table modifications it needs to make to SRAM.

Lines 170 – 173:

> If this is the first thread on this microengine to run this microblock, the CAM needs to be cleared of any stale entries. Otherwise, subsequent lookups may result in entries that have been modified by other microengines.

Line 177:

> This line of code performs the CAM lookup using the address of the RED queue information. If an entry is found, this lookup returns the entry's number and state bits. Otherwise, this lookup returns the entry number of the element that has been least recently used, which the code later overwrites.

Lines 179 – 193:

> These lines use the CAM to make sure the current thread is the only thread working on this entry in the RED queue table. One of the state bits in the CAM entry is used to indicate whether or not the entry is locked.

Lines 195 – 199:

> Once the CAM entry indicates the table entry is unlocked, this code sets the lock bit in the CAM state to lock it so we can modify it.

After this code executes, the thread is free to read the data from either local memory or SRAM based on the results of the lookup and perform whatever calculations are necessary to modify the data in local memory.

Before entering the write phase, the CAM state bit is cleared indicating the entry is no longer locked. Clearing this bit allows other threads to lock the entry and modify the data if they need to. Then the code waits for another signal. If the current thread is thread zero, this signal comes from the last thread on the current microengine to enter the read phase. The other threads are signaled by their previous thread after the previous phase has left the write state. If the signal has been received, the thread knows that all of the other threads on this microengine have either successfully locked the CAM entry they need, or are waiting in a spin loop to do so. Swapping out one more time allows any thread waiting for this thread's CAM entry to lock the entry if it needs to. Then, this thread waits for the CAM entry to be unlocked before writing the data back to SRAM.

As an optimization, only one thread needs to write back the SRAM data. Once the CAM entry has been unlocked, the thread entering the write phase can be assured that the other threads are done modifying the table entry. So the thread that read the data from SRAM can write the modified data back to SRAM. Entering the write phase is implemented in the following microengine assembly code:

start_write_phase()

File: Chapter09\ordered_signal.uc

```
225    #macro start_write_phase(in_block_sig, in_lm_index, \
226                            in_need_to_write)
227        .begin
228
229        // Clear the state bit in the CAM so that other
230        // threads know they can use the data we have
231        // written
232        cam_write_state[in_lm_index, 0]
233
234        // Wait for a signal from the previous thread.  This
235        // signal just ensures that all threads have
236        ctx_arb[in_block_sig]
237
238        // If we were the first to read this data from
239        // memory, we need to be the one to write it back
240        .if (in_need_to_write)
241            // Wait for the CAM state bit to show that the
242            // entry is unlocked
243            .reg state_info
244
245            .repeat
246                ctx_arb[voluntary]
247                cam_read_state[state_info, in_lm_index]
248            .until (!state_info);
249        .endif
250
251        .end
252    #endm
```

Line 232:

Here the code clears the CAM state bit so that other threads can lock the CAM entry.

Line 236:

This line of code waits for a signal. If the current thread is thread zero, this signal comes from thread seven entering the read phase. Otherwise, this signal comes from the previous thread exiting the write phase.

Lines 238 – 249:

If this thread read the data from SRAM, it must also write it back to SRAM (which happens external to this macro). Before doing so, it waits for the CAM entry to be unlocked.

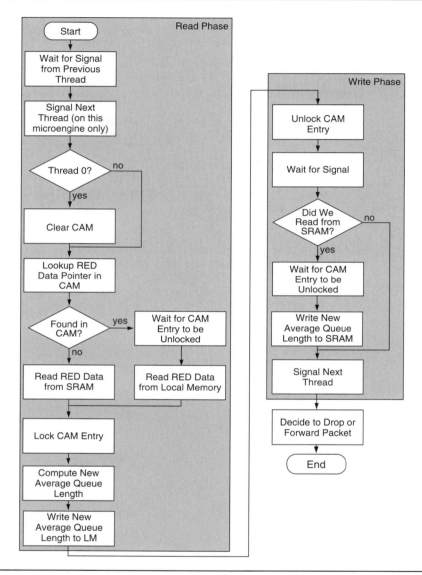

Figure 9.12 RED Algorithm using Advanced Ordered Thread Execution, with
Phases Identified

Once the write phase has been started, the code can write the modified
data to SRAM, if it needs to do so. Then, before exiting the write phase,
the thread signals the next thread. For threads 0 through 6, this signal
tells the next thread that it is acceptable to start the write phase. For

thread 7, this signal is sent to thread 0 on the next microengine, indicating that the current microengine has updated all of the table entries in SRAM.

These modifications to the basic ordered thread execution algorithm allow for a little more parallelism in your microblocks. Instead of threads being forced to wait for other threads processing unrelated packets, threads can continue to work.

Deciding between Ordered and Unordered Thread Execution

When writing packet processing code for the IXP2XXX microengines, you have to decide to use either ordered or unordered thread execution for a particular set of microblocks on a microengine. Multiple factors contribute to this decision. Sometimes, only one decision is possible. For example, if your microblock graph contains loops that have microblocks that need synchronization or packet ordering, unordered thread execution is the only option, as ordered thread execution does not support looping ordered blocks.

Many microblocks can be written to be easily adapted to both programming models, but some microblocks only work with one model or the other. For example, a microblock using folding is difficult to adapt to unordered thread execution. If you want to use a microblock targeted for a particular programming model, you either have to use its programming model or re-implement it with the other model.

If you still have a choice at this point, the prevailing decision factor is performance. If many of the microblocks have coarse granularity synchronization, ordered thread execution may be superior because of its very efficient coarse granularity synchronization. If the application requires per-flow synchronization and the device will be used in an environment where many flows go through the system at the same time, perhaps unordered thread execution is better. Also, if an application has many parallel branches of widely varying lengths, unordered thread execution tends to perform faster than ordered thread execution because the time it takes to process one packet is independent of the time it takes to process another. The ability to easily cache table data in local memory in ordered thread execution is also a factor in deciding between unordered and ordered thread execution.

In the end, the question of which programming model to use is not an easy one. No fundamental rules govern this decision. Analysis, simulation, and/or hardware testing must be used to select between unordered and ordered thread execution for a particular application.

Summary

Ordered thread execution is an alternative to unordered thread execution for implementing packet-processing code. Ordered thread execution uses inter-thread signals to achieve synchronization, end-to-end packet order, and partial packet order. With a very efficient, coarse grain synchronization and packet ordering mechanism also comes the ability to cache lookup table entries in local memory without much programming effort. When compared with unordered thread execution, ordered thread execution results in very fast code for applications with very simple microblock graphs, but may be slower for applications with complicated microblock graphs, or even impossible for graphs with loops.

Chapter 10

Rings and Queues

Y ou probably noticed that thus far in the book we have been relying on various types of rings and queues for communications between microengines. You probably also noticed the serious lack of details regarding the implementation of these rings and queues! Well, you're in luck because this chapter covers the hardware support for rings and queues on the IXP2XXX processor. Specifically, you'll learn about the software for initializing and accessing (enqueueing, dequeueing, checking the size, etc.) information in these data structures.

Both rings and queues implement a First-In-First-Out (FIFO) data structure. In the IXP2XXX literature, rings are fixed-sized, circular FIFOs, whereas queues are not fixed-sized FIFOs. FIFOs, whether implemented as rings or queues, are an extremely common concept in networking for several reasons:

- The rates of the tasks producing and consuming on the ring or queue may not be identical. Although when the producing task is faster than the consuming task the ring or queue eventually fills. Rings and queues do insulate the two tasks from temporary bursts or stalls present in either task.

- Multiple producing tasks can be coupled with a single consuming task. For example, this coupling might be used to enable multiple processing tasks to all use a single transmit task.

- Using multiple rings or queues, a single producing task can be coupled with multiple consuming tasks. This coupling might be used in a system where some packets require different processing than others.

- Different service preferences can be given to different rings or queues. For example, one ring may represent high-priority traffic— reserved for readers of this book of course—and a second ring may represent all other, best-effort traffic.

Furthermore, packet ordering on a single ring or queue is maintained due to the FIFO nature of both rings and queues.

Due to the common use of rings and queues, the IXP2XXX hardware has built-in support for these data structures. These data structures can be maintained in scratchpad memory (rings only), SRAM memory (rings and queues), or in next-neighbor registers (rings, as described in Chapter 8). The microengines contain instructions, signals, and CSRs for modifying and monitoring these FIFOs.

Scratchpad Rings

The IXP2XXX hardware supports 16 scratchpad rings. As shown in Figure 10.1, each ring is implemented as an array (of configurable size) in scratchpad memory, with pointers to the first and last entries on the ring, called the head and tail respectively.

The SHaC unit maintains the head and tail pointers, the base address, and the size (in long-words) of the ring. The head and tail pointers are modified during put and get commands on the ring, whereas the base pointer and size do not change once the ring is created. For example, as shown in Figure 10.1(b), after an entry is put onto the ring, the tail pointer is advanced. Similarly, Figure 10.1(c) shows the head pointer being advanced as the result of a get operation. Using the head and tail pointers, the hardware also implicitly maintains the count of entries currently on the ring. Thus, from a programmer's perspective, the hardware contains enough information to determine the fullness of the ring.

Both the head and tail pointers wrap around the ring so as not to exceed the size of the ring. Each ring can be configured into one of four sizes: 128, 256, 512, or 1,024 long-words. Since these rings are stored in scratchpad memory, you cannot create 16 rings of 1,024 long-words because that would require 64KB of scratchpad memory.

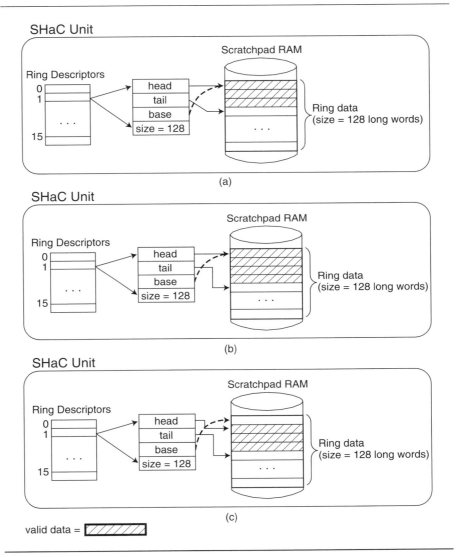

Figure 10.1 The Implementation of Scratchpad Rings

Note

Actually, the hardware does allow 16 rings of 1,024 entries to be created, but the data of the rings would overlap. The hardware does not prevent two rings from overlapping, but we cannot think of a reason for it. Thus, you should always set up the head and tail pointers and ring sizes to avoid multiple rings from overlapping.

Creating a Scratchpad Ring

To create a scratchpad ring, the software must specify the size of the ring, the starting scratchpad address where the ring data should reside, and the ring number to use. The ring number corresponds to one of the 16 rings supported by the hardware and is between 0 and 15.

All of this information is then written into several CSRs, as shown in the following code.

scratch_ring_init()

```
       File: Chapter05\scratch_rings.uc
47     #macro scratch_ring_init(IN_RING_NUM, IN_RING_BASE,
48                            IN_RING_SIZE)
49     .begin
50        .reg $ring_init_xfer $ring_head $ring_tail ring_init
51        .sig ring_init_sig ring_head_sig ring_tail_sig
52
53        immed32(ring_init, IN_RING_BASE)
54        alu_shf_left($ring_init_xfer, ring_init, OR,
55                    ((IN_RING_SIZE/128)-1),
56                    RING_BASE_SIZE_BITPOS)
57
58        cap[write, $ring_init_xfer,
59            SCRATCH_RING_BASE_/**/IN_RING_NUM],
60            sig_done[ring_init_sig]
61
62        immed32($ring_head, 0)
63        cap[write, $ring_head,
64            SCRATCH_RING_HEAD_/**/IN_RING_NUM],
65            sig_done[ring_head_sig]
66
67        immed32($ring_tail, 0)
68        cap[write, $ring_tail,
69            SCRATCH_RING_TAIL_/**/IN_RING_NUM],
70            sig_done[ring_tail_sig]
71
72        ctx_arb[ring_init_sig, ring_head_sig, ring_tail_sig]
73     .end
74     #endm
```

Lines 47 – 60:

This routine has parameters for the ring number, base address in scratchpad memory, and the size of the ring. To add to the confusion, we chose to make the base address a byte address (in scratchpad memory) whereas the size is in long-words.

The first cap[write, …] writes the size and base address of the ring for the given ring number. The size and base address are contained in the value written into the CSR, whereas the CSR itself is determined by the ring number.

The ring size required by the CSR is a value between 0 and 3, corresponding to the ring sizes of 128, 256, 512, and 1,024 respectively. For example, for rings of size 256 long-words write a size of 1.

Lines 62 – 72:

Since the above instructions already set the ring number, ring size, and base scratchpad address, what is left for initializing a scratchpad ring? Well, the head and tail pointers must be initialized to zero so the hardware knows the ring is initially empty.

To accomplish this part of the initialization, these lines write zero into two more CSRs, corresponding to the head and tail pointers for the ring number.

Finally, because each of the above CSR writes has generated a signal, all three signals are caught to ensure that the ring has been properly initialized. It would have been equally correct to catch a single signal after each CSR write. However, that process would make the time necessary to execute this code longer.

Putting Data on a Scratchpad Ring

After creating a scratchpad ring, the code to put data onto a given scratchpad ring is a single instruction, scratch[put, …]. This instruction takes the ring number and one or more transfer registers and puts them onto the given ring by writing into scratchpad memory, as shown in the following code segment extracted from the routine ring_put_buffer.

scratch_ring_put_buffer()

```
        File: Chapter05\scratch_rings.uc
149     #macro scratch_ring_put_buffer(\
150                     IN_RING_NUM, \
151                     in_handle, \
152                     in_length, \
153                     in_offset)
```

Continues

```
154    .begin
155        .reg ring_addr
156        .sig ring_signal
157
158        xbuf_alloc($ring_data, 3, write)
159
160        immed32(ring_addr, (IN_RING_NUM<<2))
161
162        move($ring_data[0], in_handle)
163        move($ring_data[1], in_length)
164        move($ring_data[2], in_offset)
165        scratch[put, $ring_data[0],
166                ring_addr, 0, 3],
167            ctx_swap[ring_signal]
168
169        xbuf_free($ring_data)
170    .end
171    #endm
```

Getting Data from a Scratchpad Ring

In a similar fashion as putting data on a scratchpad ring, the code to get data from a given scratchpad ring is a single instruction, scratch[get, ...]. This instruction takes the ring number and one or more transfer registers and retrieves the given ring by reading from scratchpad memory into the transfer registers, as illustrated in the following code segment.

scratch_ring_get_buffer()

File: Chapter05\scratch_rings.uc

```
100    #macro scratch_ring_get_buffer(\
101                        IN_RING_NUM, \
102                        out_handle, \
103                        out_length, \
104                        out_offset)
105    .begin
106        .reg ring_addr
107        .sig ring_signal
108
109        xbuf_alloc($ring_data, 3, read)
110
111        immed32(ring_addr, (IN_RING_NUM<<2))
```

Continues

```
112        scratch[get, $ring_data[0],
113               ring_addr, 0, 3],
114           ctx_swap[ring_signal]
115        move(out_handle, $ring_data[0])
116        move(out_length, $ring_data[1])
117        move(out_offset, $ring_data[2])
118
119        xbuf_free($ring_data)
120    .end
121    #endm
```

Checking for Scratchpad Ring Fullness

Because rings are of fixed size, before putting data on a ring, the fullness of the ring must be checked. What did we mean by fullness? Well, for each of the first 12 scratchpad rings, the hardware provides a fullness bit that is not an exact indication of the ring being full. Rather, this bit indicates that the ring has reached the threshold of three quarters of the total ring capacity. Table 10.1 shows the thresholds for each of the four scratchpad ring sizes.

The fullness bit is set at these thresholds because multiple micro-engine threads may simultaneously put data on the same ring. Imagine if the hardware waited to set the fullness bit exactly when a ring was full. Now imagine that a particular scratch ring has room for just one more entry. The ring is not full, so the fullness bit would not be set. Multiple threads could then check that the ring was not full and issue a put command. The result would be that the hardware would receive multiple put commands for a ring that only had room for one more entry. The hardware would be forced to discard some of the requests.

Table 10.1 Fullness Thresholds for Each Scratchpad Ring Size

Scratchpad Ring Size	Threshold When Full is Asserted
128	96
256	192
512	384
1024	768

The following code illustrates how this fullness bit is tested.

---

scratch_ring_full()

File: Chapter05\scratch_rings.uc

```
197    #macro scratch_ring_full(IN_RING_NUM, \
198                        IN_FULL_TARGET)
199       br_inp_state[SCR_Ring/**/IN_RING_NUM/**/_Full,
200                        IN_FULL_TARGET]
201    #endm
```

Lines 199 – 200:

The br_inp_state instruction tests the specified state bit, in this case the fullness indicator for a particular scratchpad ring number, and branches to the specified location (IN_FULL_TARGET) if the state bit is set.

Several conclusions can be drawn from this discussion:

■ When the fullness bit is set, the ring is not necessarily full. In our examples throughout the book, we have chosen to interpret the fullness bit as the ring being full, but you don't need to make this same assumption. You can use knowledge of the application to determine how many threads are putting data on the ring and then ignore the fullness indicator for some number of puts (according to Table 10.1) before checking again.

■ The fullness bit is not sufficient to prevent rings from overflowing. Consider the case where 128 threads are simultaneously putting two long-words of data on a scratchpad ring of size 128 long-words. Even if the ring is initially empty, the fullness bit does not prevent the ring from receiving too much data. Thus, when writing an application you must account for the number of threads that may put data onto a ring, the size of the data each thread might add, and the size of the ring itself to determine the meaning of the fullness bit. For some applications, the fullness bit may not provide any protection against ring overflow.

So is there a way to determine exact fullness of a ring? Yes, and luckily a simple solution exists. However, simple does not mean efficient. A counter can be maintained in either scratchpad or SRAM memory that corresponds to the number of long-words currently on the ring.

Any thread that performs a put operation would first atomically test and add to this counter. If the counter was originally less than the size of the ring, the thread could issue the scratch[put, …] instruction. Otherwise, the ring is full and so the thread must atomically subtract from the counter to undo the addition it originally performed.

After a thread performs the scratch[get, …] instruction, if the ring is not empty, the counter is atomically decremented. The cost of this solution is at least one extra memory operation per put (and get) operation. For the case where the ring is full, the put operation must issue two extra memory references.

An example of this code is provided in the accompanying CD-ROM in the Chapter10 directory.

SRAM Queue Array

For applications requiring a few small FIFOs, scratchpad rings are sufficient. However, scratchpad rings are not sufficient for applications requiring more than 16 FIFOs. For example, quality-of-service (QoS) applications may need hundreds, perhaps thousands, of FIFOs per port. Furthermore, scratchpad rings are not sufficient for applications requiring very large FIFOs, such as those used for freelists of buffers, which could require many thousands of entries.

For applications where scratchpad rings are not sufficient, the IXP2XXX processor's solution is to use SRAM-based FIFOs. The IXP2XXX hardware can support as many FIFOs as can fit within SRAM memory and provides access to these FIFOs through a 64-element cache (per SRAM controller), as shown in Figure 10.2. Before a new FIFO can be used, its "descriptor" must be loaded into the "cache" (queue array). A queue descriptor contains all of the necessary data to work with the FIFO, such as the head and tail pointers and current number of entries in the FIFO.

When the cache is full and a new FIFO needs to be used, one entry from the cache must be unloaded. Thus, the total number of FIFOs supported is not limited by the size of the SRAM queue arrays, but instead by the amount of SRAM dedicated to the FIFOs.

For some applications, queue descriptors may never need to be unloaded from the cache. This situation may be the case when the total number of FIFOs required is less than the total number of queue-array elements. This situation may also be true for certain FIFOs, such as freelists of buffers, which are a global resource that should never be unloaded from the queue array.

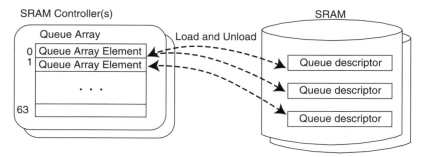

Each SRAM controller contains a 64-element queue array. Each queue-array element represents a FIFO. Queue-array elements are loaded from, and unloaded to, "queue descriptors" in SRAM memory. A queue descriptor contains all of the necessary information to represent a FIFO (e.g., head and tail pointers, size, etc.)

Figure 10.2 Using the SRAM Queue Array as a Cache

Each *queue-array element* contains enough information to add or remove an entry from a single SRAM FIFO. For example, each queue-array element contains a head pointer, a tail pointer, and a count of the number of entries currently in the FIFO.

If a new FIFO needs to be loaded and no unused queue-array elements exist, you must unload an existing queue-array element first. The unloading process writes the queue-array element into SRAM. To load a queue descriptor, you specify the SRAM controller (called a channel), queue-array element number, and SRAM memory from which the descriptor should be loaded. To unload a queue descriptor, you specify the SRAM controller and queue-array element number. The queue descriptor is written back into the same SRAM location from where it was loaded.

Just like scratchpad rings, you must keep the memory associated with the data on multiple FIFOs separate. For the SRAM queue array, it is equally important to keep the memory used for loading and unloading queue descriptors distinct from the memory used by the FIFOs themselves. Because both the data and queue descriptor values are stored in SRAM, it is possible to overwrite one with the other.

The SRAM controller implements two different types of FIFOs: a linked-list queue, and a circular ring. The usage model for these FIFOs and the format of the queue descriptors in the queue array are different depending on which type of FIFO is being used. The following subsections describe the two types of SRAM FIFOs.

Note Scratchpad rings and the SRAM FIFOs are not mutually exclusive. In fact, most applications typically use both types of FIFOs. Scratchpad rings are especially useful following the receive task and into the transmit task as neither of these FIFOs needs to be large, and each task only requires one FIFO. The SRAM FIFOs could be used within the packet-processing stages for service differentiation and is often used to maintain freelists of buffers which are inherently not fixed-length.

SRAM Rings

A queue-array element can be used to access a queue or a ring, depending on your design. When used as a ring, a SRAM ring is very similar to a scratchpad ring. Of course, instead of the data being stored in scratchpad memory, the data is stored in a contiguous block of SRAM. Also, SRAM rings can be configured into sizes of 512, 1K, 2K, 4K, 8K, 16K, 32K, and 64K long-words. Thus, one reason for using an SRAM ring instead of a scratchpad ring might be to support a larger FIFO.

When used to implement a ring, a queue-array element contains the head and tail pointers, the size of the ring, and the current number of elements (count) on the ring, as shown in Figure 10.3.

Initializing SRAM Rings

To initialize an SRAM ring, the size, head, tail, and count fields of the queue descriptor must be written with appropriate values and loaded into the queue array, as shown in the following code.

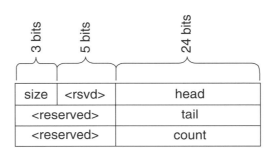

Figure 10.3 The Format of a Queue-array Element for an SRAM Ring

sram_ring_init()

File: Chapter10\sram_rings\sram_rings.uc

```
76    // Initialize the SRAM ring
77    .begin
78        .reg $q_head $q_tail $q_count
79        .xfer_order $q_head $q_tail $q_count
80        .reg addr q_desc_addr
81        .sig write_sig init_sig
82
83        // Bits 31 - 29 of the head pointer contain an
84        // encoding of the size. 000 = 512 words,
85        // 001 = 1024, etc.
86        immed32(addr,
87            ((RING_CHANNEL << 30) | RING_BASE_NO_CHAN))
88        immed32($q_head, ((RING_BASE_NO_CHAN>>2) |
89                        (((RING_SIZE/512)-1)<<29)))
90        immed32($q_tail, ((RING_BASE_NO_CHAN>>2) |
91                        (((RING_SIZE/512)-1)<<29)))
92        immed32($q_count, 0)
93
94        sram[write, $q_head, addr, 0, 3],
95            ctx_swap[write_sig]
96
97        immed32(addr, RING_BASE_NO_CHAN)
98        buf_form_q_desc_addr(q_desc_addr,
99                            RING_CHANNEL,
100                           RING_NUM,
101                           addr)
102       sram[rd_qdesc_head, $q_head,
103           q_desc_addr, 0, 2],
104           sig_done[init_sig]
105       sram[rd_qdesc_other, --, q_desc_addr, 0]
106       ctx_arb[init_sig]
107       .use $q_head // Suppress an assembler warning
108   .end
```

Lines 83 – 95:

Before the SRAM controller can initialize a queue-array element, the size, head, tail, and count values must be written into three consecutive words in SRAM memory. The head, tail, and count values must be aligned on a four long-word boundary. Thus, you cannot pack queue descriptor values one directly after another in SRAM. They must be separated by at least one long-word. This fourth long-word is not used by the queue array hardware.

For SRAM rings, the size of the ring must be encoded into the upper three bits of both the head and tail pointers. The encoding is 000_2 for 512 long-words, 001_2 for 1K long-words, and so on, through 64K long-words.

Once the size, head, tail, and count values have been formatted into transfer registers, this code writes these values into SRAM.

But at what address should you write these values? If the SRAM ring ever needs to be unloaded from the queue array hardware, these values should be written into an area of SRAM reserved for queue descriptors. In our example, we have decided that unloading this SRAM ring need never occur, so we chose to write these values directly into the first three words of the SRAM ring's data area which is located by combining the SRAM channel with the 'channel-less' address. For SRAM rings or queues that never get unloaded from the queue array, this solution is convenient because it guarantees that no other code can use this memory. If another piece of code was using this same memory, the SRAM ring's data would interfere with the other code anyway.

Lines 97 – 106:

Now that the queue descriptor values are in SRAM, they can be loaded into any queue array entry. To load the queue descriptor, the code must provide the IXP2XXX hardware with the SRAM controller number, the queue-array-element number to load, and the SRAM address where the head, tail, and count values are located. These three values are packed into the address operands of the sram instruction by the routine buf_form_q_desc_addr, shown in the following code.

```
#define QDESC_CHANNEL_BITPOS            30
#define QDESC_ENTRY_BITPOS              24

#macro buf_form_q_desc_addr(out_desc, in_channel,
in_entry, in_offset)
    shf_left(out_desc, in_entry, QDESC_ENTRY_BITPOS)
    alu_shf_left(out_desc, out_desc, OR,
                 in_channel, QDESC_CHANNEL_BITPOS)
    alu_shf_right(out_desc, out_desc, OR,
                  in_offset, 2) // Convert to SRAM words
#endm
```

Notice that the SRAM address must be converted into a long-word address before being encoded in the queue descriptor address.

The sram[rd_q_desc_head, …] instruction loads the head and count values from SRAM into the proper queue-array entry. The head pointer and count are also placed into the given transfer registers. This instruction does not load the tail pointer. Instead, a second instruction, sram[rd_q_ desc_other, …] loads the tail pointer. Actually, sram[rd_q_desc_other, …] loads either the tail or head pointer, depending on which one is not currently loaded into the given queue array entry.

So how is the tail pointer loaded without the head pointer? The sram[rd_q_desc_tail, …] instruction loads the tail pointer and count in an identical fashion as sram[rd_q_desc_head, …]. The choice of which value to load first is not usually important, unless you need the value of the head or tail pointer.

Getting Data from an SRAM Ring

Once the SRAM ring has been initialized, getting data from the ring is accomplished with the sram[get, …] instruction, as shown in the following code.

sram_ring_get()

File: Chapter10\sram_rings\sram_rings.uc

```
45    #macro sram_ring_get(out_val)
46    .begin
47        .reg addr
48        .sig ring_sig
49
50        immed32(addr, (RING_CHANNEL<<30 | (RING_NUM<<2)))
51        sram[get, out_val, addr, 0, 1],
52            ctx_swap[ring_sig]
53    .end
54    #endm
```

Lines 50 – 52:

This code is nearly identical to getting data from a scratch ring. The SRAM channel and queue-array entry are encoded in the address operand of the instruction.

Like scratchpad rings, if the SRAM ring is empty, the sram[get, …] instruction fills the transfer register with the value zero.

Putting Data on an SRAM Ring

Finally, putting data on an SRAM ring is accomplished with the sram[put, …] operation, as shown in the following code.

sram_ring_put()

File: Chapter10\sram_rings\sram_rings.uc

```
59    #macro sram_ring_put(io_val)
60    .begin
61        .reg addr
62        .sig ring_sig
63
64        immed32(addr, (RING_CHANNEL<<30 | (RING_NUM<<2)))
65        sram[put, io_val, addr, 0, 1],
66            sig_done[ring_sig]
67        ctx_arb[ring_sig]
68    .end
69    #endm
```

Lines 64 – 67:

This code, just like sram[get, …], first encodes the SRAM channel and queue-array entry into the address operand of the instruction.

Notice that instead of using ctx_swap[] at the end of the sram[put, …] instruction, a sig_done is used followed immediately by ctx_arb. The sram[put, …] operation uses a double signal, which cannot be caught with the ctx_swap[] optional token.

The double signal allows you to detect SRAM ring fullness. The first signal indicates that the SRAM controller has taken the data from the write transfer register. The second signal indicates that the SRAM controller has written status into the read transfer register.

This status information indicates whether the put operation was successful and how many entries were on the ring prior to the put operation. If the put operation is successful, bit 31 of the read transfer register is set, otherwise the bit is clear. The remaining bits of the read-transfer register contain the count field of the SRAM queue-array entry, prior to the put operation occurring.

Note | A put operation onto an SRAM ring is only successful when the current number of words on the ring is *strictly* less than the size of the ring minus sixteen. The maximum size of a put operation is 16 long-words due to the size of the transfer registers available for a single thread. So this design decision prevents any single put operation from overflowing the ring.

Thus, it is actually impossible to fill every long-word of an SRAM ring. In the best case, all but one long-word of the ring can be added before the SRAM ring no longer allows more put operations.

SRAM Queues

In addition to being used as a ring, an SRAM queue-array element can also implement a linked-list FIFO, called a queue. Like SRAM rings, the data for the queue is stored in SRAM. However, the size of this linked-list is only constrained by the size of SRAM memory, and the data itself need not be in contiguous SRAM memory. Unlike a ring, where the data is completely opaque and simply contained within one or more long-words of data, the entries on a queue have a specific format. This format tells the SRAM controller how to find the next entry on the queue (i.e., the next link in the list). The format for an entry on an SRAM queue is shown in Figure 10.4.

Each SRAM queue entry contains SOP, EOP, and segment count fields and a pointer to the next entry on the queue. When the SRAM controller dequeues a buffer from a queue-array element, the next queue entry is read from SRAM. The SOP, EOP, and segment count fields, are used to determine how the enqueue and dequeue operations work, as explained later in this section. The pointer field is used to locate any subsequent data on the queue.

To properly understand the SOP, EOP, segment count, and pointer fields of a queue entry, you must know what information is contained in

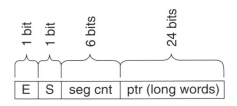

Figure 10.4 The Format of an Entry on an SRAM Queue

each queue-array element. As shown in Figure 10.5, each queue-array element representing a queue contains head and tail pointers, a count of the number of entries on the queue, start-of-packet (S), end-of-packet (E), and segment count fields.

The head and tail pointers, which are long-word addresses, point to the first and last entries in the queue, respectively. The count contains the number of entries currently on the queue. When a dequeue occurs on an SRAM queue, the SOP, EOP, and segment count fields of the next entry (as pointed to by the head pointer of the queue-array element) are copied into the queue array element, and the value of the pointer is copied into the header pointer in the queue-array element.

The SOP, EOP, and segment count fields determine exactly how enqueue and dequeue operations are performed by the SRAM controller, as shown in Figure 10.6. Specifically, you can configure the SRAM controller into three modes:

■ *Mode 0: Use EOP and use segment count.* In this mode, the enqueue operation links the new entry to the end of the linked list, updates the tail pointer in the queue-array element, and increments the count in the queue-array element.

The dequeue operation decrements the segment count value in the queue-array element. If the value is non-zero, the head pointer in the queue-array element is not removed, and the queue count is not modified. If the segment count is zero, the head pointer is removed. The queue count is decremented only when the EOP flag is set.

This mode is used to support both multi-buffer-per-packet operations as well as segmented buffers. For example, if a single packet

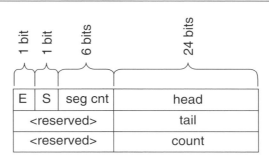

Figure 10.5 The Contents of a Queue-array Element for an SRAM Queue

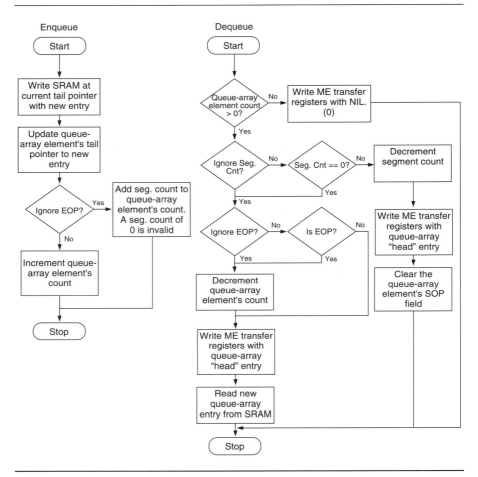

Figure 10.6 Flowcharts for the Enqueue and Dequeue Operations in the SRAM Controller

was larger than a single buffer, multiple buffers must be enqueued for a single packet with the SOP and EOP fields used to indicate the beginning and end of the packet.

Within each buffer, multiple segments may exist. This concept is used during the transmit operations to determine how many mpackets are contained within a buffer. For example, the transmit process continues to dequeue a buffer for each mpacket's worth of data in the buffer.

■ *Mode 1: Use EOP but ignore segment count.* In this mode, the enqueue operation links the new entry into the end of the linked list, updates the tail pointer in the queue-array element, and increments the count in the queue-array element.

The dequeue operation ignores the segment count in the queue-array element and always removes the entry from the head of the queue. The count in the queue-array element is decremented only when and entry with the EOP flag set is removed from the queue. You can use the segment count for any purpose. For example, some designs use the segment count as an indication of the relative size of the buffer so that the code dequeueing the buffer immediately knows the approximate size of the dequeued buffer.

This mode is used to support multi-buffer-per-packet operations. Thus, as described above, this mode is useful for situations where packets are larger than a single buffer.

■ *Mode 3: Ignore EOP and ignore segment count.* In this mode, the enqueue operation links the new entry into the end of the linked list, updates the tail pointer in the queue-array element, and adds the segment count of the entry to the count in the queue-array element. Yes, the terminology is confusing in that the segment count is used even though the mode is 'ignoring segment count'. In this mode the segment count must never be zero. Therefore, as you will learn in the next sections, the default enqueue operation must never be used in this mode since it specifies a segment count of zero. Instead, the enqueue operation should always specify the segment count using an indirect reference.

The dequeue operation ignores the segment count value in the queue-array element and always removes the entry from the head of the queue. The count in the queue-array element is decremented for every dequeue operation performed.

This mode is used to support single buffer per-packet operations, such as buffer freelists (covered at the end of this chapter).

Mode 2, or "Ignore EOP but use segment count," is not a valid configuration of the SRAM controller.

Note | The segment count is also called the cell count in some of the IXP2XXX literature.

An Illustration of Enqueuing on SRAM Queues

Since it is always easier to learn through examples, let's enqueue some packets on an SRAM queue and watch what happens. Figure 10.7 shows the sequence of operations necessary to enqueue two packets onto an SRAM queue. The first packet is represented by a single buffer (i.e., both the SOP and EOP bits are set) with a single segment. The second packet is represented with three buffers, which have three, one, and two segments.

The code for performing these operations is supplied on the accompanying CD-ROM in the `Chapter10\sram_queues_test` subdirectory if you want to watch these operations in action.

Figure 10.7 shows the same enqueue operations for each of the three modes. In this figure, the count and segment count fields are shown with three different potential values, depending on the mode of operation. The first count is the value that would be correct for the "use EOP

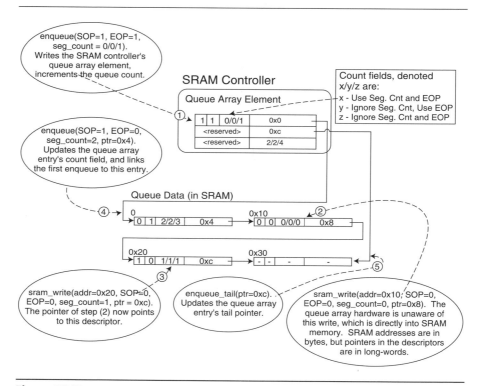

Figure 10.7 Enqueue Examples: Using the SOP, EOP, and Segment Count Fields of SRAM Queues

and use segment count" mode. The second count is the value that would be correct for the "use EOP but ignore segment count" mode. The final value is the one that would be correct for the "ignore EOP and ignore segment count" mode. For each of these modes, the steps taken to enqueue these packets are as follows:

1. Enqueue the first packet. This operation updates the queue-array element with the appropriate values for SOP, EOP, and segment count. In modes 0 and 1, these values are 1, 1, and 0, respectively. However, in mode 3, while the SOP and EOP bits are 1 and 1 respectively, the segment count is 1 instead of 0. This is because in modes 0 and 1 the segment count is treated as a zero-relative number; thus, a 0 segment count actually represents 1 segment in these modes. At the end of this step the count of entries in the queue-array element is 1 for all three modes.

2. Write the entry for the second buffer in the second packet. This step does not involve the SRAM queue array hardware at all. Instead, the descriptor for the second buffer in the second packet is written into SRAM memory. This entry has both the SOP and EOP bits set to zero, and the segment count field set to zero as well. The segment count field is zero even for mode 3 because this operation does not use the SRAM queue array hardware. The pointer field in the entry is written with a long-word-based SRAM address that indicates the (future) location of the third buffer in the second packet.

3. Write the entry for the third buffer in the second packet. In a manner identical to the second step, the entry for the third buffer in the second packet is written into SRAM memory. For this buffer, the SOP bit is zero, but the EOP bit is one. In mode 1, the segment count field is set to one (indicating two segments) and is ignored for the other modes. Again, the SRAM queue array hardware is unaware (and unaffected) by this write operation. This entry is written into the SRAM memory location indicated by the pointer field in the descriptor written in step 2.

4. Enqueue the first buffer in the second packet. This step uses the SRAM queue array hardware to enqueue the SOP buffer in the second packet. The SOP bit is one but the EOP bit is zero. The segment count field is 2 for modes 0 and 1, and 3 for mode 3. At the end of this step, the count field in the queue-array element is 2, 2, and 4 for modes 0, 1, and 2, respectively. For modes 0 and 1, this

count represents the number of packets (or enqueues) performed on the queue. For mode 3, this count represents the number of buffers on the queue. Finally, the head pointer in the queue-array element is updated to point to this first buffer descriptor.

5. Update the tail pointer in the queue-array element. This final operation is a bit tricky. At this point in the process, the queue array hardware does not have the appropriate tail pointer. It couldn't because we wrote the second and third buffer descriptors of the second packet without using the SRAM queue array hardware! Thus, we use a special operation, the enqueue-tail operation, to inform the queue array hardware of the true tail (i.e., last entry) in our linked-list. This operation only affects the tail pointer in the queue-array element, and is described in more detail in the next section.

The Enqueue-Tail Operation

To properly take advantage of the SOP and EOP fields for multi-buffer per-packet modes, SRAM queues support the notion of an enqueue-tail operation. The enqueue-tail operation allows a multi-buffer packet to be enqueued without the queue count being incremented for each buffer. As shown in Figure 10.8, the enqueue-tail operation only modifies the tail pointer in the queue-array element.

Enqueue-tail operations work in conjunction with enqueue operations. To enqueue a multi-buffer packet, first the multiple buffers are manually chained together in SRAM memory using sram[write, …] instructions. Second, the SOP buffer is enqueued onto an SRAM queue. This enqueue operation results in the count being incremented and the SOP mpacket linked into the queue. However, as shown in Figure 10.8, the enqueue-tail operation results in an incorrect tail pointer for the queue. Thus, the third and final operation is to perform an enqueue-tail operation for the EOP buffer in the packet. This operation updates the tail pointer of the queue-array element but does not modify the count.

When enqueueing a multi-buffer packet, the enqueue-tail operation must always immediately follow an enqueue operation, with no other SRAM queue operations for the queue-array entry in between the two. The reason for this restriction should be obvious. Imagine an additional enqueue operation occurring before the enqueue-tail operation. The SOP buffer entry would be linked to the new entry being enqueued and the rest of the multi-buffer packet would be lost.

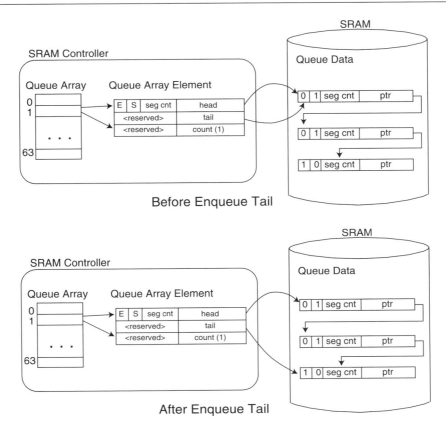

Before the enqueue-tail operation is performed, a multi-buffer packet has been created in SRAM memory and the SOP buffer has been enqueued. At this point, the tail pointer in the queue-array entry points to the head entry and the queue count is one.

After the enqueue-tail operation, the tail pointer is updated to point to the EOP buffer in the packet. This modification occurs without any modification to the count, as desired.

Figure 10.8 An Illustration of the Enqueue-Tail Operation

This race condition may not seem like a big deal, but if multiple microengines are enqueuing buffers onto the same queue, extra synchronization mechanisms are required to prevent this issue. Chapter 12 discusses a queue manager design that solves this issue.

Dequeuing from a SRAM Queue

So now you have two buffers on an SRAM queue, let's dequeue them! Figure 10.9 shows the results of repeatedly dequeuing, in each of the three modes, from the SRAM queue-array element created in the previous example.

The results of the repeated dequeue operations depend on the mode of operation, as follows:

■ *Mode 0: Use EOP and use segment count.* The first time an entry is dequeued in this mode, the SOP bit in the returned entry is set according to the SOP bit in the queue-array element. For all subsequent dequeue operations, the SOP bit is clear.

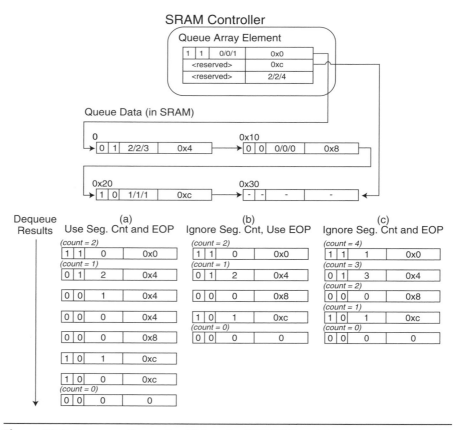

Figure 10.9 Dequeue Examples: Using the SOP, EOP, and Segment Count Fields of SRAM Queues

This mode is illustrated in Figure 10.9(a), where the results of repeated dequeue commands on the example queue are shown. The first element dequeued has SOP and EOP set and no segment count. Thus, this entry is immediately removed from the queue and the count is decremented.

The second entry dequeued has SOP set, EOP clear, and a segment count of two. The next two dequeue operations continue to return this same entry, only with the SOP field clear and the segment count decremented. The count is never modified for this element.

The third entry dequeued has SOP and EOP clear and a segment count of zero. This entry is immediately removed from the linked list, but again the queue count is not decremented.

The final entry dequeued has SOP clear, EOP set, and a segment count of one. The next dequeue returns this same entry and, because the EOP flag is set, decrements the queue count.

■ *Mode 1: Use EOP but ignore segment count.* This mode is illustrated in Figure 10.9(b) where the results of repeated dequeue commands on the example queue are shown. The first entry dequeued has SOP and EOP set and no segment count and is immediately removed from the queue. The count is decremented.

The second entry dequeued has SOP set, EOP clear, and a segment count of two. This entry is also immediately removed from the queue, but the queue count is not modified.

The third entry dequeued has SOP and EOP clear and a segment count of zero. Like the previous entry, this entry is immediately removed from the queue and the queue count is not modified.

Finally, the fourth entry dequeued has SOP clear, EOP set, and a segment count of one. This entry is removed from the queue and the queue count is decremented.

■ *Mode 3: Ignore EOP and ignore segment count.* This mode is illustrated in Figure 10.9(c) where the results of repeated dequeue commands on the example queue are shown. All of the dequeue operations result in the entry being removed from the queue and the count being decremented.

In our examples, the first enqueue operation was modified to specify a segment count of one and the second enqueue operation was modified to specify a segment count of three. Recall, in this mode the segment count is directly added to the count, and thus, each of these segment counts needs to be one larger than in the previous examples.

Creating a Buffer Freelist with SRAM Queues

To further illustrate the usage of SRAM queues, this section shows how to put them to use for buffer management. In this section you'll learn about how the Intel IXA SDK 3.0 implements a buffer management library using SRAM queues.

Buffers are used throughout the book—as well as throughout networking applications—so managing them is a nearly-universal theme. It turns out that SRAM queues provide a nice solution to the problem of buffer management, but before jumping to that conclusion, consider the desirable properties of a buffer-management library. Our requirements are as follows:

■ The allocate and free routines must be O(1) in complexity. For performance reasons, the buffer-allocation routine shouldn't perform long searches of memory to find an empty buffer.

■ The allocate and free routines must be thread safe. Because the receive driver typically allocates buffers and the transmit driver frees them, we fully expect that multiple threads may be allocating and freeing buffers at the same time.

■ The buffer-allocating mechanism must allocate buffers from DRAM memory. This requirement enables the receive (and later on transmit) code to take advantage of the direct RBUF-to-DRAM (or DRAM-to-TBUF) transfers available on the IXP2XXX hardware.

■ The allocate routine must allocate buffers at least as large as the largest packet possibly received from any MSF device. This requirement implies that the size of the buffers allocated must be configurable since the largest packet size of the next latest-and-greatest MSF device can't be known a-priori.

Ignoring the thread safety requirement, a myriad of solutions exist that would meet these requirements. A linked-list, stack, or queue, of pointers to free packets would all work nicely, assuming that the size of the buffers was somehow configurable.

To meet the thread safety requirement, a mutex could be implemented using some of the atomic operations available from the SRAM unit or scratchpad memory, as shown in Chapter 7.

If we ignore the third requirement for a moment, SRAM queues could be a solution. Building a freelist with a queue is easy. By definition all buffers on the queue are free, or unallocated. For initialization, the queue is enqueued with the complete list of free buffer handles. When a new buffer is required, like when an SOP mpacket is received, the buffer handle is dequeued from the queue. When a previously allocated buffer is to be freed, the buffer handle is enqueued onto the queue.

Unfortunately, SRAM queues are in SRAM not DRAM. So either a new solution is needed, like a linked-list of buffers in DRAM with mutual exclusion coming from operations in SRAM or scratchpad memory, or a mapping from SRAM queues onto DRAM memory is needed.

It turns out mapping from SRAM queues to DRAM memory can be done quite efficiently, as we show in the next section. This fact, coupled with the fact that the hardware can implement thread safety, it should not be surprising to learn that the Intel IXA SDK 3.0 uses SRAM queues for its buffer-allocation mechanism.

Mapping SRAM Freelists to DRAM Buffer Data

The problem with the SRAM queue solution for freelists is that SRAM queues are in SRAM and buffers need to be in DRAM. One solution would be to put all buffers in SRAM, but SRAM is expensive, and comes in limited sizes. Besides, placing packets in DRAM allows the code to take advantage of the direct data path to and from RBUFs and TBUFs.

The software solution to this problem employed by the Intel IXA SDK 3.0 is to have a parallel freelist in DRAM, as shown in Figure 10.10. Consider the SRAM freelist to actually be an array of free buffers. Then a second array in DRAM is created with the same number of elements as the SRAM array. Each index in the SRAM array corresponds to the same index in the DRAM array. However the DRAM array entries can be much larger than the SRAM, and are thus capable of holding an entire packet. The SRAM-array entries are overlaid with the SRAM-queue linked-list for allocation purposes. When an SRAM entry is allocated, so is the corresponding DRAM entry.

This solution's advantages are that SRAM queues are used for allocating and freeing buffers while the actual packet data is stored in DRAM. Better yet, the mapping function between the two compiles to only a few arithmetic operations.

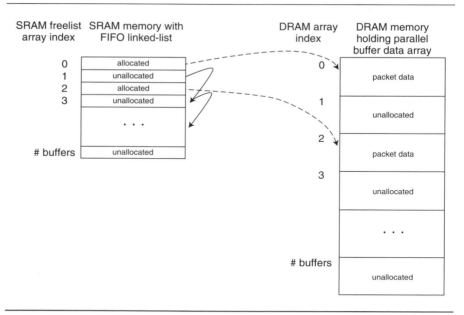

Figure 10.10 The Parallel SRAM and DRAM Freelists

Converting a DRAM address after dequeing an entry from the SRAM queue is a two-step calculation:

1. First, compute the array index of the SRAM entry.

2. Then, using the array index, compute the address for this index in the DRAM array.

To illustrate the efficiency of this conversion, the following code segment shows the microengine code generated by the dl_buf_get_data() macro, which converts an SRAM buffer handle (dl_buf_handle) into a DRAM address (cur_mpacket_addr) for the buffer's data.

```
alu_shf[10010!cur_mpacket_addr, dl_buf_handle, and~,
    0xff, <<24]
alu_shf[10010!cur_mpacket_addr, --, b,
    10010!cur_mpacket_addr, <<8]
```

This conversion is implemented in just two instructions! The first line computes the index of the SRAM entry by extracting certain bits from the buffer handle. The second line converts this index into an address by shifting the index by an amount that corresponds to the size of the buffer. This value is compile-time configurable.

A Special Note about Enqueue

If you dig deep enough into the Intel IXA SDK 3.0 buffer library, you'll find the key operation used to implement freeing a buffer is:

```
sram[enqueue, --, SRAM_ADDR_REG, 0]
```

Notice that the `sram[enqueue, …]` instruction has no signals associated with it! Because all of the information needed to perform the enqueue is encoded in the queue-descriptor address, no signal is needed to protect a write-transfer register. Moreover, because queues have no maximum length, no signal is needed to return success or failure of the enqueue operation.

Having no signal on the enqueue command can prove problematic when unloading a queue array entry. Consider an application that enqueues data onto a queue and then decides than the queue-array entry should be unloaded because the application has more queues that queue-array entries. The unload operation cannot be performed until the enqueue command is complete. However, there is no way to guarantee that the enqueue command has completed!

The heart of the problem is that the `sram[enqueue, …]` and `sram[wr_q_desc_addr, …]` operations are not ordered. So the unload operation could occur before the enqueue operation even when the unload operation is issued after the enqueue operation. The result would be an incorrect unloaded queue descriptor.

Three solutions exist: first, never unload the queue descriptor. Of course, this solution only applies to certain applications, and even then, usually is reserved for those queues that must be always available, such as buffer freelists.

Second, always perform a dequeue operation after the enqueue and before unloading the queue-array entry. Dequeue and enqueue commands are ordered. Because the dequeue operation contains a signal and is ordered after the enqueue command, you can be sure that the enqueue command has completed. Of course, it may not always be reasonable to assume a dequeue operation occurs before the queue-array entry needs to be unloaded.

The second solution is to simply wait some amount of time before unloading the queue-array entry. Unfortunately, we don't have any concrete values for how long to wait, however, in Chapter 12 we discuss a general queue manager design that provides a reasonable answer for how long to wait.

Summary

First-in-first-out data structures, whether they are implemented with rings or queues, are critical to packet-processing applications. The IXP2XXX hardware supports both rings and queues by supporting atomic get, put, enqueue, and dequeue commands on these data structures. Rings, which are circular fixed-size FIFOs, can be created and accessed in next-neighbor registers, scratchpad, and SRAM memory. The use of next-neighbor-based rings is covered in Chapter 8. Queues, which are variable-length FIFOs, can be created and accessed in SRAM memory.

Scratchpad rings, of which there can be 16, are useful for situations where only a few rings are necessary, such as from the receive driver and into one or more processing microengines. Scratchpad rings can be created in a variety of sizes ranging from 128 long-words to 1024 long-words.

Each SRAM controller contains a 64-element queue array. These arrays are typically treated as a cache of queue descriptors. Any entry can be 'loaded' or 'unloaded' depending upon the needs of the application. Each queue-array element can be configured to implement either a ring or a queue. When used as a ring, a queue-array element can be configured with ring sizes ranging from 512 long-words up to 64K long-words. When used as a queue, a queue-array element provides atomic access to a linked-list of data. The semantics associated with the enqueue and dequeue operations are controlled by one of three modes, which allow you to choose to treat queue elements with or without segment counts and EOP markers.

Chapter 11

Multithreaded Receive and Transmit Drivers

Now that you have read all about using multiple threads to process packets, let's apply this knowledge to the receive and transmit tasks. In Chapter 5, we developed single-threaded receive and transmit drivers that, while functionally correct, won't likely be as fast as they could be. So, multithreaded versions of receive and transmit drivers represent an excellent example of how to apply the multithreaded programming techniques discussed in previous chapters and boost performance of the sample code. Besides, it just does not seem right to have the other threads of the receive and transmit microengines doing nothing.

Writing multithreaded receive and transmit drivers is also valuable for another reason: it illustrates some of the subtle ordering issues when performing receive and transmit tasks on multiple threads. By covering these tasks in this chapter, we can hopefully eliminate some common logic errors in multithreaded receive and transmit code.

Multithreaded Receive Driver

Chapters 2 and 5 described the process of receiving a packet on the IXP2XXX processor. Recall that the basic challenge is the reassembly of multiple mpackets into one packet. The code in Chapter 5 performs this reassembly but ignores the issues of mpacket and packet ordering, as well as sharing the reassembly state between the threads of the microengine. The single-threaded nature of the code in Chapter 5 guarantees these ordering constraints are met without any explicit ordering constructs and makes state sharing between threads unnecessary. To make a multithreaded receive driver, both issues must be addressed.

Sharing Reassembly State: Absolute Registers

Previous chapters discuss many different forms of intra- and inter-microengine communication mechanisms, including shared memory (local, scratchpad, SRAM, and DRAM), next-neighbor registers, and rings and queues. In all of this discussion, we skipped perhaps the simplest form of intra-microengine communication: absolute registers.

Recall, each thread in a microengine has its own unique slice of the global register set. However, certain instructions allow one thread to access any register in the global set, even those outside of its normal slice. Accessing registers in this way is done through absolute register addressing. Absolute registers do not come from a special reserved pool; instead they take away normal, thread-specific, register space. Regardless, absolute registers represent a relatively efficient form of intra-microengine communication, assuming that the information shared between the threads of a microengine fit in the available absolute registers because their access is (almost) as fast as any register access.

Note | Absolute registers can only be used with a subset of the instructions in the microengine's instruction set. Because of this, it is common when using an absolute register to first have to copy the value of the absolute register into a thread-local register, perform the desired operations on the thread-local register, and then write the value of thread-local register into the absolute register. This overhead is acceptable if the desired operations require many instructions—say five or more—but is probably unacceptable otherwise. In situations where this overhead of accessing absolute registers is unacceptable, consider using local memory. If the information can fit within an absolute register it can probably fit in local memory. However, this solution does assume that the local memory address registers can be setup once, in advance, otherwise the overhead of writing these register may be no better than copying absolute registers into thread-local registers.

Absolute registers represent a good container for the receive reassembly state. The state fits within a modest number of absolute registers (three), and can be accessed directly, and atomically, by any thread. However, if the receive code is handling multiple ports, the size of the reassembly state may grow beyond an acceptable size for absolute registers. In that case, local memory is the next-best choice for storing this information.

Maintaining Mpacket and Packet Ordering

In multithreaded receive code, both mpacket and packet ordering must be considered. Mpacket ordering ensures that the reassembled packet contents are not scrambled. Packet ordering is required for some applications (e.g., Ethernet bridging) and highly desirable in almost all applications, even those that do not require it (e.g., the performance of IP and TCP reassembly operations improves when packet order is maintained).

Conveniently, both mpacket and packet ordering can be maintained with the same inter-thread signaling scheme used in the functional pipelines of Chapter 9. (You'd think we planned it that way.) To illustrate this, Figure 11.1 shows how the multithreaded receive driver uses inter-thread signaling to ensure the order of mpackets is maintained. As shown in Figure 11.1 (a), the RX_THREAD_FREELIST is shown holding all of threads of the receive microengine. These threads are added into the freelist in order using inter-thread signaling.

Threads are 'removed' from the RX_THREAD_FREELIST in FIFO order to service arriving mpackets (Figure 11.1 (b) and (c)). Thus, thread 0 services the first mpacket, thread 1 the second, and so on, through all eight threads in the microengine and then back to thread 0. So, for example, after thread 0 finishes with an mpacket, it adds itself back into the RX_THREAD_FREELIST. Because of the inter-thread signaling, thread 0 always comes after thread 7 (and before thread 1) in the RX_THREAD_ FREELIST as shown in Figure 11.1 (d).

Sounds simple enough, however, adding threads into the RX_THREAD_ FREELIST in order only solves half of the ordering problem. The threads must also maintain ordered access to the shared reassembly state. For example, thread 0 and thread 1 could receive the first and second mpackets, respectively, only to then have thread 1 win the race for access to the shared reassembly state.

How is this possible? Well, the RX_THREAD_FREELIST only ensures that the mpacket assignment is made in order. The thread arbiter on the

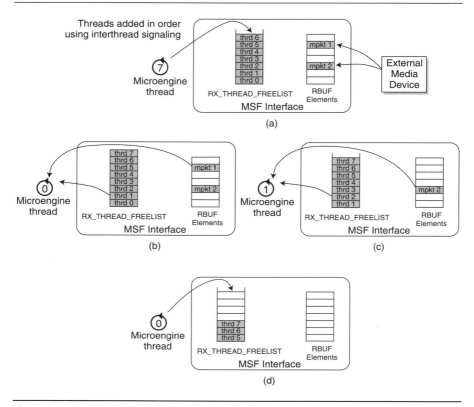

Figure 11.1 Using Inter-thread Signaling to Control Access to the RX_THREAD_ FREELIST, and thus Ensure Mpacket Ordering

microengine determines the order in which threads execute, so it is entirely possible for thread 1 to be granted control of the microengine before thread 0, even if thread 0 has the signal from the MSF available.

Solving this second issue requires another inter-thread signal chain that ensures access to the shared reassembly state happens in order. For those following along closely, we have created a context pipeline stage that internally has two strictly ordered phases, much like the critical sections in ordered thread execution. As shown in Figure 11.2, the first phase controls adding threads into the RX_THREAD_FREELIST, and the second phase controls access to the shared reassembly state. The shaded boxes in the figure represent the changes from the receive flow-chart in Chapter 5.

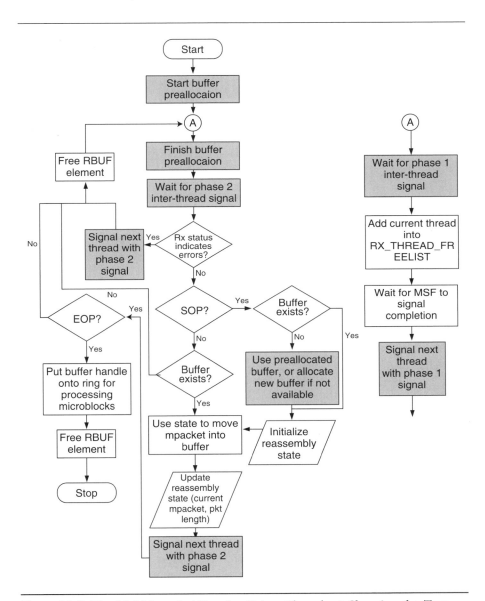

Figure 11.2 The Multithreaded Receive Driver Flowchart, Showing the Two Ordered Phases of Execution

In the flow chart, the first signaling phase is completely contained in the _spi4_rx_get_mpacket routine—the code that accesses the RX_ THREAD_FREELIST. The second phase is within the spi4_rx routine and surrounds the access to the shared reassembly state.

You probably noticed that we snuck in one further optimization. Specifically, the flowchart now shows buffer allocation occurring 'during' the time an mpacket is received. The latency associated with buffer allocation, which is an SRAM dequeue operation, is overlapped with the access to the MSF to receive an mpacket.

The Receive Code

Finally, putting these details into code is the easy part! First, the shared reassembly state and inter-thread signals used to control the two phases of execution are declared globally, as shown in the following microengine-C code.

```
volatile SIGNAL rx_get_mpacket_sig;
volatile SIGNAL rx_read_state_sig;
volatile SIGNAL rx_init_sig;

__declspec(shared) dl_buf_handle_t rx_buffer_handle;
__declspec(shared) unsigned int rx_buffer_length;
__declspec(dram) unsigned char *
            __declspec(shared) rx_cur_mpacket_addr;
```

First, notice that all of the variables are declared shared. The microengine C compiler will attempt to put shared variables into absolute registers and if that fails due to a lack of space, local memory. In this example, the microengine C compiler does indeed place the reassembly state into absolute registers.

Second, the declaration of the rx_cur_mpacket_addr variable may force you to dust off your favorite C book. This declaration reads as follows: rx_cur_mpacket_addr is a shared variable containing a pointer to an unsigned character in DRAM memory. Notice the difference between this, and the following, which is a declaration of a pointer to an unsigned character to a *shared* memory location in DRAM. In this case, each thread in the microengine would have its own copy of this pointer in a GPR, not an absolute register.

```
__declspec(dram shared) unsigned char *rx_cur_mpacket_addr;
```

Now, the modified portion of the _spi4_rx_get_mpacket routine can be explored, and is shown in the following code with a brief explanation of the new inter-thread signaling afterward.

_spi4_rx_get_mpacket()

File: Chapter11\spi4_rx.c

```
227     // Wait for the previous thread to signal that
228     // the fast_wr can occur
229     wait_for_all(&rx_get_mpacket_sig);
230
231     // Signal that the next thread can run. This can
232     // occur before the write because no ctx_arb's
233     // happen in between the instructions
234     signal_same_ME_next_ctx(
235         __signal_number(&rx_get_mpacket_sig));
236
237     msf_fast_write(rx_tfl_addr_and_val);
238     __implicit_write(&rsw);
239     wait_for_all(&rx_complete_sig); // wait for an mpacket
```

Line 229:

In the above code, before the RX_THREAD_FREELIST is written with the current thread's information, the thread waits for the appropriate inter-thread signal.

Lines 234 – 239:

Likewise, 'after' the RX_THREAD_FREEELIST is written, the signal is delivered to the next thread in the microengine. Notice that the signal is actually sent before the msf_fast_write instruction, but because the thread does not release control of the microengine between the two statements, the semantics of ordering are preserved.

Finally, the modified portions of the rx_packet routine are shown in the following code, with a discussion afterward.

spi4_rx()

File: Chapter11\spi4_rx.c

```
347         // Preallocate a buffer, if necessary
348         if (next_buf_handle.value == 0)
349         {
```

Continues

```
350                     Dl_BufAlloc(&temp_buf_handle,
351                             BUF_FREE_LIST0,
352                             BUF_POOL,
353                             &buf_alloc_sig,
354                             SIG_NONE,
355                             ___);
356             }
357
358         // Get the next mpacket
359         rsw = _spi4_rx_get_mpacket();
360
361         // Preallocate a buffer, if necessary
362         if (next_buf_handle.value == 0)
363         {
364             wait_for_all(&buf_alloc_sig);
365             next_buf_handle = temp_buf_handle;
366         }
367
368         // Wait for a signal from the previous thread
369         // and then get the global reassembly state.
370         wait_for_all(&rx_read_state_sig);
371         dlBufHandle = rx_buffer_handle;
372         dlMeta.bufferSize  = rx_buffer_length;
373         cur_mpacket_addr   = rx_cur_mpacket_addr;
374
375         // Check for errors in the packet
376         // These indicate that the current buffer, if
377         // any, should be discarded
378         if (rsw.w1.parts.err)
379         {
380             signal_same_ME_next_ctx(
381                 __signal_number(&rx_read_state_sig));
382             if (dlBufHandle.value != 0)
383             {
384                 // Drop the packet
385                 Dl_BufDrop(dlBufHandle);
386             }
387
388             _spi4_rx_free_rbuf(rsw.w1.parts.element);
389             rx_buffer_handle.value = 0;
390             rx_buffer_length = 0;
391             continue;
392         }
393
394         // If this is the EOP, then send the signal
395         // now (early) so the next SOP mpacket can be
396         // processed immediately
```

Continues

```
397                 if (rsw.w1.parts.eop == 1)
398                 {
399                     signal_same_ME_next_ctx(
400                         __signal_number(&rx_read_state_sig));
401                     rx_buffer_handle.value = 0;
402                     rx_buffer_length = 0;
403                 }
```

Lines 347 – 366:

These lines illustrate the latency-hiding of the buffer allocation. A new per-thread global variable, next_buf_handle, is filled with a new buffer handle with the latency associated with the underlying SRAM dequeue hidden by the rx_get_mpacket routine.

Lines 370 – 373:

The thread waits for the appropriate signal before the shared reassembly state is accessed. After the signal is received, the shared reassembly state is copied into local variables.

Lines 378 – 392:

These lines are an example of how the second phase of processing is completed. Once the code determines how the shared reassembly state should be updated (e.g., by clearing out the state), the next thread is signaled and the shared state is updated. The signal is sent as early as possible while ensuring that the shared state is updated before control of the micro-engine is released.

Lines 397 – 403:

When an EOP mpacket is received, the shared state is immediately updated and the next thread is signaled. This optimization allows the next thread to immediately begin processing the next SOP mpacket. The state information for the current packet is safely stored in the local variables of the current thread (lines 371 – 373).

The rest of the routine proceeds in an analogous fashion. Once the new values for the shared state are known, the inter-thread signal for phase 2 is delivered, and the state is updated. Complete microengine C and microengine assembly versions are available on the accompanying CD-ROM.

Keeping the Pipeline Flowing Using the MSFs Freelist Timeout Mechanism

For applications that use ordered thread execution and that are stimulated by more than just packets (e.g., applications that uses timers or buffer packets), keeping the stages of the pipeline continuously executing is critical. Consider what might happen to such applications if one pipeline stage (e.g., the source stage) stopped indefinitely waiting for a packet from the network. First, all threads would quickly stop executing waiting for a signal that the source stage was complete. Then, if, say, a timer fired or one of the buffered packets was available for servicing, no thread would be able to service the timer or the buffered packet.

These types of applications require some way to continuously "keep the pipeline flowing." On the IXP2XXX processor, one of the simplest ways to keep the pipeline flowing is to keep receiving packets. In the situation where no physical packets are present, the receive driver can fake it and inject bogus packets to ensure the ordered thread execution pipeline continued to execute.

On the IXP2XXX hardware, such bogus packets are easy to create using timers available in the MSF. Each of the RX_THREAD_FREELISTs in the IXP2XXX processor has an associated configurable timer. When configured, the timer for a particular RX_THREAD_FREELIST represents the maximum amount of time the MSF allows the first thread on the freelist to wait before receiving a signal. Thus, if packets are flowing slowly into the system, this timer ensures that the threads of the receive task will still be awoken. When a thread on a RX_THREAD_FREELIST is awoken due to the associated timer, a NULL receive status word is pushed into the appropriate transfer registers of the thread. The thread can check whether this NULL bit is set and, if so, ignore the mpacket and instead inject a bogus packet into the system. Of course, the rest of the system must be implemented to ignore such bogus packets.

The timeout period for each of these timers is configurable, ensuring that you can keep the pipeline flowing at a rate corresponding to the performance requirements of your application. In general, the timeout is configured to a value slightly larger than the maximum packet arrival rate supported by the application (e.g., slighter larger than the minimum-size packet arrival rate). Such a configuration ensures that the pipeline is always executing at its maximum rate, regardless of the packet arrival rate.

Multithreaded Transmit Driver

Just like with the receive code, extending the single-threaded transmit code from Chapter 5 to multiple threads requires maintaining mpacket order and providing shared segmentation state. And just like with the receive code, inter-thread signals are a great mechanism for maintaining mpacket ordering and absolute registers are a good mechanism for sharing the segmentation state.

Figure 11.3 shows the updated transmit flowchart with extensions to ensure mpacket ordering. In an analogous fashion to the receive code,

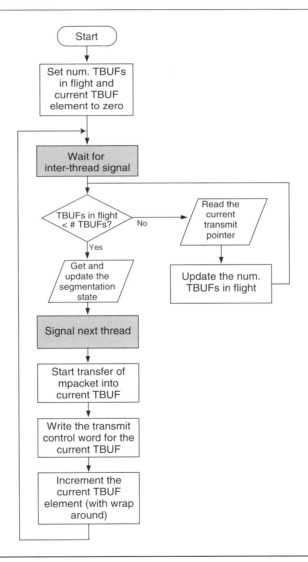

Figure 11.3 The Multithreaded Transmit Flowchart

we add inter-thread signals to protect and order access to the shared segmentation state. This accomplishes the task of maintaining mpacket ordering because the threads segmenting packets into mpackets execute in strict thread order.

We removed an optimization made in the single-threaded code so as to simplify the multithreaded example. We noticed that by removing the second check of the transmit pointer, all of the accesses to shared segmentation state were neatly contained in the first two steps of the transmit algorithm. This makes the critical section (implemented by the inter-thread signals) much smaller, and thus more of the threads can be executing in parallel. The original optimization could certainly be added back into the multithreaded code, but to do so most efficiently, a separate critical section must be created to protect access to the available number of TBUFs. An interesting experiment would be to see whether this optimization is even helpful in the multithreaded example since it represents another critical section for which multiple threads must contend.

The Transmit Code

The following code shows the new declarations of the transmit segmentation state. Like the receive code, a new signal is defined to implement the ordered critical section in the transmit code, and the segmentation state is declared as shared.

Shared Segmentation Stage

```
        File: Chapter11\spi4_tx.c
38      typedef struct s_tx_state
39      {
40          // 1 if the current mpacket is SOP/EOP respectively
41          unsigned int sop, eop;
42          // A pointer to the current mpacket
43          __declspec(dram) unsigned char *cur_mpacket_addr;
44          // Length remaining, in bytes, of the current mpacket
45          unsigned int remaining_length;
46          // The handle of the current buffer
47          dl_buf_handle_t cur_buf_handle;
48      } tx_state_t;
49
50      static __declspec(shared) tx_state_t tx_state;
51
```

Continues

```
52    // . . .
53    //
54    //
55    //
56    __declspec(shared) unsigned int tx_last_tx_seq;
57         // The value of the last read to the
58         // tx_sequence number
59    __declspec(shared) unsigned int tx_tbufs_in_flight;
60         // The number of TBUFs currently being
61         // transmitted. Based on the the last
62         // time the tx sequence number was read
63
64    volatile SIGNAL tx_init_sig;
65    volatile SIGNAL tx_get_state_sig;
```

The main transmit-processing loop is modified, as shown in the following code, to include the inter-thread signals so as to protect access to the shared state. Because all of the shared state is contained in the two routines _spi4_x_get_and_update_state and _spi4_tx_update_tbufs_in_flight, the scope of the inter-thread signals is relatively small.

spi4_tx()

File: Chapter11\spi4_tx.c

```
426    while(1)
427    {
428        // Wait for the signal indicating valid state
429        wait_for_all(&tx_get_state_sig);
430
431        tx_tbufs_in_flight++;
432
433        // Check that the TBUF is available for use
434        while (tx_tbufs_in_flight == NUM_TBUFS)
435        {
436            // We are out of TBUFs, wait for the
437            // sequence number to increase
438            _spi4_tx_update_tbufs_in_flight(
439                (unsigned int *)&tx_tbufs_in_flight,
440                (unsigned int *)&tx_last_tx_seq);
441        }
442
443        // Get the state (next mpacket) for the current
444        // TBUF element.
```

Continues

```
445            cur_state = _spi4_tx_get_and_update_state(
446                               cur_tbuf_elem);
447
448            // Signal the next thread to run.
449            signal_same_ME_next_ctx(
450                __signal_number(&tx_get_state_sig));
451
452            // Move the next portion of the packet into
453            // the next tbuf
454            _spi4_tx_move_dram_to_tbuf(
455                cur_tbuf_elem,
456                cur_state.cur_mpacket_addr,
457                cur_state.remaining_length,
458                &dram_to_tbuf_sig);
```

Lines 429, 449 – 450:

> These lines implement the critical section used to protect the shared trans-
> mit segmentation state. Once the shared state is safely stored into thread-
> local registers (line 445), the next thread is allowed to run while the cur-
> rent thread operates on the local copy (lines 454 – 458).

Finally, the `_spi4_tx_get_and_update_state` and `_spi4_tx_update_`
`tbufs_in_flight` routines are both trivially modified to access the
shared segmentation state. The illustrative lines from the `_spi4_tx_`
`get_and_update_state` routine are shown in the following code.

_spi4_tx_get_and_update_state()

File: Chapter11\spi4_tx.c

```
346        if (tx_state.eop)
347        {
348            while (1)
349            {
350                // Dequeue a packet from the processing task
351                dl_source();
352
353                // Check for an empty queue
354                if (dlBufHandle.value != 0)
355                {
356                    // The queue was not empty
357                    tx_state.sop = 1;
358                    tx_state.cur_buf_handle   = dlBufHandle;
```

Continues

```
359                    tx_state.cur_mpacket_addr =
360                        (__declspec(dram) unsigned char *)
361                        Dl_BufGetData(dlBufHandle);
362                    tx_state.remaining_length =
363                        dlMeta.bufferSize;
364                    break;
365                }
366            }
367        }
368        ret_state.cur_mpacket_addr =
369                        tx_state.cur_mpacket_addr;
370        ret_state.cur_buf_handle   = tx_state.cur_buf_handle;
371        ret_state.sop              = tx_state.sop;
```

Lines 357 – 363:

> Notice that the global shared state is used to store information about a new packet and to retrieve information about a partially transmitted packet in the exact same way GPRs were used in the single-threaded code.

■ Summary

Extending the single-threaded versions of receive and transmit to multi-threaded versions requires attention to two key things: maintaining ordering of both mpackets and packets, and providing shared reassembly and segmentation states between the multiple threads.

Maintaining ordering is easily accomplished with inter-thread signals, in a similar fashion to the ordered thread execution model of Chapter 9. In the receive driver, two different inter-thread signals are used to ensure ordered access the RX_THREAD_FREELIST and the shared reassembly state, respectively. In the transmit driver, a single inter-thread signal is used to ensure ordered access to the shared segmentation state.

Certain instructions allow any thread to access any GPR in the microengine. When a GPR is used in such a manner, it is called an absolute register. State sharing in both the receive and transmit drivers is accomplished with absolute registers. For intra-microengine state sharing that only requires a few long-words of size, such as the reassembly and segmentation states, absolute registers represent a good intra-microengine-communication mechanism. They are fast to access (usually as fast as any register access), and critical sections can be created by simply taking advantage of the non-preemptive thread arbiter.

Chapter **12**

Advanced Programming Topics

This chapter covers some advanced IXP2XXX programming topics. specifically, timers, CRC calculations, queue managers, CSIX interfaces, and the crypto unit.

You can read, or skip, the sections of this chapter as they relate to your needs. The details of this chapter are probably best read as a reference after you discover you need to take advantage of them. The details of the CSIX operations in this chapter assume a familiarity with the receive and transmit operations covered in Chapters 5 and 11.

This chapter covers the following five programming topics:

■ *Programming with microengine timers:* In addition to timestamps (covered in Chapter 8), the IXP2XXX microengines have a per-thread timer, which can be configured to send a signal to the appropriate microengine thread after a configurable amount of time. Timers can be useful in many applications that hold 'soft-state' or have buffering and retransmission requirements.

■ *Using the Cyclical Redundancy Check (CRC) unit on the microengines:* The IXP2XXX microengines contain special instructions, and dedicated hardware, for computing CRC checks on data. For applications that require CRC calculations, such as ATM SAR, using this hardware feature can significantly enhance performance.

- *Accessing the crypto unit on the IXP2850:* As explained in Chapter 2, the IXP2850 contains two cryptographic units that can encrypt and decrypt data using AES and 3DES algorithms, and compute SHA-1 message digests and HMAC-SHA1 authentication codes. This unit is useful for applications, such as VPNs and security offload.

- *Receiving and transmitting frames over a CSIX interface:* CSIX is a standard interface for sending cells to, and receiving cells from, a switch fabric. All IXP2XXX processors can receive or transmit packets from a CSIX interface, and while the code for doing this is similar to the SPHY4 receive and transmit code of Chapters 5 and 11, CSIX receive and transmit presents a few new challenges.

- *The Queue Manager Design for the SRAM queue array:* Thus far, our example applications have limited the number of SRAM queues used to fewer than 64, the size of one SRAM controller's queue array. However, IXP2XXX designs are not limited to fewer than 64 SRAM queues. Instead, the SRAM queue array should be thought of as a cache for queue descriptors. One good design of code to manage this cache is captured in the Queue Manager driver supplied with the IXA SDK 3.0.

Timers

Some data-plane packet-processing applications require events to occur at well-defined time intervals. For example, a device routing IP packets over Ethernet must execute the Address Resolution Protocol (ARP) to determine the Ethernet media access control (MAC) address of the next-hop device. ARP requests are transmitted at a particular maximum rate and if no ARP response is seen within a certain amount of time, an Internet Control Message Protocol (ICMP) packet is generated to indicate an error. Additionally, buffering and reordering, and many quality-of-service functions (e.g., metering and scheduling) involve timers.

To better support such applications, each microengine thread on the IXP2XXX processor contains two timer registers as follows:

- *Future count:* Each thread's future-count register contains a 16-bit value indicating when the timer expires. When the least significant 16-bits of the TIMESTAMP_LOW microengine CSR match the value in this register, the signal number in the associated *future-count-signal* register is sent to the thread.

Writing to this CSR enables the timer. After the timer 'fires' (i.e., the future count signal is sent), the timer is automatically disabled by the hardware. Thus, periodic timers are constructed by re-writing this register every time a timer expires.

■ *Future-count signal:* Each future-count-signal register contains a signal number to send to the thread when the future-count value matches the value of the TIMESTAMP_LOW CSR.

The actual coding of timers is simple and fast since all accesses are to microengine-local CSRs. In the following example, the current thread initializes its timer and then waits for it.

timer main()

File: Chapter12\timers.uc

```
37        .if (ctx() == 0)
38            // Setup the signal to send when
39            // the timer expires
40            immed[tmp, &timer_sig]
41            local_csr_wr[ACTIVE_FUTURE_COUNT_SIGNAL,
42                        tmp]
43            .set_sig timer_sig
44
45            // Read the current time
46            local_csr_rd[TIMESTAMP_LOW]
47            immed[timestamp, 0]
48            add(timestamp, timestamp, 200)
49            alu_op(timestamp, timestamp, AND, 0xffff)
50            local_csr_wr[ACTIVE_CTX_FUTURE_COUNT,
51                        timestamp]
52
53            // Wait for the signal
54            ctx_arb[timer_sig]
55
56            // Read the current time
57            local_csr_rd[TIMESTAMP_LOW]
58            immed[new_timestamp, 0]
59
60            // Can now inspect timestamp and
61            // new_timestamp
```

Lines 40 – 43:

Before setting and enabling the timer, the future-count-signal register must be written with the signal number to send when the timer fires. The future-count-signal register for the currently executing thread can be accessed using the ACTIVE_FUTURE_COUNT_SIGNAL mnemonic, and in this example, is written with the signal number for timer_sig.

Lines 46 – 51:

These lines first read the current timestamp and then set and enable the current thread's timer for 200 'ticks' in the future. Recall each tick represents 16 clock cycles. The currently executing thread's future-count register is accessed with the ACTIVE_CTX_FUTURE_COUNT mnemonic.

Only the least significant 16 bits of the timestamp are used for comparison to the future count register, so the code masks off all but the least significant 16 bits from the timestamp.

The previous example illustrated how a thread could establish a timer for itself. Additionally, one thread can set and enable a timer for another thread on the same microengine. The basic steps involved are identical to those of the previous example except the future-count signal and future-count registers are accessed indirectly, as shown in the following code.

Using Indirect-Context Future-Count Registers

File: Chapter12\timers.uc

```
63          .elif (ctx() == 1)
64              // One thread can also write the
65              // timer count for another thread
66              immed32(tmp, 2)
67              local_csr_wr[CSR_CTX_POINTER, tmp]
68
69              immed[tmp, &timer_sig]
70              local_csr_wr[INDIRECT_FUTURE_COUNT_SIGNAL,
71                              tmp]
72
73              // Read the current time
74              local_csr_rd[TIMESTAMP_LOW]
75              immed[timestamp, 0]
76              add(timestamp, timestamp, 200)
77              alu_op(timestamp, timestamp, AND, 0xffff)
78              local_csr_wr[INDIRECT_CTX_FUTURE_COUNT,
79                              timestamp]
80
81          .elif (ctx() == 2)
82              // Wait for the signal
83              .set_sig timer_sig
84              ctx_arb[timer_sig]
85          .endif
```

Lines 63 – 79:

In these lines, thread number 1 writes both the future-count signal and future-count registers for thread number 2. To access another thread's CSRs, first the CSR_CTX_POINTER CSR is written with the thread number to access. Once the CSR_CTX_POINTER CSR is written, the future-count signal and future-count CSRs are setup as in the previous example with one difference: the mnemonic to access the CSRs is prefixed with INDIRECT instead of ACTIVE. The INDIRECT prefix instructs the hardware to use the CSR_CTX_POINTER CSR value to access the associated CSR.

Lines 81 – 85:

In these lines of code, thread number 2 waits for the timer signal established by thread number 1. In this manner then, one thread can set and enable a timer for another thread on the same microengine.

Perhaps a better design would have thread number 2, in this example, write the future-count-signal register and have thread number 1 only set and enable the future-count register. In this approach, the thread setting and enabling the timer does not need knowledge of the signal number the receiving thread is using.

The CRC Unit

In Chapter 6 you saw how the CRC unit can be used to perform hashes as part of a hash-table lookup algorithm. In this chapter, you'll see how the CRC unit can be used to verify data in packets encapsulated in some protocols. Many applications require CRC calculations to be performed to validate the incoming data. Typically, incoming packets contain a CRC value that must be recomputed and verified to ensure no corruption has occurred, and outgoing packets must have a new CRC calculated and appended to the packet data so that the process can begin again at the next network device.

Unlike the relatively simple checksums commonly employed in IP packets, CRCs can be complicated to compute. Computing a CRC requires calculating the remainder resulting from the division of the input data by a *generator* value. Different generator values are used to define different types of CRCs. This remainder, which is the CRC value, has the property that different input data very likely produces different CRC values, thus any corruption in input data results in a change in the CRC value.

To alleviate the need to implement the complicated CRC calculations in the microengine software, each IXP2XXX microengine contains a CRC unit and instructions for accessing this unit to calculate CRCs over an arbitrary length of data. Each CRC unit can calculate one of two different CRC types: CRC-CCITT and CRC-32. CRC-CCITT generates a 16-bit remainder and is found in applications such as wireless networks and disk drives. CRC-32 generates a 32-bit remainder and is found in applications, such as Ethernet and ATM AAL5.

The CRC unit on each microengine maintains a running remainder in a microengine local CSR. On any instruction, the CRC unit can be provided one long-word of data from a GPR, transfer register, or local memory, and using the current remainder, the unit updates the remainder CSR. The microengines can also read and write the remainder CSR at any time for both verification and initialization purposes. So, the basic steps in calculating a CRC are as follows:

1. Initialize the remainder by writing the microengine-local CSR.

2. For each long-word in the input data, run the CRC calculation, updating the CRC remainder.

3. Read the remainder and verify the CRC associated with the input data matches the remainder, or update the outgoing CRC associated with the input data.

Note

Just like with the T_INDEX register, each microengine contains only one CRC-remainder CSR. Thus, if multiple threads are computing CRCs, the CRC remainder must be managed carefully to avoid one thread corrupting the CRC of another thread. Typically the CRC-remainder CSR must be saved and restored into either a thread-local GPR or local memory every time a thread releases control of the microengine. If you know the other threads are not accessing the CRC unit, for example in a context pipeline stage, this extra save-and-restore is not necessary.

Also, you cannot have back-to-back CRC accumulate instructions on the IXP2XXX processor. So, something to consider when writing a loop to calculate a CRC over a range of data is what other operations you can intersperse between consecutive CRC accumulate instructions.

As an example of using the CRC unit, we extended the Chapter 5 receive code to compute a CRC-32 over each incoming packet. The value is then compared to the last four bytes of the packet itself, which is presumed to be a CRC-32. If the CRC results match, the packet is accepted (i.e., a counter is incremented), otherwise the packet is dropped (i.e., a second counter is incremented).

To test the code, we inject several different Ethernet frames which, by definition, contain a CRC-32 as the last field in the frame. It should be noted that normally the Ethernet MAC hardware would verify this CRC and this calculation would not be necessary in software. Nevertheless, by using Ethernet in this example, we can focus on the CRC calculation and not some additional application details.

First, as shown in the following code, the CRC remainder register is initialized to 0xFFFFFFFF at the beginning of each packet.

spi4_crc_rx()

```
        File: Chapter12\spi4_crc_rx.uc
464                     // Initialize the CRC remainder
465                     .begin
466                         .reg init
467                         immed32(init, 0xffffffff)
468                         local_csr_wr[crc_remainder,
469                                          init]
470                     .end
```

Lines 467 – 469:

The initial value of 0xFFFFFFFF, which is established by Ethernet standards, is written in the CRC_REMAINDER microengine-local CSR using the now-familiar `local_csr_wr` instruction.

Reading the final CRC value is just the reverse process as shown in the following code.

spi4_crc_dl()

```
        File: Chapter12\dispatch_loop\spi4_rx_dl.uc
71                      // Read the resulting CRC remainder
72                      local_csr_rd[crc_remainder]
73                      immed[remainder, 0]
74
75                      // Make sure the remainder is zero
76                      .if (remainder == 0)
77                          // Do normal packet processing,
```

Continues

```
78                              // Here we simply count
79                              // the packet
80                              scratch[incr, --, good_crc_addr, 0]
81                          .else
82                              scratch[incr, --, bad_crc_addr, 0]
83                          .endif
```

Line 76:

In these lines, the same CSR as above is read and checked against zero. Later we show code that adds the logical compliment of the frame's CRC into the CRC calculation itself. The result is that the final remainder is zero only if the two CRCs match.

Finally, the following code is executed for each incoming mpacket and updates the CRC.

_spi4_rx_update_crc()

```
      File: Chapter12\spi4_crc_rx.uc
255   #macro _spi4_crc_rx_update_crc(\
256                        in_rbuf_elem, \
257                        in_size,\
258                        in_eop)
259   .begin
260       .reg rbuf_addr bytes_remaining bytes_to_compare
261       .sig rbuf_read_sig
262
263       move(bytes_remaining, in_size)
264
265       // Compute the RBUF address.
266       immed32(rbuf_addr, MSF_RBUF_BASE_ADDR)
267       alu_shf_left(rbuf_addr, rbuf_addr, +,
268                    in_rbuf_elem, 6)
269
270       xbuf_alloc($$data, 16, read)
271
272   again#:
273       // Read in the RBUF element information
274       // (up to 64 bytes)
275       msf[read64, $$data[0], rbuf_addr, 0, 8],
276           ctx_swap[rbuf_read_sig]
277
278       // Set up the T_INDEX register to cycle
279       // through the data
```

Continues

```
280        .begin
281            .reg t_idx_addr
282            immed[t_idx_addr, &$$data[0]]
283            local_csr_wr[T_INDEX, t_idx_addr]
284        .end
285
286        // Typically would also restore the CRC
287        // remainder, but because this is
288        // single-threaded code, the remainder
289        // is valid
290
291        // Establish the number of bytes to
292        // compare
293        move(bytes_to_compare, bytes_remaining)
294        .if (bytes_remaining > 64)
295            immed32(bytes_to_compare, 64)
296        .elif (in_eop && (bytes_to_compare > 3))
297            sub(bytes_to_compare,
298                bytes_remaining, 4)
299        .endif
300
301        // Add the bytes to the CRC.
302        .while (bytes_to_compare > 3)
303            crc_be[crc_32, --, *$$index++], bit_swap
304            sub(bytes_to_compare,
305                bytes_to_compare, 4)
306        .endw
307
308        // Check if more information is available
309        .if (bytes_remaining > 64)
310            sub(bytes_remaining,
311                bytes_remaining,
312                64)
313            add(rbuf_addr,
314                rbuf_addr, 64)
315            br[again#]
316        .endif
317
318        // If this is the end of the packet, read
319        // the CRC off the end, invert it and add
320        // it to the CRC. The result should be a
321        // zero remainder.
322        .if (in_eop)
323        .begin
324            .reg tmp crc
325            immed32(tmp, 0xffffffff)
326
```

Continues

```
327              // It may be that the last 4 bytes are not
328              // aligned. This code almost, but not
329              // entirely, deals with that situation.
330              // This code breaks when the trailing CRC
331              // is not contained within the mpacket.
332              // Extra state would be necessary to
333              // remedy this deficiency.
334              move(crc, *$$index)
335              local_csr_wr[byte_index, bytes_to_compare]
336              nop
337              nop
338              nop
339              .if (bytes_to_compare == 1)
340                  crc_be[crc_32, --, *$$index],
341                      bit_swap, byte_0
342                  byte_align_be[--, *$$index++]
343                  byte_align_be[crc, *$$index]
344              .elif (bytes_to_compare == 2)
345                  crc_be[crc_32, --, *$$index],
346                      bit_swap, bytes_0_1
347                  byte_align_be[--, *$$index++]
348                  byte_align_be[crc, *$$index]
349              .elif (bytes_to_compare == 3)
350                  crc_be[crc_32, --, *$$index],
351                      bit_swap, bytes_0_2
352                  byte_align_be[--, *$$index++]
353                  byte_align_be[crc, *$$index]
354              .endif
355              alu[tmp, tmp, XOR, crc]
356              crc_be[crc_32, --, tmp], bit_swap
357          .end
358      .endif
359
360      xbuf_free($$data)
361  .end
362  #endm
```

Lines 263 – 276:

These lines pull up to 64 bytes of the current mpacket from the RBUF into DRAM transfer registers. The address of the RBUF is calculated as it was in Chapter 5.

In addition, the size of the mpacket is saved into the bytes_remaining register. This register is used to deal with the fact that a single mpacket may be larger than the 64 bytes available in DRAM transfer registers.

Lines 280 – 284:

Once the mpacket data is in the DRAM transfer registers, the T_INDEX register is set to point to the first of these transfer registers. This allows subsequent code to cycle through all of the transfer registers adding their value into the CRC remainder calculation.

At this point if we were running multi-threaded code, we would also need to restore the value of the CRC remainder register based on some per-port reassembly state. Because we have used the single-threaded receive code from Chapter 5, this is unnecessary.

Lines 293 – 299:

These lines compute the number of bytes in the mpacket, accounting for the cases where we are limited by the size of the transfer registers and, in the case of an EOP mpacket, the fact that we want to treat the last four bytes of the payload as the CRC to compare with.

You might have noticed that this is one problem with this code. Namely, it does not correctly handle the situation where the Ethernet CRC spans two mpackets. To deal with this, the code would need additional reassembly state information to buffer the last four bytes of the previous mpacket. These previous bytes would be used to properly construct the Ethernet CRC. In our example, we use the bug in the code to show how the CRC calculation can produce a non-zero remainder. In particular, we inject one out of every seven packets with a packet length such that the Ethernet CRC spans two mpackets.

Lines 302 – 306:

These lines update the CRC remainder by incrementally 'feeding' each long-word of the packet into the CRC unit. Several items of interest are:

■ First, the instruction mnemonic, crc_be, calculates the CRC assuming the byte ordering of the long-word is in big-endian format. A similar mnemonic, crc_le, is also available for little-endian byte ordering.

■ Second, the CRC instruction can swap the order in which the bits of each byte are fed into the CRC calculation. The optional token bit_swap performs this transformation. In this case, the Ethernet specification requires the bit ordering within each byte to be fed into the CRC calculation in reverse order, so we use the bit_swap option here.

Lines 309 – 316:

> These lines of code handle the situation where the size of the mpacket was larger than the size of the DRAM transfer registers. The code simply updates the RBUF element address and repeats all of the steps described above.

Lines 322 – 357:

> The final step of the CRC verification is to extract the Ethernet CRC from the frame, logically invert it, and add it into the CRC calculation. The end result is that if the calculated CRC remainder equals the Ethernet CRC, the result is a zero remainder.
>
> The main difficulty in extracting the CRC is dealing with the byte alignment. That is, the CRC may be spread across two different transfer registers. To deal with this, the byte_align instruction comes in handy. We first set up the byte align size using the byte offset of the CRC in the last two transfer registers (line 345), then, depending on this same offset, we add any final bytes of payload into the CRC calculation and extract the CRC (lines 349 – 364).
>
> Notice in these lines we take advantage of another optional token of the CRC instruction: bytes_X_Y. These optional tokens allow you to specify which bytes within the long-word should be fed into the CRC unit.

The Crypto Unit

The IXP2850 processor contains two identical crypto units specifically designed for security-related applications. Chapter 2 contains a description of the IXP2850[1] crypto-unit hardware. Each unit can offload the work associated with symmetric-key encryption and decryption as well as calculating message digests, message authentication checks (MACs), and checksums. For applications requiring bulk ciphers, such as VPN gateways and SSL accelerators, the crypto unit can perform the bulk of the packet transformations at high speeds, freeing up the microengines to perform other packet-processing tasks.

Because a complete VPN or IPsec implementation could fill an entire book, in this section we show a contrived example of using a crypto unit to encrypt some plain text and then decrypt the resulting cipher

---

[1] Since you probably read Chapter 2 quite a while ago, feel free to peek back at Figure 2.11 if you can't remember the components and basic flow of operations in the crypto-unit.

text to restore the original plain text. This may not expose all of the issues involved with building a complete security offload application, but it will at least make you more familiar with the crypto hardware.

The flow of the example application is illustrated in Figure 12.1. A single microengine uses both crypto units: one for encrypting data and the other for decrypting data. We chose to use both crypto units for illustration purposes; each crypto unit can perform both encryption and decryption.

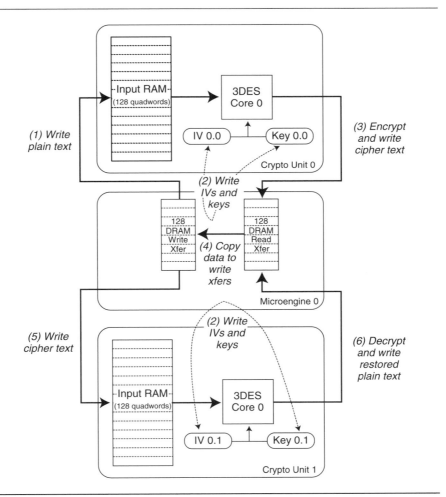

Figure 12.1 Crypto Example Application Data Flow

The steps shown in Figure 12.1 are:

1. Write the plain (unencrypted) text from DRAM write transfer registers into the input RAM of crypto unit 0. Recall from Chapter 2 that each crypto unit has an input RAM where data to be encrypted and decrypted can be written. In addition, input RAM can be used to load other crypto states including keys and initialization vectors.

2. Write the initialization vector (IV) and key into both crypto units. These writes occur directly from DRAM transfer registers into the associated crypto state. However, we could have first written the IV and key into the input RAMs of each crypto unit and then requested a write of the crypto state from these values in input RAM.

3. Encrypt the plain text. This step instructs crypto unit 0 to write the resulting cipher text into DRAM read transfer registers on the microengine.

4. Copy the cipher text into DRAM write transfer registers. Before we can write the cipher text into the input RAM of crypto unit 1, we have to move the data into write transfer registers. And, for the record, we remembered this step even during our first pass at this code.

5. Write the cipher text from DRAM transfer registers into the input RAM of crypto unit 1.

6. Decrypt the cipher text. Like we did in step 3, the resulting (new) plain text is written into DRAM read transfer registers, which we can compare to the original plain text to make sure everything worked properly.

Before we show you the code, keep in mind the following notes when you are programming the crypto unit:

■ The crypto unit is accessed with a single instruction of the following format:

```
crypto[command, xfer, src_op1, src_op2, ref_cnt], opt_tok
```

Depending on the source address (i.e., src_op1 + src_op2) and command (e.g., read, write, etc.), a different action is taken. The source address is a bit field containing, among other things, an encoding of the crypto unit (i.e., 0 or 1), the input RAM address, the *algorithm* (e.g., AES, 3DES, SHA-1), the *bank* (e.g., 3DES block 0 or 3DES block 1), and the state (e.g., IV0.1 or Key0.1, etc.) to use.

■ The crypto unit always deals in units of quad-words. Both addresses and sizes are specified in quad-words. Most instructions can be indirectly overridden to extract individual bytes, but by default everything is specified in quad-words

The easiest way to access the crypto unit is through a set of macros provided with the IXA SDK 3.0. These macros, such as `crypto_write_ram` and `crypto_load_iv`, properly format the command's source address to perform the desired action.

Step1: Writing the Plain Text into Input RAM

The first step in the example involves writing the plain text into input RAM of the first crypto unit, as shown in the following code example.

---

crypto_example() Step 1

```
        File: Chapter12\crypto_example.uc
35    // First, write the plain text into crypto input RAM
36    xbuf_alloc($$orig_plain_text, 16, write)
37
38    // Some contrived plain text
39    immed32($$orig_plain_text[0], 0x00010203)
40    immed32($$orig_plain_text[1], 0x04050607)
41    immed32($$orig_plain_text[2], 0x08090a0b)
42    immed32($$orig_plain_text[3], 0x0c0d0e0f)
43    immed32($$orig_plain_text[4], 0x10111213)
44    immed32($$orig_plain_text[5], 0x14151617)
45    immed32($$orig_plain_text[6], 0x18191a1b)
46    immed32($$orig_plain_text[7], 0x1c1d1e1f)
47    immed32($$orig_plain_text[8], 0x20212223)
48    immed32($$orig_plain_text[9], 0x24252627)
49    immed32($$orig_plain_text[10], 0x28292a2b)
50    immed32($$orig_plain_text[11], 0x2c2d2e2f)
51    immed32($$orig_plain_text[12], 0x30313233)
52    immed32($$orig_plain_text[13], 0x34353637)
53    immed32($$orig_plain_text[14], 0x38393a3b)
54    immed32($$orig_plain_text[15], 0x3c3d3e3f)
55
56    // Perform and wait for the write
57    crypto_write_ram(
58        $$orig_plain_text[0],
```

Continues

```
59        DATA_RAM_ADDR,
60        8,
61        ENCRYPT_UNIT,
62        ram_sig)
63   ctx_arb[ram_sig]
```

Lines 57 – 63:

These lines invoke a macro, `crypto_write_ram`, supplied with IXA SDK 3.0 that writes some data into input RAM of a crypto unit. This macro properly formats the source address to perform a write of input RAM, at the given address and on the given crypto unit. In this case, the code is writing input RAM with data contained in transfer registers. However, input RAM can also be written with data from the MSF's RBUF memory.

Step 2: Write IVs and Keys

The next step in the example is to write the IV and key (both contrived) into both crypto units. The following example shows how this is performed for crypto unit 0. Analogous code for writing in crypto unit 1 is available on the supplied CD-ROM.

crypto_example() Step 2

```
     File: Chapter12\crypto_example.uc
67   // Create a key and initialization vector.
68   // 3DES uses a 64-bit IV and a 192-bit
69   // key (with every 8-th bit ignored)
70   xbuf_alloc($$iv, 2, write)
71   xbuf_alloc($$key, 6, write)
72
73   // Some contrived IV data
74   immed32($$iv[0], 0x42424242)
75   immed32($$iv[1], 0x42424242)
76   crypto_load_iv(
77        $$iv[0],
78        1,
79        ENCRYPT_UNIT,
80        CRYPTO_BANK,
81        ENCRYPT_STATE,
82        iv_sig)
83
84   // Some contrived key
85   immed32($$key[0], 0xa55aa55a)
86   immed32($$key[1], 0x12345678)
```

Continues

```
87      immed32($$key[2], 0xa55aa55a)
88      immed32($$key[3], 0x12345678)
89      immed32($$key[4], 0xdeadbeef)
90      immed32($$key[5], 0xcafebabe)
91      crypto_load_key(
92          $$key[0],
93          3,
94          ENCRYPT_UNIT,
95          CRYPTO_BANK,
96          ENCRYPT_STATE,
97          key_sig)
98
99      // Wait for both the key and IV to
100     // be written
101     ctx_arb[iv_sig, key_sig]
```

Lines 74 – 82:

> In these lines, the initialization vector (which we made up) is first written into DRAM write transfer registers and from there into the IV registers of the crypto hardware. The `crypto_load_iv` macro properly formats the operands for the underlying `crypto[...]` instruction.

Lines 85 – 97:

> In a manner similar to writing the initialization vector, we first load the key into DRAM transfer registers and then let the `crypto_load_key` macro write this value into the crypto unit hardware.

Line 101:

> Finally, the code waits for both the IV and key to be taken from the DRAM write transfer registers before proceeding.

Step 3: Encrypt the Data

Encrypting the data is now extremely simple, as shown in the following code.

crypto_example() Step 3

```
        File: Chapter12\crypto_example.uc
125     // Now encrypt the data and write the results
126     // into transfer registers
127     xbuf_alloc($$encrypt_data, 16, read_write)
128
```

Continues

```
129   crypto_cipher(
130       $$encrypt_data[0],
131       DATA_RAM_ADDR,
132       8,
133       CRYPTO_CIPHER_ENCRYPT,
134       CRYPTO_CIPHER_NO_CBC,
135       CRYPTO_CIPHER_3DES,
136       ENCRYPT_UNIT,
137       CRYPTO_BANK,
138       ENCRYPT_STATE,
139       cipher_sig)
140   ctx_arb[cipher_sig]
```

Lines 129 – 140:

This macro call instructs crypto unit 0 to use 3DES along with the IV and key written previously to encrypt the data in input RAM. The resulting cipher text is written into transfer registers on the microengine, but could have also been written directly into TBUF memory.

The code waits for the transfer registers to be updated with cipher-text before proceeding.

Steps 4 and 5: Write the Cipher Text into Input RAM

In a manner identical to step 1, the next steps take the cipher text (in transfer registers) and write it into the input RAM of crypto unit 1. We could have just as well used crypto unit 0 for this step. The only trick is the copy from read-transfer registers into write-transfer registers; something you should certainly be used to by now.

crypto_example() Steps 4 and 5

> File: Chapter12\crypto_example.uc

```
143   // Write the encrypted data into input RAM
144   // Here we overwrite the plain text for
145   // convenience
146   #define_eval IDX 0
147   #while (IDX < 16)
148       move($$encrypt_data[IDX], $$encrypt_data[IDX])
149   #define_eval IDX (IDX+1)
150   #endloop
151
```

Continues

```
152     crypto_write_ram(
153         $$encrypt_data[0],
154         DATA_RAM_ADDR,
155         8,
156         DECRYPT_UNIT,
157         ram_sig)
158     ctx_arb[ram_sig]
```

Lines 146 – 150:

> In these lines we use the preprocessor to do the work of copying all sixteen transfer registers. The resulting code is no different than that tried-and-true, cut-and-paste approach, but this code might impress your coworkers more.

Step 5: Decrypting the Data

Finally, we decrypt the data as shown in the following code.

crypto_example() Step 6

File: Chapter12\crypto_example.uc

```
162     // Now decrypt the encrypted data to restore
163     // the plain text. The resulting plain text
164     // is written into transfer registers
165     xbuf_alloc($$new_plain_text, 16, read)
166     crypto_cipher(
167         $$new_plain_text[0],
168         DATA_RAM_ADDR,
169         8,
170         CRYPTO_CIPHER_DECRYPT,
171         CRYPTO_CIPHER_NO_CBC,
172         CRYPTO_CIPHER_3DES,
173         DECRYPT_UNIT,
174         CRYPTO_BANK,
175         DECRYPT_STATE,
176         cipher_sig)
177     ctx_arb[cipher_sig]
```

Lines 166 – 177:

> Decrypting the data is identical to encrypting except the command requested is CRYPTO_CIPHER_DECRYPT as opposed to CRYPTO_CIPHER_ENCRYPT. So, if you've properly setup the IVs and keys, the resulting data, which is placed in transfer registers, will match the original plain text!

The CSIX Interface

The Common Switch Interface (CSIX) defines a physical and logical standard for transferring information, called CFrames, between two devices, typically a network processor[2] and a switch fabric. For example, in Figure 12.2(a), a group of network processors are connected to a

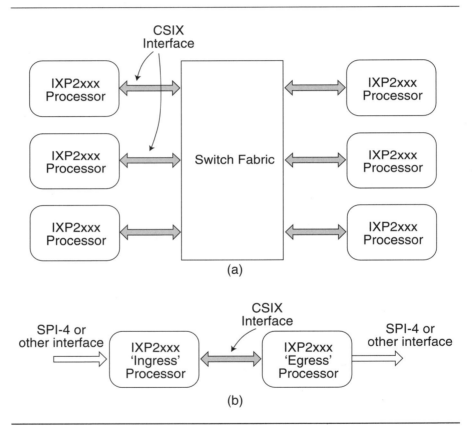

Figure 12.2 Example CSIX Usage Topologies

---

[2] The CSIX-L1 specification refers to traffic managers as opposed to network processors, but the distinction is irrelevant. CSIX is the interface and any two devices can use the interface to transfer information.

central switch fabric through a set of CSIX interfaces. Such a topology might be found in a multi-blade chassis, where each network processor resides on a blade and the switch fabric represents the backplane connecting the blades. Each of the network processors can address CFrames to any other network processor.

Figure 12.2(b) shows another example, where two network processors are directly connected through a CSIX interface. Such a topology might be found in a single-blade design where one network processor performs 'ingress processing' and the other performs 'egress processing'. In this section, we build code for exactly this second example. Our code receives packets from a SPHY-4 device on one IXP2800 processor and transmits these packets via a CSIX interface to another IXP2800 processor, which, in turn, transmits the packets out a second SPHY-4 interface. To accomplish this, we need to understand how to transmit and receive CFrames on the IXP2XXX processor, but first, let's cover the definition of a CFrame.

Flow Control and Multiple Ports

By not implementing CSIX receive and transmit code for Figure 12.2(a), we are ignoring two critical issues in our CSIX implementation: flow control and retrieving receive context state. Solutions to both of these issues can be found in the CSIX receive and transmit drivers on the Intel IXA SDK 3.0, but we discuss them briefly here so that you are aware of these complications.

The CSIX interface defines a mechanism for exchanging flow control information from the receiving entity to the transmitting entity. Roughly speaking, the receiver of data can request the transmitter to stop sending data if the receiver becomes congested. On the IXP2XXX processor, such flow control information can be both transmitted and received via the CSIX interface and a special side-band bus called the C-Bus. CSIX receive and transmit drivers should use, and honor, these mechanisms. In particular, the receive driver needs to read flow control requests and stop sending data to any recipient that requests it. This requirement can complicate the design and implementation of a transmit driver as the code must maintain state about which recipients are able to receive data.

In addition, when receiving from, or transmitting to, more than one port, the receive and transmit drivers must be able to retrieve multiple instances of state. For a small number of ports, the solution is simply to use an array of reassembly state in local memory. However, for a large number of ports, such as the four thousand supported by CSIX, local memory is not an option. In such designs, SRAM or scratchpad memory can be used to hold the reassembly and segmentation state, but at the cost of larger access latencies. To minimize the effects of these access latencies, caching recently-used state in local memory (i.e., through "folding") can help boost the performance of the drivers.

CFrames

All information transmitted across a CSIX interface is encapsulated in CFrames. A CFrame is a variable-sized packet where the maximum size is defined by the switch fabric vendor. The CSIX standard allows for CFrames up to 256 bytes, however the IXP2XXX processor restricts the maximum size of a CFrame to 128 bytes.

Figure 12.3 shows the format of a CFrame. A CFrame consists of a base header, an (optional) extension header, a payload, and a vertical parity trailer. The base header contains flow control information, the type of the Cframe, and the length of the payload. The contents of the extension header, when present, depend on the type of CFrame. For example, the extension header for a unicast CFrame contains traffic class and destination address fields, whereas the extension header for a broadcast CFrame contains only a traffic class field. The payload contains a variable amount of data between the two communicating endpoints, and the vertical parity trailer allows the endpoints to verify the integrity of the CFrame.

For more information on CSIX and CFrames, including details on flow control, read the official CSIX-L1 standard (CSIX 2000).

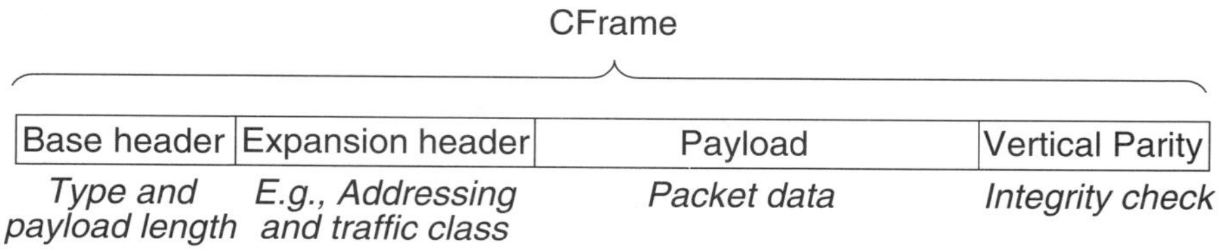

Base header	Expansion header	Payload	Vertical Parity
Type and payload length	E.g., Addressing and traffic class	Packet data	Integrity check

Figure 12.3 The Format of a CFrame

The Need for a CSIX-L2 Header

Nowhere in a CFrame are fields for segmentation and reassembly. You might be wondering, then, whether or not you can pass a packet larger than 128-bytes across a CSIX interface. Indeed, in our example we do just that since the code receives large packets from a SPHY-4 interface and then transmits these packets across a CSIX interface.

The answer is you can, but you need another header to hold the segmentation and reassembly information. Such a header is referred to as the CSIX-L2, or traffic manager (TM), header. Unfortunately, at the time of writing this book, the NPF has yet to publicly release a specification for such a header. So, we are forced to make up our own header.

Figure 12.4 shows the simple header we add to the beginning of every CFrame payload to enable reassembly of larger packets. The header contains SOP and EOP bits to mark the start and end of a packet, respectively. The header also contains a 6-bit source identifier. This source identifier could be used by the reassembly routine to correlate incoming CFrames from the same packet. Because all of the examples in this book have dealt with only a single port, such a field is not used in our examples, but is necessary in general (see the sidebar "Flow Control and Multiple Ports").

Following the SOP, EOP, and source ID fields, our CSIX-L2 header has seven empty bytes. These bytes add extra overhead to the switch fabric, but make the reassembly process more efficient on the IXP2XXX processor receiving the CFrames. These extra bytes ensure the data being reassembled is aligned on a quad-word boundary and thus is efficiently

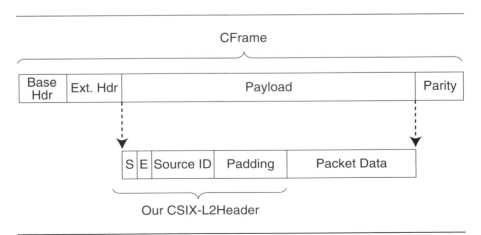

Figure 12.4 Our CSIX-L2 Header

transferred between RBUF and DRAM memory. As for the extra band-width consumed, some designs use these extra bytes to store metadata about the packet, such as flow treatment identifiers and destination port and host information, so you may be able to use these extra bytes anyway.

CSIX Transmit

The code to transmit CFrames on the IXP2XXX processor differs from the SPHY-4 transmit code in Chapters 5 and 11 in three ways:

- The TBUF element size must be as large as the maximum CFrame transmitted. Thus, we must use a TBUF element size of 128 bytes.

- The segmentation process now includes a new step to insert our CSIX-L2 header into the TBUF.

- The TBUF control word must be formatted to match the requirements of the CSIX interface.

Changing the TBUF element size from 64-bytes to 128-bytes is easily accomplished by setting the appropriate bits in the MSF_TX_CONTROL_VAL CSR.

Updating the segmentation process is only a bit more involved in that the code to transfer packet data from DRAM into TBUFs must make room for the CSIX L2 header. Additionally, the CSIX-L2 header must be inserted into the TBUF element in front of the packet data, which is illustrated in the following code segment.

_csix_tx_write_l2a_header()

```
        File: Chapter12\csix_tx.uc
221  #macro _csix_tx_write_l2a_hdr( \
222      in_tbuf_elem, \
223      in_sop, \
224      in_eop, \
225      in_sid)
226  .begin
227      .reg indir tbuf_addr
228      .reg $l2a_hdr_xfer l2a_hdr
229      .sig msf_sig
230
231      // Form the L2A header
232      move(l2a_hdr, in_sid)
```

Continues

```
233        alu_shf_left(l2a_hdr, l2a_hdr, OR,
234                    in_eop, L2A_HDR_EOP_BITPOS)
235        alu_shf_left(l2a_hdr, l2a_hdr, OR,
236                    in_sop, L2A_HDR_SOP_BITPOS)
237        move($l2a_hdr_xfer, l2a_hdr)
238
239        // Compute the TBUF address. This is the base TBUF
240        // address in the MSF plus the element number times
241        // 64.
242        immed32(tbuf_addr, MSF_TBUF_BASE_ADDR)
243        alu_shf_left(tbuf_addr, tbuf_addr, OR,
244                    in_tbuf_elem, 6)
245
246        msf[write, $l2a_hdr_xfer, tbuf_addr, 0, 1],
247            ctx_swap[msf_sig]
248    .end
249    #endm
```

Lines 232 – 237:

The L2 header is first formatted into write transfer registers. This involves setting the SOP, EOP, and source ID fields in the first byte of a general purpose register and then copying the resulting value into an SRAM transfer register.

Lines 242 - 247:

Unlike the previous transmit code which always wrote a TBUF element with data from DRAM, this code performs the write of the CSIX-L2 header directly from the microengine's SRAM transfer register(s). The end result is that both the packet data and the CSIX-L2 header are properly formatted in the same TBUF element.

This code only writes one long-word of data into the TBUF element. The other four bytes of data in the CSIX-L2 header are left uninitialized because the CSIX receive code ignores these bytes anyway.

The final change necessary for CSIX transmit is to properly format the TBUF control value. Recall that the SPHY-4 control word contained, among other things, a packet length field, and SOP and EOP markers. The CSIX control word, on the other hand, contains the information necessary to build the CSIX base and extension headers. The following code shows how the CSIX control word is formed and written into the TBUF control word memory.

_csix_tx_validate_tbuf()

File: Chapter12\csix_tx.uc

```
274   #macro _csix_tx_validate_tbuf(\
275       in_tbuf_elem, in_class, \
276       in_dest_addr, in_size)
277   .begin
278       .reg $tbuf_control_xfer $extension
279       .reg tbuf_control extension size_w_hdr
280       .xfer_order $tbuf_control_xfer $extension
281       .reg tbuf_addr
282       .sig msf_sig
283
284       // Set the mpacket length
285       add(size_w_hdr, in_size, 8)
286       shf_left(tbuf_control, size_w_hdr, 24)
287
288       // Set the cframe type to unicast
289       alu[tbuf_control, tbuf_control, OR,
290           1]
291
292       // Fill in the extension header
293       shf_left(extension, in_class, 24)
294       alu_shf_left(extension, extension, OR,
295                   in_dest_addr, 0)
296
297       immed32(tbuf_addr, MSF_TBUF_CONTROL_BASE_ADDR)
298       alu_shf_left(tbuf_addr, tbuf_addr, OR,
299                   in_tbuf_elem, 3)
300
301       move($tbuf_control_xfer, tbuf_control)
302       move($extension, extension)
303       msf[write, $tbuf_control_xfer, tbuf_addr, 0, 2],
304           ctx_swap[msf_sig]
305   .end
306   #endm
```

Lines 285 – 286:

The CSIX base header packet length is the size of the packet payload plus the eight bytes for our CSIX-L2 header. This field is stored in the first transmit control word, as it was for the SPHY-4 transmit code.

Lines 289 - 290:

In addition to the length of the payload, the CSIX base header includes a field that specifies the type of the CSIX payload. Our code always sends unicast CSIX frames.

Lines 293 - 302:

> These lines format the unicast extension header and place the resulting value into the appropriate transfer register to be written into the second transmit control word. The unicast extension header contains a class of service as well as a destination address. In our example, both fields are ignored because our hardware is arranged in a point-to-point topology. These fields would be used by a switch fabric to properly route and service the CFrame.

CSIX Receive

The code to receive CFrames on the IXP2XXX processor differs from the SPHY-4 receive code in Chapters 5 and 11 in two ways:

■ The reassembly process now includes a new step to extract our CSIX-L2 header from the RBUF.

■ The RBUF control word must be interpreted in a manner appropriate for the CSIX interface.

We don't have to adjust the size of the RBUF elements because the code from previous chapters uses 128-byte RBUF elements. Thus, the changes necessary in the receive reassembly process are to extract the L2A header and use it to determine the SOP and EOP state information instead of the receive status words. These changes are illustrated in the following code.

csix_rx()

```
        File: Chapter12\csix_rx.uc
383         // Extract the RBUF element number and size
384         alu_shf_right(rbuf_elem,
385                     RSW_CSIX_ELEMENT_MASK, AND,
386                       $rsw0, RSW_CSIX_ELEMENT_BITPOS)
387         alu_shf_right(elem_size,
388                     RSW_CSIX_BYTECOUNT_MASK,
389                     AND, $rsw0,
390                     RSW_CSIX_BYTECOUNT_BITPOS)
391         // Subtract the L2A header size
392         sub(elem_size, elem_size, 8)
393
```

Continues

```
394              // Read the L2A header
395              .begin
396                  .reg rbuf_addr
397
398                  immed32(rbuf_addr, MSF_RBUF_BASE_ADDR)
399                  alu_shf_left(rbuf_addr, rbuf_addr, +,
400                               rbuf_elem, 6)
401                  msf[read, $l2a_hdr, rbuf_addr, 0, 1],
402                       sig_done[l2a_hdr_sig]
403              .end
404
405              // Wait for a signal from the previous thread
406              // and then get the global reassembly state.
407              ctx_arb[l2a_hdr_sig, rx_read_state_sig]
```

Line 392:

The receive status word payload size is the sum of our CSIX-L2 header (eight bytes) and the packet data itself. Here we subtract out the length of the CSIX-L2 header as part of the process of not reassembling it into the final packet.

Lines 395 – 403:

Once the mpacket is in the RBUF element, and before the code can begin the actual reassembly process, these lines extract our CSIX-L2 header from the RBUF element. This is accomplished by reading from the RBUF element directly into a SRAM read transfer register on the microengine. The remaining code that checks for SOP and EOP markers use this new transfer register instead of the receive status word transfer register.

The Queue Manager Design

In Chapter 8, we seemingly built a scheduler to prioritize the servicing of multiple queues in our example application. In actuality, we built a dual-purpose context pipeline stage: a scheduler and queue manager. At the time, this approach allowed us to focus on context pipeline stages, but in practice, most IXP2XXX designs separate these two functions as shown in Figure 12.5.

As illustrated, the queue manager driver executes on a single microengine and manages a (potentially large) set of queues. The management of these queues consists of enqueuing data onto the queues based on enqueue requests from a processing pipeline and dequeuing

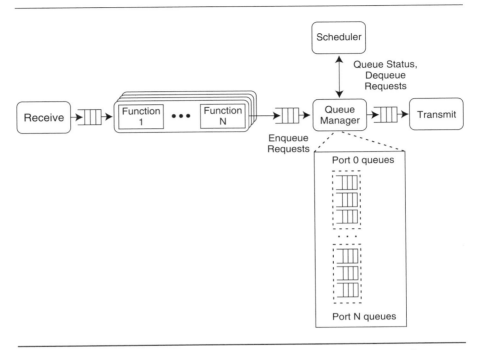

Figure 12.5 A Typical Usage of a Queue Manager in a Processing Pipeline

data based on dequeue requests from a separate scheduler. But before we get into all of these details, let's review the motivations for a queue manager to see why this design is appropriate.

Managing Queues

Some applications, especially quality-of-service applications, require more than the fixed number of queue array entries available in the IXP2XXX SRAM controllers. If you happen to develop such applications, you don't need to abandon the SRAM queueing hardware. Instead, you need to deal with the SRAM queue array entries as a cache, evicting and storing queue descriptors as the need arises, even per-packet if necessary.

Any caching mechanism needs several inter-related algorithms and policies:

■ Loading and unloading algorithms for retrieving an item from some backing storage, such as memory or a disk drive, into the cache and vice-versa. On the IXP2XXX processor, this equates to reading and writing queue descriptors.

■ A lookup algorithm for determining whether a given entry exists in the cache, and if so, its location. In our example, we must determine where, if at all, a queue descriptor is in the SRAM queue array.

■ An eviction policy for determining which entry to remove from a full cache when a new entry must be added. In our example, we must determine the best candidate queue descriptor to write back into SRAM memory.

■ A policy for when to write cache entries to their backing storage. Both write-back and write-through mechanisms are found in cache designs today.

Loading and unloading are the easy part on the IXP2XXX processor because the hardware performs these functions, as detailed in Chapter 10. However, the mechanisms described in Chapter 10 for reading and writing queue descriptors do not provide solutions to the other problems listed above.

Using the CAM to Manage the Cache

The lookup algorithm needs to search the queue array for a given queue, but the SRAM controller does not provide such a capability. Indeed, the SRAM unit precludes such a search because the SRAM unit does not expose the association between a queue array entry and the SRAM address for the queue descriptor. Instead, you must maintain such a mapping.

One possible lookup algorithm might maintain a hash table whose keys are the queue numbers and whose values indicate presence and location in the queue array. The problem with such an approach is the extra time needed to access memory to perform the lookup.

A better solution is to take advantage of the CAM on the microengine. If we placed queue numbers in the CAM and we associated CAM entry numbers with queue array entry numbers, then with a single CAM lookup operation both the presence and location information can be obtained. This approach is highly efficient, but does have two drawbacks:

■ The CAM is only 16 entries in size, so some queue entries are unused.

■ The CAM is local to a microengine, so the queue manager must run on exactly one microengine.

Nevertheless, the extra efficiency of using the CAM can be worth the size and microengine restrictions. Typically, an application has some number of other queue array entries that are not cached anyway, such as buffer freelists, which can occupy some of the unused queue array entries. Also, limiting the queue manager to a single microengine fits the model of a context-pipeline stage perfectly.

Given the choice of the CAM for our lookup algorithm, the eviction policy becomes easy: use the least-recently used algorithm built into the CAM. When a CAM lookup fails, the CAM returns the least-recently used CAM entry. If the lookup requests exhibit any kind of temporal locality, the least-recently used entry represents the ideal choice for eviction. If these requests do not exhibit any temporal locality, the least-recently used policy represents a choice as good as any other.

Finally, the choice of write-back or write-through is also influenced by the decision to use the CAM. In particular, by restricting the queue manager to a single microengine, a write-back policy is possible. Because no other microengines access the queues managed by the queue manager, the design can safely write the queue descriptors back to SRAM memory when the cache entry is evicted.

Note

> The choice of using a single microengine and the CAM for the Queue Manager also solves the two issues of the SRAM queue array controller discussed in Chapter 10. Specifically, enforcing the requirement that `enqueue_tail` operations immediately follow associated enqueue operations is possible because all of the queue-related commands are originating from the same microengine.
>
> Additionally, the LRU eviction policy greatly increases the chances that an enqueue operation completes before the queue descriptor is written back to SRAM, thus minimizing the chances of misordering queue descriptor writes with enqueue commands.

Integrating the Queue Manager in the Packet-Processing Pipeline

Figure 12.5 illustrates how the queue manager design described in the previous section is integrated with a packet-processing pipeline. Figure 12.6 provides an additional level of detail to show how the queue manager interacts with the scheduler and surrounding packet processing functions.

The queue manager dequeues enqueue requests from a scratchpad ring or SRAM ring. These enqueue requests originate from the packet

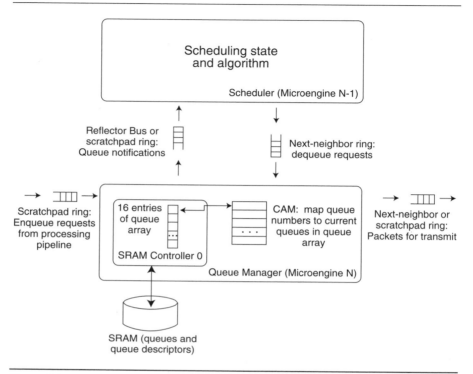

Figure 12.6 The Basic Queue Manager Design

processing pipeline and contain a packet (handle) and a queue number on which to enqueue the packet.

After the queue manager dequeues an enqueue request, it checks its CAM to see whether the requested queue number is already loaded in the queue array. If the queue descriptor is in the queue array, the queue manager performs the enqueue operation. If the descriptor is not in the queue array, the queue manager loads the queue descriptor for the requested queue number into the queue array, updates the CAM, and performs the requested enqueue operation. This process may include the eviction of an existing queue array entry.

Regardless of the initial state of the queue array, after the enqueue operation has been fulfilled, the queue manager informs the scheduler, through a the reflector bus or scratchpad ring, of the newly enqueued packet.

The scheduler dequeues queue notifications from the queue manager and uses this information to schedule, according to any scheduling algorithm, the next queue from which to dequeue. Once the scheduler determines the next queue to be serviced, it sends a dequeue request to the queue manager. These dequeue requests arrive from either a next-neighbor ring or from a scratchpad ring.

Note

The scheduler and queue manager are likely to be context-pipeline stages and can, thus, utilize next-neighbor rings for communications. However, the asymmetric, unidirectional nature of next-neighbor rings means that only one direction of the scheduler and queue manager communications can be via a next-neighbor ring. Typically the communications from the scheduler to the queue manager use a next-neighbor ring to avoid making the queue manager perform two scratchpad accesses: one for enqueue requests and one for dequeue requests.

Finally, the queue manager services the dequeue requests from the scheduler in a manner nearly identical to the servicing of the enqueue requests. Specifically, the queue manager first ensures the requested queue is in the cache, performs the dequeue operation, and enqueues the dequeued packet to the next processing stage, which is typically transmit. In addition, the queue manager sends queue empty notifications to the scheduler when it dequeues the last packet from a queue.

Chapter 13

Tips and Tricks

The tips and tricks in this chapter are categorized by topic: debugging, optimizing, or pitfalls. Depending on your background and previous involvement with the IXP12XX processor and the IXP2XXX processor, some of the tips and tricks might seem obvious, while others may surprise you. Some of the tips and tricks apply to writing in a particular language, microengine C or microengine assembly, and some are independent of the implementation language. So feel free to skip around through this chapter to suit your needs.

To help you quickly understand the tip or trick, a summary note is placed at the beginning of each section. You can scan these summaries to determine whether the information is useful to you. These tips and tricks can be read in any order.

Using ctx_arb[kill] for Debugging

Summary: The `ctx_arb[kill]` instruction (and `ctx_wait(kill)` intrinsic) can be used to implement a simple assert statement for debugging.

We have found no substitute for the workbench, simulator, and breakpoints for debugging microcode. But, occasionally we have found that some form of an assert statement for microcode helpful in debugging. For example, we have used an assert statement when debugging code on the hardware without the workbench. Assert statements are also convenient in that they reduce the number of breakpoints we have to set.

The `ctx_wait(kill)` intrinsic can be used to implement a simple assert statement as follows in microengine C:

```
#ifdef MICRO_DEBUG
#define micro_assert(__e) \
    if (!(__e)) \
       ctx_wait(kill);
#else
#define micro_assert(__e)
#endif

/* An example usage */
void main(void) {
   unsigned int x;

   x = ctx();
   micro_assert(x <= 3);

   x = ctx();
   micro_assert(x == 3);/* The threads 0 - 2 will be
                           stuck here */
}
```

If `MICRO_DEBUG` is defined, the `micro_assert` macro halts the current thread when the provided expression does not evaluate to true. Without `MICRO_DEBUG` defined, the `micro_assert` macro expands to no code at all.

To use this macro, you can watch the program counters on your threads. If any thread's program counter stops changing, it has likely hit an assert statement. You can then take the value of the stuck program counter and work backwards to find which assert statement failed. To locate the appropriate assert statement, search for the desired program counter in the intermediate `.list` file generated by the compiler. The comments indicate the corresponding microengine C or microengine assembly statement. The same result can be obtained by flipping between the microengine C and assembly views in the workbench.

Using Infinite Loops for Debugging

Summary: An infinite loop can be used to implement an assert statement that freezes the current state of all threads on a microengine. This option can be particularly useful when you have multiple threads on a single microengine all accessing some shared state, as is common in a context-pipeline stage.

In the previous tip, we used `ctx_wait(kill)` to implement a simple assert statement for debugging. The result was a macro that would halt the execution of a single thread, while allowing all other threads on the microengine to continue normal execution. An alternative approach to creating an assert macro is to use an infinite loop. The difference is that, if the infinite loop does not release control of the microengine, the assert macro effectively freezes the state of all threads on the microengine. Our version of such a macro, in microengine C, is shown in the following code.

```
#ifdef MICRO_DEBUG
#define micro_assert_all_threads(__e) \
    if (!(__e)) \
        while(1) ;
#else
#define micro_assert_all_threads(__e)
#endif
```

The `while(1)` infinite loop does not release control of the microengine, and, thus, all other threads in the microengine never again get a chance to execute. This macro can prove particularly useful when dealing with intra-microengine programming interactions, such as in a context-pipeline stage because it allows you to examine the state of any shared variables precisely at the time the assertion failed.

Executing Junk at the End of the Instruction Store

Summary: When writing microengine assembly code that does not use all available threads on a microengine, be sure to properly terminate the unused threads with the `ctx_arb[kill]` instruction.

Context pipeline stages sometimes use fewer than the eight (or four) threads available on a microengine. The microengine assembly code that limits the number of threads in execution typically looks like the following code:

```
br!=ctx[0, end_of_program#]
start#:

// Do the normal processing here, assume 1 (or fewer
// than 8 threads
br[start#]

end_of_program#:
```

This code stops executing after the first context release operation in the normal processing code. The problem is that threads, which were supposed to be doing nothing, are actually never releasing control of the microengine. For example, in the code above, once thread 1 jumps to the end_of_program# label, it never releases control of the microengine.

The solution is to ensure unused threads are removed from the execution context using the ctx_arb[kill] instruction for all unused threads as follows:

```
end_of_program#:
ctx_arb[kill]
nop
```

Checking for the Presence of Signals

Summary: The br_signal, br_!signal instructions (and signal_test intrinsic) can be used to check for the presence of a signal without releasing control of the microengine. These instructions can help when fine-grained control of microengine thread execution is required. In addition, when combined with one of the previous debugging assert routines, spurious signals sent to a microengine can be detected.

The br_signal (br_!signal) instruction checks for the presence (absence) of the provided signal on the calling microengine thread. If the signal is present, these instructions consume the signal and branch accordingly. Otherwise, these instructions just branch appropriately. In either case, neither instruction releases control of the microengine thread.

In most cases, using `ctx_arb` to wait for, and consume, a signal is sufficient. However, `ctx_arb` releases control of the microengine even if the given signal is present. While optimizing our code, we have occasionally run across a critical path through the microcode where a thread needs to wait for a signal that, due to the overall timing of the code, is almost always already present. To prevent such a critical thread from needlessly releasing control of the microengine, we often combine these instructions and `ctx_arb` into a macro that guarantees that the given signal is consumed, but does not release control if the signal is already present. The result is shown in the following code.

```
// MicroC
#define CHECK_AND_WAIT(signal_name) \
    if ( !signal_test(signal_name) ) \
        wait_for_all(signal_name);

// Microassembly
#macro CHECK_AND_WAIT(signal_name)
    br_signal[signal_name, skip#]
    ctx_arb[signal_name]
    skip#:
#endm
```

These macros can be used in place of any `ctx_arb` instruction (or `ctx_wait` intrinsic in microengine C). The `br_signal` instruction determines whether the signal is present or not. If the signal is present, it consumes the signal, and skips the `ctx_arb`. If signal is not present, the `ctx_arb` instruction is executed.

Replacing all `ctx_arb` instructions with this macro would be a mistake. Not only would such a blanket change increase the overall code store size, but also, in general, the microengine threads perform the best when they are occasionally releasing control to each other. We always write our code with the `ctx_arb` instruction until we determine that using `br_signal` helps in a particular instance.

These instructions can also be used to track down spurious signals on the hardware. In the simulator, tracking down spurious signals is a snap. The thread history capability on the simulator allows the originator and recipient of every signal to be known. But what do you do if you suspect that, due to interactions with the core or other hardware devices, the hardware signals are behaving differently than the simulator? If you place `ctx_arb` instructions in a section of code that you suspect occasionally receives a spurious signal, the code blocks until that signal is received. This trick works great unless the spurious signal only arrives as a result of the thread performing its normal operations! One solution is to combine these instructions with one of our previous assert macros, something like in the following microengine C code.

```
#define CHECK_SPURIOUS_SIGNAL(signal_name) \
    if ( signal_test(signal_name) ) \
        micro_assert(0);
```

This macro allows the calling thread to continue execution as normal, unless the specified signal is present, in which case the thread halts.

Bit-fields, Structures, and Write-only Transfer Registers

Summary: Bit-fields in microengine C structures are a convenient way to pack data, but their use can be problematic when the structure is placed in write transfer registers. The solution is to first operate on a copy of the structure in general-purpose registers before finally copying the structure to write transfer registers.

Consider the following benign-looking code that attempts to write a given bit-field structure into memory.

```
typedef struct {
    unsigned int a_bit : 1;
    unsigned int the_rest : 30;
} bit_s;

void main(void) {
    volatile __declspec(sram_write_reg) bit_s w_struct;
    SIGNAL sig;

    w_struct.a_bit = 1;
    sram_write(
      (__declspec(sram_write_reg) void *)&w_struct,
      (void __declspec(sram) *)0,
      1,
      ctx_swap,
      &sig);
}
```

You might be surprised to find out that this code does not compile. The compiler complains that, in the w_struct.a_bit = 1 assignment statement, the code is reading a write-only register! The problem is that the compiler generates code that first reads the entire structure, sets the appropriate bit, and then writes the result back to the structure. The first read of the entire structure is not allowed because the structure is in write transfer registers.

The solution is to always operate on bit-fields in general-purpose registers, and copy the final value of the structure into the write transfer registers as the last step before writing the results to memory. Thus, to fix the above code, we would write the following code.

```
void main(void) {
    volatile __declspec(sram_write_reg) bit_test w_struct;
    SIGNAL sig;

    bit_test gpr_struct;
    gpr_struct.a_bit = 1;
    w_struct = gpr_struct;
    sram_write(
        (__declspec(sram_write_reg) void *)&w_struct,
        (__declspec(sram) void *)0,
        1,
        ctx_swap,
        &sig);
}
```

The same problem can arise for those writing microengine assembly. In microengine assembly don't forget that a single transfer register variable represents both a read-only and a write-only transfer register. Pay particular attention when using the ld_field[] instruction because the implementation of this instruction on the microengines performs a read-modify-write operation like the one discussed above. For example, consider the following assembly instruction:

```
ld_field[$xfer, 0011, some_gpr]
```

This instruction first takes the value of the read-only transfer register $xfer and replaces the lower two bytes with the corresponding values from the some_gpr register. The result is written back into the write-only transfer register $xfer. The upper two bytes of the write-transfer register are modified, even though these bytes are not part of the byte-mask of the instruction.

Using Out Parameters in C Functions

Summary: Returning values through the parameter list of micro-engine C functions causes the argument to be placed in memory. To avoid unwanted memory accesses for these functions, use return values or __forceinline as a modi-fier to the function.

The compiler places arguments passed to microengine C functions as pointers, into memory. Should you happen to be using the pointer as a means of expressing an out parameter, this extra memory access is probably undesirable. Consider the following contrived example that contains a function to initialize its parameter to the value one.

```
void function1(volatile unsigned int *out) {
    *out = 1;
}

void main(void) {
    volatile unsigned int x, y;

    function1(&x);
    y = x;
}
```

This code compiles into the following assembly.

```
<cut out initialization of address variables>

/******/ function1(&x);
br[_function1#], defer[1]
load_addr[a1, l_9#]

/******/y = x;
l_9#:
sram[read, $0, b0, 0, 1], ctx_swap
alu[y_87$1$1:a0, --, B, $0]

<cut out code jump to the exit routine>

_function1#:
/******/*out = 1;
nop
sram[write, $0, out_86_V$5b$1$2:a0, 0, 1], ctx_swap,
defer[1]
immed[$0, 1, <<0]
rtn[a1]
```

This code first jumps to function1, which then generates an SRAM write operation to set x to one and return. Following the return by function1, the code reads the same SRAM memory location previously written to retrieve the value of x. Finally, this value is assigned to y.

Unless you actually want this behavior, a few solutions exist. One solution is to use the return value of the function instead of an out parameter. We could re-write function1 to return an integer, and the compiler would then not generate any memory references for the call to function1. Of course, it often happens that a function is already using its return value for something else, like an error condition. In these situations, we could use a macro to solve the problem. Within a macro, we don't have to pass the address of a variable to modify the value of the variable. The downside of using macros is that we lose all of the type-safety, which is probably one of the main reasons we wanted a compiler instead of an assembler anyway.

Another solution is to use the auto-in-line optimization of the microengine C compiler. On the code above, the auto-in-line optimization in the compiler determines that the function is appropriate (i.e., small enough) to be in-lined and automatically in-lines the routine, eliminating the extra memory references. However, this size restriction may not be true for more realistic functions.

Finally, another solution is to use the __forceinline modifier. Declaring a function with __forceinline forces the function to be in-lined by the compiler. When a function is in-lined, the compiler optimizes out any unnecessary memory reads or writes like those shown in the above example. The following assembly shows the result of compiling the above example with a __forceinline modifier before function1!

```
immed[x_87$1$1:a0, 1, <<0]
```

Caution
__forceinline does not work if the in-lined function and the function invocation are in different compilation units. The compiler cannot in-line a function for which it only has a declaration and no definition. You need to place the implementation of __forceinline functions in header files, as opposed to source files, to ensure that the compiler can in-line the functions you declare _ _forceinline.

Scripting with the Transactor

Summary: The IXP2XXX transactor has a scripting language that allows developers to do many of the functions in the simulator that would normally be done by the XScale core in the hardware. These functions include setting up lookup tables, and starting and stopping microengines.

When running microengine code on the IXP2XXX hardware, the XScale core handles many necessary functions, such as setting up lookup tables, and starting and stopping microengines. These same functions are needed to simulate running code in the transactor as well. Unfortunately, the transactor does not have a way to run XScale code, so instead it offers a scripting language to do the things in the simulator that the XScale core would normally do in hardware. The full documentation for the transactor's scripting language can be found in the "Intel IXP2400/ IXP2800 Network Processor Development Tools User Guide", which is listed in the References. In this section, you'll get a quick introduction.

Transactor commands can be run in two ways. They can be run from a file, typically with the .ind extension, or they can be run from a command prompt in the Developer's Workbench. To run a series of commands from a the command line, open the Command Line window using the View > Debug Windows > Command Line menu option. Selecting this option opens a window similar to the one shown in Figure 13.1. The bottom portion of this window is where commands are entered. The top portion shows the results of the commands. To have the transactor run a file with commands in it, either type @<file name> on the command line, or set the file up as a start-up script using the Startup tab in the window opened by selecting the Simulation > Options from the menu.

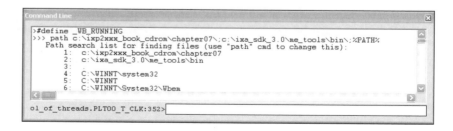

Figure 13.1 Transactor Command-Line Window

Setting up lookup tables is simple with transactor scripting. Using the `sat_sram` command helps to set up lookup tables. For example, the following command sets the four bytes starting at the address 0xa0b8 to be 0x0000a800:

```
set_sram(0xa0b8, 0x0000a800);
```

The transactor has similar commands for DRAM, scratch, and local memory. The transactor scripting language interpreter interprets basic C header files as well, including #define statements. Developers often create header files to be used in the microengine code as well as in the transactor scripts, so that they both get the same constants.

The transactor allows developers to define functions in the scripting language as well. The syntax for these functions and the syntax for their usage is the same as C syntax.

One transactor command is essential to using the transactor with the built-in packet generator. To start packets flowing to in the transactor, use the `ps_start_packet_receive()` command.

Differences between Receive and Transmit on the IXP2400 and the IXP2800

Summary: The MSF interface for receiving and transmitting packets differs slightly between the IXP2400 and the IXP2800. Just updating the format of the receive and transmit control words to accommodate the differences in media types does not suffice to make receive and transmit code written for one processor execute properly on the other.

The example receive and transmit code in Chapters 5, 11, and 12 works properly on the IXP2800 (and IXP2850), but requires two tweaks to run properly on the IXP2400. These changes are in addition to changes for the different media types supported on the IXP2400.

The first change is to initialize the RBUF freelist on the IXP2400. On the IXP2800, the initial state of this freelist is 'full'. All RBUFs are on the freelist when the chip initializes. On the IXP2400, however, the opposite is true. So, during the initialization process on the IXP2400, be sure to 'free' all of the RBUF elements or your code will never receive any mpackets.

The second change is in the numbering of RBUF and TBUF elements. On the IXP2800, RBUF and TBUF element numbering is not dependent upon the size of the RBUF and TBUF elements, respectively. For example, when using 128-byte TBUFs on the IXP2800, only even TBUF numbers are used. The odd TBUF numbers, which are present in 64-byte TBUF configuration, are not valid.

However, on the IXP2400, the RBUF and TBUF element numbering is always 0, 1, 2, 3, etc. regardless of size of the RBUF and TBUF elements. This numbering scheme has an impact on the computation of RBUF and TBUF addresses because RBUF and TBUF addresses are always byte addresses. Thus, on the IXP2800, you can always just scale the RBUF or TBUF number by 64, whereas on the IXP2400, you must scale the RBUF or TBUF number by 64, 128, or 256, depending on the configured size of the element.

Writing Efficient Microengine C Code

Summary: Writing efficient microengine C sometimes involves a few tricks.

Here are a few tips and tricks for writing efficient microengine C code:

- Use unsigned integers where possible. The use of signed integers sometimes results in the generation of extra instructions.

- Use structure fields that are a multiple of 8 bits in size. Fields that are not a multiple of 8 bits take more instructions to extract.

- Put the common conditional case in the `if` clause, and not the `else` clause. The IXP2XXX instruction pipeline predicts that branches will not be taken, and hence no pipeline stalls occur when the `if` clause is executed.

- Make small, commonly executed functions in-line. To force a function to be in-lined, use `static __forceinline` in the declaration and definition of the function. Of course, you can take this advice too far and end up exceeding the instruction store size.

I'm out of Registers! Now what?

Summary: Sometimes microengine code runs out of general-purpose registers and needs to use other slower memories to store variables. In many cases this problem can be avoided, and the tips for doing so are different for microengine C code and microengine assembly code.

Even with each microengine's 256 general-purpose registers, sometimes microengine code runs out of registers. The alternatives for storing variables are local memory, scratch, SRAM, and DRAM. These alternatives are all slower than registers, so efficient use of these registers is very important. Handling issues related to register shortages is different for microengine C code than for microengine assembly code.

Microengine C Code

When the microengine C compiler runs out of registers for variables, it begins to allocate variables in local memory, then SRAM. While this behavior is correct for the compiler, your code can take a significant performance hit as a result.

Detecting when the compiler runs out of registers is easily accomplished with the –Qperfinfo=1 command line option. This option causes the compiler to print out any instance in which a variable is spilled to memory due to a lack of available registers. The variable name can be used to track down where in the code you have exhausted the register space. Unfortunately, as easy as it is to detect spilled registers, reducing register usage to avoid the problem is sometimes frustratingly hard. We don't have a silver bullet for this problem, other than a lot of careful inspection of the code, looking for places where multiple variables could be packed as bit-fields in a single structure, or where the scope of variables can be reduced.

Microengine Assembly Code

When microengine assembly code runs out of registers, you must resolve the issue before the code can assemble. As with micorengine C code, no one thing resolves this problem. And again, careful inspection of code is required.

It often helps to look for scopes that can be narrowed. In other words, try to make the `.begin` and `.end` statements as close to each other as possible. The assembler is good at detecting the active range of registers, but sometimes better placement of scoping statements can help.

As was covered in Chapter 2, microengine general-purpose registers are split between A and B banks. Sometimes register shortages are actually just a shortage in one of the two banks. The .list files created for each microengine image lists the registers and the banks to which they are allocated. Inspection of this file as well as the code can often provide clues as to how best to modify the code to solve register shortages.

References

Carlson, Bill. *IXA Network Architecture*, Intel Press, 2003.

CSIX-L1: Common Switch Interface Specification-L1, CSIX, 2000.

Floyd, Sally and Van Jacobson. "Random Early Detection Gateways for Congestion Avoidance" In *August 1993 IEEE/ACM Transactions on Networking*, IEEE/ACM, 1993.

Internet Engineering Task Force (IETF). www.ietf.org.

Intel 2800 Network Processor Hardware Reference Manual, Intel Corporation, 2002.

Intel IXP2400/IXP2800 Network Processor Programmer's Reference Manual, Intel Corporation, 2002.

Intel IXP2400/IXP2800 Network Processor Development Tools User Guide, Intel Corporation, 2002.

Intel Internet Exchange Architecture (IXA) Portability Framework Reference Manual, Intel Corporation, 2002.

Intel IXP2400/IXP2800 Network Processors Microengine C Compiler Language Support Reference Manual, Intel Corporation, 2002.

Network Processor Forum (NPF). www.npforum.org.

Schneier, Bruce. *Applied Cryptography*, Second Edition, John Wiley & Sons, Inc., 1996.

Glossary

Advanced Encryption Standard (AES) is a cryptographic algorithm initiated by the National Institute of Standards and Technology (NIST) to replace DES and its variations. The IXP2850 processor implements this algorithm in the IXP2850 crypto unit.

Arbiter is also referred to as the thread arbiter. On the IXP2XXX microengines, the arbiter selects the next thread to execute in a round-robin fashion.

Asynchronous Insert/Synchronous Remove (AISR) is a data structure that serves as a mechanism to ensure packet ordering in the unordered thread execution programming model.

Atomic Memory Operation is a multi-access, Read-Modify-Write (RMW) memory operation in which no other memory accesses are interleaved between the separate memory accesses of the RMW. Atomic memory operations are important when updating critical data so software mechanisms aren't needed to lock the data during updates.

Cbus is a CSIX flow control bus used to connect an egress IXP2XXX network processor that receives flow control messages to an ingress IXP2XXX network processor that is responsible for scheduling the data to be transmitted.

Cframe is a CSIX frame. The three categories of Cframes are: data, control, and flow control.

Common Switch Interface (CSIX) defines an interface between a traffic manager and a switch fabric for data communications applications. The Network Processor Forum (NPF), controls the CSIX-L1 specification. The traffic manager in CSIX refers to any device using the CSIX-L1 interface, including a network processor, such as the IXP2XXX processor.

Content Addressable Memory (CAM) is a memory technology that allows the parallel search of the memory's contents. Each IXP2XXX microengine contains a 16-entry CAM, which is typically used for maintaining locks, or in folding, or for caching (in conjunction with local memory).

Context, often called a thread, is the state associated with one execution thread. On the IXP2XXX microengines, this state includes the program counter, GPRs, transfer registers, and local memory address pointers. The IXP2XXX microengines can maintain up to eight contexts.

Context Pipeline Stage is a processing function written to execute exclusively on one microengine.

Control Plane Platform Development Kit (CP PDK) is an implementation of APIs defined by the Network Processor Forum (NPF) that runs on the Intel® XScale™ core and an optional external control plane processor.

Control Plane is the abstraction for a functional area of an application that controls and configures the data plane and handles control packets, such as routing protocol updates.

Core Component is the counterpart of the microblock running on the Intel XScale core handling exception packets and microblock configuration.

Critical Section is a section of code executed by one processing thread that requires exclusive access to a data structure so it can update that data without concern that other threads will simultaneously update the same data, causing data corruption errors.

Cyclic Redundancy Check (CRC) is a name for a group of algorithms for checking the consistency of transmitted data. Each IXP2XXX microengine contains a CRC unit, which can compute CRCs over any sized data.

Data Encryption Standard (DES) is a 64-bit block cipher that uses a 56-bit key. DES is a crypto algorithm used in the IXP2850 processor.

Data Plane is the abstraction for the functional area of an application where the bulk of packet data is processed within a system. In IXP2XXX systems the microengines and the Intel XScale core typically run data plane software.

Deficit Round Robin (DRR) is a scheduling algorithm that allows for different priorities between queues and variable length packets.

Deli-Ticket Server is a method to insure ordered locking in critical sections when using the unordered thread execution programming model.

Developer's Workbench is an integrated development environment for developing, simulating, and debugging microengine code for the IXP2XXX processors.

Dispatch Loop is the code that combines microblocks on a microengine and implements the data flow between them. The dispatch loop may also cache commonly used variables in registers or local memory.

Driver is microengine code that is closely coupled to the hardware, such as receive code, transmit code and queue management. Drivers supplied by Intel are available in the IXA SDK 3.0.

Egress Path When used in the context of a full-duplex, IXP2XXX-based line card, the egress path is from the switch fabric to the network.

End-to-end Packet Order is one type of packet ordering that ensures packets in the same flow leave a device (e.g., network processor) in the order in which they arrived at the network processor.

Flow is a group of related packets as defined by the application consuming the packets. For example, all packets with the same destination address might constitute a flow in a forwarding application.

Whereas, all packets with the same source and destination addresses, source and destination ports, and protocol type might constitute a flow in a quality-of-service application.

Flow Control is a mechanism for managing congestion in a network system in which downstream components throttle upstream components.

Folding is a software technique used by threads running on the same microengine to optimize read-modify-writes in a critical section. The technique uses the CAM and strict thread ordering enforced via inter-thread signaling to fold the read/modify/write into a single read, multiple modifies, and one or more writes.

Generalized Thread Signaling (GTS) is a design feature of the IXP2XXX microengines allowing them to wait for asynchronous events, such as memory references, while consuming a minimal amount of resources.

Hardware Abstraction Library (HAL) provides operating system-like abstraction of hardware assisted functions. It is composed of two sub-libraries: Instruction simplification library and OS emulation library.

Hash Function is a mapping from a key to a (usually smaller) value. Hash functions are used to generate a smaller index than the original key, which then can be used to index into a hash table. Good hash functions, like those provided in the IXP2XXX SHaC unit, give a uniformly distributed set of values.

Hash Table is a data structure used for high-speed lookups of exact-matched data. Hash tables use a hash function to guide and speed the lookup process.

Ingress Path—when used in the context of a full-duplex, IXP2XXX based line card, the ingress path is from the network to the switch fabric.

Intel Internet Exchange Architecture (Intel IXA) is an architecture that allows for software reprogrammable silicon and open APIs.

Intel IXA SDK 3.0 is the Intel IXA Software Development Kit for assembling, compiling, linking, and simulating MEv2 microengine code and XScale code for IXP2XXX network processors.

Intel XScale core is a general purpose processor core based on the ARM V5TE instruction set.

Intrinsic is a microengine C primitive used to access a feature of the IXP2XXX hardware that is not accessible with conventional C syntax.

Local Memory is a per-microengine memory store of 640 long-words.

Long-word is a 32-bit word.

Media & Switch Fabric Interface (MSF) is the primary packet interface between IXP2XXX network processors and the network (via MACs and framers) or switch fabrics.

Media Access Control (MAC) is a protocol layer responsible for providing access to a shared communications medium.

Media Access Controller (MAC) is a device used to interface with the physical layer medium.

MEv2 are the microengines used in the IXP2XXX family of network processors.

Microblock is a discrete unit of IXP2XXX microengine code written in microengine assembly or microengine C according to the guidelines specified in the IXA Software Framework. Typically, a microblock has an Intel XScale core component that is used to configure and manage the microblock.

Microblock Group is one or more microblocks that have been combined, using a dispatch loop, into a thread executable on a microengine. Typically, all threads on the microengine execute the same microblock group, but it is not required.

Microengine is a programmable processor designed specifically for high-speed packet processing functions. The IXP2400 processor contains eight microengines, the IXP2800 processor and IXP2850 processor contain sixteen microengines. The IXP2XXX family has version 2 microengines (MEV2).

Microengine Assembly is a language for programming the IXP2XXX microengines. Microengine assembly adds symbolic register and signal names and many structured programming constructs on top of a traditional assembly language.

Microengine C is a language for programming the IXP2XXX microengines. Microengine C provides standard C syntax and adds intrinsics for access to the special features of the IXP2XXX hardware.

Microengine Cluster is a group of microengines that uses the same internal buses on the IXP2XXX processor.

Mpacket is an IXP2XXX media bus interface data transfer unit that can be configured to be 64, 128, or 256 bytes in length.

Network Address Translation (NAT) is a technique for modifying the addresses and port numbers of packets for the purpose of hiding or reusing network addresses.

Network Processor Forum (NPF) is a standards body that "encourages the growth and effective use of network processing technology through standards, testing, benchmarking, and education."

Next Neighbor Registers are IXP2XXX registers that receive data from the previous neighbor via a direct, low latency data path. These registers allow for efficient message and data passing from one microengine to its nearest downstream neighbor.

n-tuple is a collection of n packet fields that uniquely identifies a packet as being part of a flow. For example, the IPv4 five-tuple consists of the IP source and destination addresses, IP protocol number, and the source and destination port numbers from the next layer header.

Operating System Services Library (OSSL) is an OS abstraction API used within the Intel IXA SDK to achieve portability.

Ordered Thread Execution is a method of microengine programming in which multiple microblocks run on the same microengine such that the threads execute each microblock in strict order.

Partial Packet Ordering is a requirement imposed by microblocks that must process packets in particular flows in the order in which they arrive at the device.

Policing is a mechanism to force traffic to comply with certain quality-of-service metrics, such as constant bit rate and maximum burst size.

Quad-word is a 64-bit word.

Quality-of-Service (QoS) is a networking term that specifies a preferential treatment for different traffic classes or flows.

Queue is a first-in-first-out data structure implemented in the IXP2XXX SRAM unit with a linked list.

Queue Array Controller is a data structure and associated control logic integrated within each channel of the IXP2XXX SRAM unit. The queue array controller allows for atomic linked list and ring operations.

Queue Manager is an IXP2XXX driver, implemented as a context pipeline stage, that receives enqueue messages from a packet processing stage and dequeue messages from a traffic scheduler.

Random Early Detection (RED) is an algorithm invented by Sally Floyd and Van Jacobsen used for detecting congestion in a network device. For more information, refer to their book (Floyd and Jacobsen 1993).

Receive Buffer (RBUF) is memory in the IXP2XXX MSF unit used to receive mpackets.

Reflector Bus is a SHaC function that supports reading from a device on the pull bus and writing the data to a device on the push bus (reflecting the data from one bus to the other). A typical implementation of this mode is to allow a microengine to read or write the transfer registers or CSRs in another microengine.

Resource Manager is a library used between XScale core applications and the microcode running on the microengines for IXP2XXX network processors.

Ring is a circular first-in-first-out data structure consisting of a base address, length, head address, and tail address.

Scratchpad Memory is an IXP2XXX processor on-chip memory resource for applications to use in addition to SRAM, DRAM, and local memory.

Scratchpad, Hash, and CAP (SHaC) is a functional unit in IXP2XXX network processors that contains the scratch memory, hash unit, and chip wide CSR registers. The SHaC also controls reflector read and writes.

Secure Hash Algorithm (SHA-1) is a keyed message digest algorithm used in the IXP2850 processor's crypto unit.

Sequence Number is a number assigned to a packet identifying the order in which the packet arrived, with respect to the other packets in the same flow.

Synchronization is a concept used to describe the coordination of multiple threads. On the IXP2XXX microengines, synchronization between threads can be achieved through inter-thread signals, atomic memory operations, the thread arbiter, or other mechanisms.

Thread is also referred to as a context.

Transfer registers are I/O registers in the microengine that store data transferred to and from a microengine. Transfer registers attach to the internal S and D push and pull buses of the IXP2XXX processor.

Transmit Buffer (TBUF) is memory in the IXP2XXX MSF unit used to transmit packets.

Triple Data Encryption Standard (3DES) is a variation of DES that is used in many security-enabled network protocols. The IXP2850 processor implements this algorithm in the IXP2850 crypto unit.

Universal Test & Operations Interface for ATM (UTOPIA) is the standard chip-chip interface for interfacing ATM traffic shapers, SARs, and framers.

Unordered Thread Execution is a method of microengine programming in which multiple microblocks run on the same microengines such that the threads execute the microblocks independently.

Weighted Random Early Detection (WRED) is a congestion avoidance algorithm that randomly discards packets based on current queue depth for the packet. WRED discards a packet based on its relative priority.

Index

66 As the pace of technology introduction increases it's difficult to keep up. Intel Press has established an impressive portfolio. The breadth of topics is a reflection of both Intel's diversity as well as our commitment to serve a broad technical community.

I hope you will take advantage of these products to further your technical education.99

Patrick Gelsinger
Senior Vice President and Chief Technology Officer
Intel Corporation

Turn the page to learn about titles from Intel Press for system developers

Meet the Challenges of Network Packet Processing

Intel® Internet Exchange Architecture and Applications

A Practical Guide to Intel's Network Processors

By Bill Carlson

ISBN 0-9702846-3-2

Every week, Bill Carlson explains the IXP2XXX network processor family to leading equipment manufacturers across the western US. In this invaluable developer resource, he provides an overview of Intel Internet Exchange Architecture (IXA) that comes straight from the experts to you, providing an in-depth technical view of the standards required by hardware and software developers of next-generation OEM networking equipment. The book is not only for hardware and software engineers. It also explains to support professionals, management, and salespersons how the IXP2XXX processors are replacing ASICs. Intel® Internet Exchange Architecture and Applications describes the architecture of a typical network core or edge to provide a context for the network processor architecture and provides a detailed example of a DSLAM using the multi-protocol software framework.

Inside you will learn about the internal and external architecture of the Intel® IXP2400/2800 network processor family. Specifically, this book describes:

- Performance estimation techniques

- Multiprocessing and multithreading techniques to maximize performance

- Ways of mapping tasks to multiple microengines using Hyper Task Chaining or Pool of Threads programming models

- How the programming framework supports modular and portable software applications

Accelerate development and improve product quality

● *IXP1200 Programming*

The Microengine Coding Guide for the Intel® IXP1200 Network Processor Family
By Erik J. Johnson and Aaron Kunze
ISBN 0-9712887-8-X

As very deep submicron ASIC design gets both more costly and time-consuming, the communications industry seeks alternatives providing rich services with higher capability. The key to increased flexibility and performance is the innovation incorporated in the IXP1200 family of network processors. From engineers who were there at the beginning, you can learn how to program the microengines of Intel's IXP12xx network processors through a series of expanding examples, covering such key topics as receiving, processing, and transmitting packets; synchronizing between hardware threads; debugging; optimizing; and tuning your program for the highest performance.

Increase performance with this hands-on coding guide

● *Introduction to PCI Express†*

A Hardware and Software Developer's Guide
By Adam Wilen, Justin Schade, and Ron Thornburg
ISBN 0-9702846-9-1

Written by key Intel insiders who have worked to implement Intel's first generation of PCI Express chipsets and who work directly with customers who want to take advantage of PCI Express, this introduction to the new I/O technology explains how PCI Express is designed to increase computer system performance. The book explains in technical detail how designers can use PCI Express technology to overcome the practical performance limits of existing multi-drop, parallel bus technology. The authors draw from years of leading-edge experience to explain how to apply these new capabilities to a broad range of computing and communications platforms.

❝This book helps software and hardware developers get a jumpstart on their development cycle that can decrease their time to market.❞

Ajay Kwatra, Engineer Strategist, Dell Computer Corporation

● InfiniBand† Architecture Development and Deployment
A Strategic Guide to Server I/O Solutions
By William T. Futral
ISBN 0-9702846-6-7

InfiniBand, a contemporary switched fabric I/O architecture for system I/O and inter-process communication, offers new and exciting benefits to architects, designers, and engineers. Intel I/O Architect William Futral was a major contributor to InfiniBand architecture from its inception. Currently, he serves as Co-Chair of the InfiniBand Application Working Group. His comprehensive guide details the InfiniBand architecture, and offers sound, practical expert tips to fully implement and deploy InfiniBand-based products, including deployment strategies, InfiniBand-based applications, and management.

**Develop
leading edge server
I/O solutions**

● The Virtual Interface Architecture
A Guide to Designing Applications for Systems Using VI Architecture
By Don Cameron and Greg Regnier
ISBN 0-9712887-0-4

The VI architecture addresses the long-standing problem for systems that need an efficient interface between general-purpose computers and high-speed switched networks. In this book, Intel architects outline the motivation, benefits, and history of the Virtual Interface Architecture. Code examples guide you through the syntax and semantics of the VI Provider Library API. With this reference, hardware and software engineers can apply the VI Architecture to development of scalable, high-performance, and fault-tolerant systems.

**Design scalable,
high-performance,
fault-tolerant systems**

About Intel Press

Intel Press is the authoritative source of timely, highly relevant, and innovative books to help software and hardware developers speed up their development process. We collaborate only with leading industry experts to deliver reliable, first-to-market information about the latest technologies, processes and strategies.

Our products are planned with the help of many people in the developer community and we encourage you to consider becoming a customer advisor. If you would like to help us and gain additional advance insight to the latest technologies, we encourage you to consider the Intel Press Customer Advisor Program. You can **register** here:

www.intel.com/intelpress/register.htm

For information about bulk orders or corporate sales, please send email to **bulkbooksales@intel.com**.

Other Developer Resources from Intel

At these Web sites you can also find valuable technical information and resources for developers:

developer.intel.com	general information for developers
www.intel.com/IDS	content, tools, training, and the Early Access Program for software developers
www.intel.com/software/products	programming tools to help you develop high-performance applications
www.intel.com/idf	world-wide technical conference, the Intel Developer Forum